D1605277

A Course in Semantics

A Course in Semantics

Daniel Altshuler, Terence Parsons, and Roger Schwarzschild

The MIT Press
Cambridge, Massachusetts
London, England

This book was set in Times New Roman by Westchester Publishing Services. Printed and bound in the United States of America.

Library of Congress Cataloging-in-Publication Data

Names: Altshuler, Daniel, 1981- author. | Parsons, Terence, author. | Schwarzschild, Roger, author.
Title: A course in semantics / Daniel Altshuler, Terence Parsons, and Roger Schwarzschild.
Description: Cambridge, MA : The MIT Press, 2019. | Includes bibliographical references and index.
Identifiers: LCCN 2018056265 | ISBN 9780262042772 (hardcover : alk. paper)
Subjects: LCSH: Semantics.
Classification: LCC P325 .A4248 2019 | DDC 401/.43—dc23
LC record available at https://lccn.loc.gov/2018056265

10   9   8   7   6   5   4   3   2   1

Contents

List of Exercises Labeled as "Important Practice and Looking Ahead"
Chapter 1: Exercises (1.5); (1.10)–(1.16); (1.22)–(1.23)
Chapter 2: Exercises (2.5); (2.13); (2.15); (2.20)
Chapter 3: Exercises (3.4); (3.21)
Chapter 4: Exercises (4.5); (4.17)
Chapter 5: Exercise (5.19)

List of Exercises Labeled as "Thinking About"
Chapter 3: Exercises (3.10); (3.14); (3.35); (3.43)–(3.44)
Chapter 4: Exercises (4.7); (4.11)–(4.16)
Chapter 5: Exercises (5.2); (5.6); (5.9); (5.13)–(5.14); (5.18); (5.23); (5.26)–(5.29)

Preface

This is a textbook for a course that develops *semantic intuition* and *semantic methodology*. After completing the course, students will be able to: (i) form intuitions about a set of data, (ii) explain how well an analysis of the data accords with their intuitions, and (iii) extend the analysis or seek an alternative. No prior knowledge in linguistics is required. Students who have some background will have the opportunity to build on that knowledge.

In order to achieve these ambitious goals, we have borrowed the strategy employed in successful textbooks we are familiar with: reduce the empirical phenomena typically covered in an introductory course. Moreover, since our textbook is for undergraduates, the formalism is basic. Finding the right balance between empirical coverage and formalism, on the one hand, and development of intuition and methodology, on the other, is what makes this textbook unique.

Chapter 1 introduces basing concepts such as *truth conditions* and *compositionality*, as well as assorted technical background. This sets the stage for the second chapter which presents a basic symbolic logic with negation, conjunction, and generalized quantifiers, but without disjunction or the material conditional. The textbook assumes an *indirect method of interpretation*, and the logic presented in chapter 2 serves as the basis for translation throughout. In chapters 3–5, a compact set of translation rules take syntactic structures into symbolic logic formulas, which are then interpreted by semantic rules. With these tools, the textbook takes the reader through quantifier scope ambiguity, pronouns, tense, aspect, and modifiers. There is close attention to pragmatics with rules for interpreting deictic pronouns and narrative progression. Topics not covered include: plurals, presupposition, implicature, and intensionality.

Throughout the textbook, we use generalized quantifier notation[1] as in the formulas below:

Every dog barked $\leadsto$ $[\forall x: \text{Dog}(x)](\text{Barked}(x))$.

Some dog barked $\leadsto$ $[\exists x: \text{Dog}(x)](\text{Barked}(x))$.

We opted for this notation over the various notations based on unary quantification, which are found in other popular textbooks. These include:

$$\forall x \, [\text{Dog}(x) \rightarrow \text{Barked}(x)] \qquad \exists x \, [\text{Dog}(x) \, \& \, \text{Barked}(x)]$$

$$[\forall x \, . \, [\text{Dog}(x) \rightarrow \text{Barked}(x)]] \qquad (\exists x)[\text{Dog}(x) \wedge \text{Barked}(x)]$$

$$(\forall x)(\text{Dog}(x) \rightarrow \text{Barked}(x)) \qquad (\exists x)(\text{Dog}(x) \, \& \, \text{Barked}(x))$$

$$\forall x(\text{Dog}(x) \rightarrow \text{Bark}(x)) \qquad \exists x(\text{Dog}(x) \, \& \, \text{Barked}(x))$$

There are two problems with the unary regimentation. First, understanding the syntactic difference between the natural language sentences and their translations entails extensive training and practice, and it engenders an incorrect feeling that one is studying "logician's English." Second, as is well known, some quantifiers cannot be understood in terms of unary quantification. We would like students to immediately be in a position to explore the full range of quantifiers.

While we feel it is crucial for students of semantics to be conversant in the language of symbolic logic based on unary quantification, achieving that goal shouldn't come at the expense of topics in natural language semantics; nor does it need to come at the beginning of their careers.

Another technical choice made in the interest of cutting to the natural language chase concerns the lambda calculus. It doesn't get introduced until late in chapter 3, and then only for use in relative clauses. By that point, the mechanics of variable binding is well-trodden territory. We think this gives the student a deeper understanding of how the lambda operator works, and it does so at the point at which they have a natural language guide and goad. Lambdas are not employed later on, but the concept is on the table for instructors to build upon if they so wish (see further discussion in "Tips for the Instructor"). We also include an optional exercise for advanced students to figure out how to give a set of sets extension for quantificational DPs in subject position.

Since 2013, this textbook has been used successfully at Hampshire College, the Massachusetts Institute of Technology, Rutgers University, Heinrich Heine University, Humboldt University, Leiden University, the Yerevan Academy for Linguistics and Philosophy, the Crete Summer School in Linguistics, and the New York–St. Petersburg Institute of Linguistics, Cognition, and Culture. It has been revised each year, up to and including the current version. At the end of each chapter, there is a list of further reading for students who wish to learn more about the phenomena discussed in the chapter. Each chapter contains a wealth of exercises strategically interspersed throughout the text, creating a journey of discovery for the student. Some exercises have the label "Important practice and looking ahead" or "Thinking about____." These exercises are highly recommended. The former provide practice that is especially relevant to phenomena discussed in subsequent sections and chapters. The latter empower the student to think beyond the basic content of the textbook.

The textbook can be taught, cover to cover, in one term (quarter, trimester, or semester) or in multiple terms. Teaching a subset of the chapters is also possible. We recommend that the instructor read "Tips for the Instructor" and "Sample Schedule" to help decide how to best use this textbook.

Tips for the Instructor

There are five aspects of the textbook that are worth considering when planning to use it in your course: (1) Not all chapters have to be taught, though some presuppose others; (2) chapter 2 employs a particular methodology to teach symbolic logic; (3) there are two advanced sections in chapter 3 that are optional; (4) the teaching of this textbook differs slightly if the course does not require prior exposure to syntax; and (5) there are many ways to incorporate the exercises into your course instruction.

(1) Chapters 1–3 constitute a *mini-course* in semantics. Chapters 1–5 constitute a *full course* in semantics. One may choose to teach chapters 1–3 as part of a more general course (such as "Semantics and Pragmatics" or "Introduction to Linguistics"). Teaching all five chapters is possible in a quarter, a trimester, a semester, or even multiple semesters. See discussion below, in (4), as well as in "Sample Schedule," for some suggestions.

(2) In chapter 2, we present the syntax and semantics of symbolic logic, taking care to explain why the rules look the way they do. Exercises are then provided to allow students to practice using the rules and eventually develop their own intuitions about what a grammatical sentence looks like and what it says. We think this is a rewarding experience for the student. However, we acknowledge that this is not the route taken in most introductory logic classes. In those settings, time is often spent on translation to and from a natural language before rolling out the formal system. Some instructors may prefer that approach. In that case, we recommend that the instructor read chapter 2 and then choose standard predicate logic materials to supplement the course.

(3) There are two advanced sections in chapter 3, which may be skipped without loss of continuity. The first is §3.3.3, "Constraints on Quantifier Raising," which briefly discusses wh-movement, negative and positive polarity items, as well as ellipsis, in order to show that quantifier raising is syntactically constrained. The other optional section is §3.5, "Relative Clauses," which (for the first and only time in the textbook) makes use of the λ operator. Both sections discuss phenomena that are ubiquitous in the literature on natural language semantics. The latter section also employs a formal tool (the λ operator), which is vital in more advanced semantics courses. A decision to include these sections will partly depend

on whether the course has a prerequisite that will enable students to engage with them. This question is directly related to (4).

(4) For courses that have no prerequisites, there are a few important disclaimers about using this textbook. To begin with, when covering the first half of chapter 1, it is important to devote additional time to discuss *constituent structure*. The natural trigger for this discussion is the attachment ambiguity discussed in §1.1. We note that the tree structures in chapter 1 do not have labels, which signifies that *constituent structure* is the only theoretical construct needed at this point.

The opening pages of chapter 3 introduce two labeled phrase structures (verb phrase and negation phrase). While it is not necessary for students to understand the motivation for these particular structures, some understanding will enhance the experience. We recommend Howard Lasnik's 1995 chapter on "The Forms of Sentences," in *An Invitation to Cognitive Science*, 2nd edition, edited by Lila R. Gleitman and Mark Liberman, Vol. 1, *Language,* pp. 283–310 (Cambridge, MA: MIT Press). This chapter does not presuppose any linguistic background. We provide references to relevant parts of it throughout chapters 3–5.

The discussion of scope ambiguity in §3.3 motivates the distinction between base and LF structures. Students with no prior background in syntax will be exposed for the first time to movement. It is important to cover this part of the chapter slowly, enabling the students to realize why movement is necessary, given the theoretical assumptions of the grammar being developed. Moreover, it is recommended that the two advanced sections noted in (2) above be skipped. On the other hand, if students have some background in syntax, teaching the two advanced sections will enable them to build on their knowledge from previous courses.

The syntactic innovations in chapters 4 and 5 are conceptually easy for students to grasp after completing chapter 3 and can be covered in full regardless of whether the course has a prerequisite.

(5) When planning to teach from this textbook, instructors should consider which exercises they will assign for homework (or some other assessment task, such as a quiz, exam, group-work or project) and which exercises they aim to cover in class and/or in discussion/recitation/lab sessions. There are 141 exercises to choose from, some longer and/or conceptually more demanding than others, some directly pertinent to the text, some more tangential. The extent and diversity of exercises offers the instructor a great deal of flexibility. For example, there are enough exercises to cover a year-long or a semester-long course that meets frequently (with additional discussion/recitation/lab sessions). Such a course could have the aim of using class time to work through the longer, conceptually more demanding exercises and exposing students to current research on natural language semantics. On the other hand, one can assign a small number of exercises in a shorter course (such as a quarter long), while still allowing the students to get sufficient practice with

the core concepts. Regardless of the course length, we recommend spending ample time on exercises labeled as "Important practice and looking ahead." For example, exercise (2.7) goes through the steps in calculating the truth conditions for a formula with two quantifiers, while exercise (3.21) enables students to discover a technical innovation that will be crucial for building LFs with tense and aspect. It is essential that students complete these exercises satisfactorily. Moreover, for longer courses that aim for broader coverage, we recommend exercises labeled "Thinking about____," which empower the student to think beyond the basic content of the textbook. See contents for a list of all labeled exercises.

Sample Schedule

Below is a sample schedule for a 15-week semester course that meets twice a week. There are 26 (rather than 30) classes due to holidays and breaks (not listed). Classes are distributed between those that introduce new content (in bold) and those that are based on selected exercises. We suggest assigning for homework those exercises that develop technical skills, while discussing in class exercises labeled as "Important practice and looking ahead" and "Thinking about____."

Table 0.1
Sample schedule

Class theme	Assignment for next class
First day of class	§1.1–§1.4
Syntax/semantics interface, truth-conditions, truth-values	§1.5–§1.6
Set theory, lexicon	Selected exercises from chapter 1
Discussion of selected exercises	§2.1–§2.2
Atomic sentences, connectives	Selected exercises from chapter 2
Discussion of selected exercises	§2.3–§2.6
Generalized quantifiers, predicate conjunction	Selected exercises from chapter 2
Discussion of selected exercises	§3.1–§3.2
Indirect interpretation	§3.3
Quantifier raising, negation, scope	Selected exercises from chapter 3
Discussion of selected exercises	§3.4–§3.5
Modifiers	§3.6
Narrative progression	§3.7–§3.10
Pronouns, semantics/pragmatics interface	Selected exercises from chapter 3
Discussion of selected exercises	§4.1–§4.2
Events, thematic roles, event phrases	§4.3–§4.5
Thematic uniqueness, states	Selected exercises from chapter 4
Discussion of selected exercises	§4.6–§4.8

(continued)

Table 0.1 (continued)

Class theme	Assignment for next class
Adverbial modifiers	Selected exercises from chapter 4
Discussion of selected exercises	§5.1
Tense	Selected exercises from chapter 5
Discussion of selected exercises	§5.2
The progressive	Selected exercises from chapter 5
Discussion of selected exercises	§5.3–§5.5
The perfect	Selected exercises from chapter 5
Final day of class	

As noted in "Tips for the Instructor," there are 141 exercises to choose from, empowering the instructor with a great deal of flexibility. For example, one could extend the sample schedule above to a year-long or a semester-long course that meets more frequently (such as one with additional discussion/recitation/lab sessions) by incorporating more exercises into the classroom discussion. On the other hand, one can also adapt the sample schedule above to a shorter course (such as a quarter long) by reducing the number of exercises that are covered in class (and/or by teaching a *mini-course* version of the textbook; see "Tips for Instructor").

Acknowledgments

The genesis of this textbook can be traced to the undergraduate course "Linguistics 120C: Semantics 1," which was regularly taught at UCLA by Terry Parsons for over a decade. Daniel Altshuler took this course in 2000. The textbook that was used in the course became a bible throughout his undergraduate studies. In 2003, Daniel met Roger Schwarzschild, who was visiting UCLA. This meeting had a great impact on Daniel's decision to go to Rutgers University for his graduate studies. In 2010, Daniel defended his dissertation, with Roger as his chair, on temporality in narrative discourse—a topic that Daniel was introduced to by Terry's textbook. When writing the dissertation, Daniel mentioned to Roger that his dream was to revise and publish Terry's textbook (an online manuscript at the time) so that future generations of undergraduates could be inspired by its innovative pedagogical techniques. In 2013, this dream became reality. Daniel and Roger began to revise the textbook and teach it in their undergraduate semantics classes. This textbook is the 2018 version.

There are many individuals who helped along the way. We would like to thank the TAs who assisted in our teaching: Walden Avery, Nadja Bart, Itai Bassi, Paul Gaus, Maya Gilmore, Sophie Greene, Michael Jacques, Paloma Jeretič, Fabian Koglin, Nicholas Longenbaugh, Lile Merrell, Despina Oikonomou, Grusha Prasad, Ivy Skinner, and Benjamin Storme. The section on relative clauses is based on Nicholas Longenbaugh's handout. Some of the exercises were refined based on insight from Lile Merrell and Ivy Skinner, who—for multiple semesters—taught the exercises (and their refined versions) during their lab sessions. Mariam Asatryan was also helpful in discussing the solutions to the exercises.

Thanks to the students in the course 24.903 at MIT from 2014 to 2018, the students in the courses "What Is a Theory of Meaning Like?" and "Semantics" at Hampshire College from 2015 to 2018, the students in the course "Introduction to Semantics" at the Yerevan Academy for Linguistics and Philosophy in 2017, and the students in the course "Introduction to Formal Semantics" at the New York–St. Petersburg Institute of Linguistics, Cognition, and Culture in 2018. Special thanks to the students in the course "Introduction to Semantics" at the Heinrich Heine University, Düsseldorf, Summer 2014, as well as the students in the Fall 2013 and Spring 2014 course 01:615:325 at Rutgers, where the joint project got started.

Thanks to Rajesh Bhatt, Lisa Bylinina, Simon Charlow, Markus Egg, Wataru Uegaki, Károly Varasdi, and Beibei Xu for teaching earlier versions of our textbook and offering helpful feedback. Thanks to Jessica Rett, Simon Charlow, and anonymous reviewers for detailed comments. Finally, thanks to Marc Lowenthal and Anthony Zannino at MIT Press for helping us realize the current version of the textbook.

1 Introduction

1.1 Syntax and Semantics

When people are asked how they come to know the meanings of sentences in a language they learn in school or even in their native language, they will usually say something like the following:

Words have meanings, they are listed in the dictionary, and you get the meaning of a sentence by putting together the meanings of the words in that sentence.

This idea has a very important consequence: whatever meanings are, they have to be combinable somehow, and the combinations have to be meanings as well. This is true at the level of sentences, but it's also true for phrases that make up a sentence and the words that make up the phrase. For example, the meaning of the phrase *near the house* comes from combining the meanings of the three words that make it up.

While it is true that the meaning of a sentence is determined in part by the words in the sentence, as the quotation above indicates, there is another important ingredient. To see that, compare these two example sentences:

(1) a. The triangle is above the square.
    b. The square is above the triangle.

(1)a and (1)b contain the same six words, and yet they don't say the same thing. Clearly, the meaning difference arises from the fact that their word order is different. This suggests that there are **semantic rules** that produce meanings using as ingredients: (i) the meanings of words and (ii) the order in which they occur.

There are other ingredients as well. Examples of **syntactic ambiguity** are especially revealing. Before turning to syntactic ambiguity, we should say a few words about **ambiguity** in general. Suppose Nadir remarks to Gadarine:

(2) The soup is very hot.

That sentence is **ambiguous**. It can mean either (3) or (4):

(3) The temperature of the soup is very high.

(4) The soup is very spicy.

If Gadarine is uncertain about which meaning Nadir intended when he uttered (2), she can use (3) and (4) to clarify. These sentences are possible **paraphrases** of Nadir's remark. Furthermore, they are **unambiguous paraphrases**—each one captures one (and only one) of the meanings of the sentence it is paraphrasing. It is because the paraphrases are unambiguous that they are useful for clarifying which meaning is intended. Notice that the word *hot* doesn't appear in either paraphrase. That's because the very source of the ambiguity in Nadir's original remark is the word *hot*, which has at least two meanings. The paraphrases manage to be unambiguous precisely because they do not contain that word. Since the source of the ambiguity is a word, we say that Nadir's remark in (2) is **lexically ambiguous**.

The two paraphrases in (3) and (4) are distinct in a sense that will be important in this course—namely, that there are possible situations in which one of the sentences is true and the other false. If Nadir's soup is cold and very spicy, then (3) is false and (4) is true.

Exercise (1.1)

Describe a situation in which (3) is true and (4) is false.

The two paraphrases in (3) and (4) represent different **readings** of (2). We say that in a situation where the soup is cold and very spicy that Nadir's remark is false on the reading paraphrased in (3) and true on the reading paraphrased in (4). We will be using *ambiguous* as a technical term. To say that a sentence is ambiguous is to say that it has at least two readings and that there are situations in which it is true on one reading and false on the other.

Exercise (1.2)

Provide a sentence of your own that is lexically ambiguous. For each reading of your sentence, provide an unambiguous paraphrase that captures that reading. Describe a situation in which your sentence is true on one reading and false on the other.

• Make sure you do not include more information in your paraphrase than is in the original sentence. The sentence *The soup that he ordered is spicy* is not an adequate paraphrase for *The soup is hot*. The latter sentence says nothing about ordering the soup.

• Make sure your situation is complete, so that the sentence is false/true on the relevant reading. It is not enough that the sentence <u>could</u> be false/true. For example, consider a situation in which I put soup on the stove ten minutes ago. In that situation, the sentence

The soup is hot <u>could</u> be true. But it could also be false. Not enough information is provided to be sure.

Now consider the sentence below:

(5) Natchaya talked about the wedding in the church.

This sentence is ambiguous. One of the readings is captured in the unambiguous paraphrase below, in (6), and the other, in the unambiguous paraphrase in (7):

(6) Natchaya talked about the wedding, which took place in the church.

(7) Natchaya talked about the wedding, while she was in the church.

If the wedding in question took place on the beach and then Natchaya talked about it in the church, the sentence is false on the reading paraphrased in (6) and true on the reading paraphrased in (7).

Exercise (1.3)

Describe a situation in which *Natchaya talked about the wedding in the church* is true on the reading paraphrased in (6) and false on the reading paraphrased in (7).

The source of the ambiguity in (5) is not a particular word, but rather the way the words are put together. Figure 1.1 presents two possible syntactic structures for the example sentence. The one on the right corresponds to the reading in (6) and the one on the left to the reading in (7).

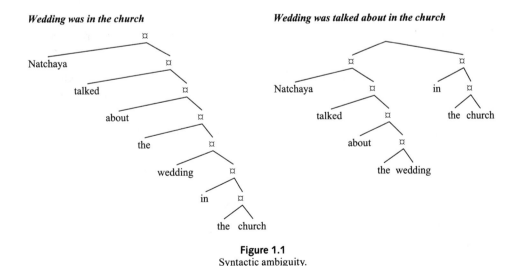

Figure 1.1
Syntactic ambiguity.

The source of the ambiguity in (5) is the attachment site of the phrase *in the church*. In the structure on the left, *in the church* forms a **constituent** with *wedding*, resulting in the phrase *wedding in the church*, while in the structure on the right, *in the church* forms a constituent with the sentence *Natchaya talked about the wedding*. A **syntactic ambiguity** is an ambiguity that arises when a string of words can be formed in two or more different ways and the results lead to differences in meaning. This leads to the following hypothesis, called **compositionality**: The meaning of a sentence is determined by the words used as well as by how they are combined. The study of how words are combined is called **syntax**. A central aim of this course is to explain how syntactic differences like those depicted in the structures above can lead to differences in meaning.

Exercise (1.4)

Provide a sentence that is ambiguous due to the possibility of some constituent being attached in different places. For each reading of your sentence, provide an unambiguous paraphrase that captures that reading. Describe a situation in which your sentence is true on one reading and false on the other.

Conclusions

• Meanings can be combined to form new meanings.

• The meaning of a complex expression is determined by the meanings of the words in that expression, as well as by its syntax (how it was put together).

• Syntactic input to meaning includes word order and constituent structure.

Evidence

We looked at two kinds of evidence for the view that semantic rules make reference to syntactic structure in addition to word meaning.

• A group of words can be combined in two different orders to produce two sentences with different meanings (*The triangle is above the square* ≠ *The square is above the triangle*).

• The same string of words might have been assembled in two different ways. The two constituent structures may give rise to different meanings (*Natchaya talked about [the wedding in the church]* ≠ *[Natchaya talked about the wedding] in the church*).

New Terminology

• semantics rules
• syntactic ambiguity

- lexical ambiguity
- paraphrases
- unambiguous paraphrases
- readings
- constituent
- compositionality
- syntax

Applications

• A particular reading of an ambiguous sentence can be singled out by using an unambiguous paraphrase.

• To show that two readings are distinct, we describe a situation in which one reading is true and the other false.

Something to Think About

Recall the quotation with which we started:

Words have meanings, they are listed in the dictionary, and you get the meaning of a sentence by putting together the meanings of the words in that sentence.

Although this hypothesis suffers from leaving out the role that syntax plays in interpretation, it is generally correct that you get the meaning of a sentence by somehow combining the meanings of the words making it up. But there is a bit of a puzzle here if your idea of a word meaning is a dictionary definition. One does not get the meaning of a sentence by combining dictionary definitions. Here is what we got by stringing together the definitions in dictionary.com for the morphemes *a*, *fish*, *jump*, and *-ed* , which make up the sentence *A fish jumped:*.

Not any particular or certain one of a class or group; any of various cold-blooded, aquatic vertebrates, having gills, commonly fins, and typically an elongated body covered with scales; to spring clear of the ground or other support by a sudden muscular effort; a suffix forming the past tense of weak verbs.

✪ Important Practice and Looking Ahead ✪

Below you will find an exercise that provides practice with ambiguity and paraphrase. The source of the ambiguity comes from the interaction between the **quantifier** expression *every* and **negation**, expressed by *not*. Such an interaction will be an important theme in the chapters ahead. This exercise gives you the opportunity to develop your own intuitions now.

Exercise (1.5)

Consider the two following passages:

(SCAN) A House subcommittee on Wednesday lambasted body scanners and pat-downs used by the Transportation Security Administration. Earlier in the meeting, some members of the panel said the scans were ineffective because every passenger was not examined. Former Department of Homeland Security Assistant Secretary for Policy Stewart Baker defended the randomization, saying that knowing a scan was possible acted as a deterrent for would-be terrorists.[1]

(MEDICAL) He couldn't figure out why there were so many complaints about the medical care on the ship. He assumed that some passengers may not have been examined after the outbreak, but surely most of them were. Then he went back to the records, and he was horrified to learn that every passenger was not examined.

[A] The sentence *every passenger was not examined* occurs in both passages, but with different readings. Provide two unambiguous paraphrases, one for each reading. The paraphrase that corresponds to the first passage should be labeled (SCAN) and the paraphrase that corresponds to the second one should be labeled (MEDICAL). Your paraphrases should capture the meaning of the sentence and nothing more. So it should describe passengers and examining but not other information contained in the discourse—such as ships or scanning. Your paraphrases should be unambiguous. The point of the paraphrase is to single out a particular reading.

[B] Describe a situation in which *every passenger was not examined* is true on one reading and false on the other.

[C] Above we defined two types of ambiguity: lexical and structural. Do you think the ambiguity felt in *every passenger was not examined* is lexical, structural or neither? Explain your answer.

[D] One idea about what's going on in this example is that the ambiguity has to do with the order in which different parts of the sentence are interpreted. To see what's behind this idea, try to produce unambiguous paraphrases of the sentence using these methods:

(i) Paraphrase sentences with quantifier expressions using the *such-that* construction:
   Akna saw every cat ⇒ Every cat is such that: Akna saw it.
   No cat scratched Akna ⇒ There is no cat such that: it scratched Akna.

(ii) Paraphrase negation using *it is not the case that*:
   Akna didn't see Natchaya ⇒ It is not the case that Akna saw Natchaya.

The sentence *every passenger was not examined* contains a quantifier expression, *every passenger*, as well as a negation, *not*. Therefore, your two paraphrases, labeled (SCAN) and (MEDICAL), will each make use of both method (i) and method (ii).

1.2 Semantic Rules and Grammar

As we have just seen, the meaning of a sentence is determined partly by the meanings of the words in the sentence and partly by the way in which the words are put together. This suggests that there are semantic rules that take as input: (a) the meanings of two or more expressions and (b) the syntactic structure in which they are combined. The semantic rules give as output the meaning of the combination. Our goal throughout this book is to discover what these rules are. Semantic rules together with syntactic rules will be called a **grammar**. The grammar generates a set of sentences paired with meanings.

Our rules are like Newton's Laws in physics or Mendel's Laws in genetics. They are precise descriptions of the subject matter. They are arrived at by generalizing based on what one takes to be representative examples. The rules or laws then make predictions about situations beyond those that motivated the rules and, by combining laws, we are able to make further predictions. These predictions can be tested. For semantic rules, that means comparing our intuitions about the meaning of a sentence with what the rules predict. If the predictions turn out to be incorrect, then the rules need to be revised. That is one way that progress is made.

New Terminology

• grammar

Applications

• The goal of semantic theory is to specify what the semantic rules are. These rules, along with syntactic rules, make up a grammar that generates a set of expressions paired with meanings.

• Grammars are tested by comparing the meanings they assign with speakers' intuitions.

1.3 Truth Conditions

Biology is a science concerned with the study of life. That doesn't mean that biologists begin their research by asking what life is. Instead they develop theories about phenomena that are related to life. Similarly, while semantics is the study of meaning, we will not start our investigation by directly asking what meaning is or what meanings are. Instead we will begin by focusing on a property of sentences that depends on their being meaningful, namely, that a sentence is something that can be TRUE or FALSE, unlike a vowel or a table or a neutrino, which aren't the kinds of things that can be assessed for truth and falsity.

Let's briefly explore the connection between truth and meaning. Whether a sentence is true or not depends in part on what the facts are in the situation being described. For

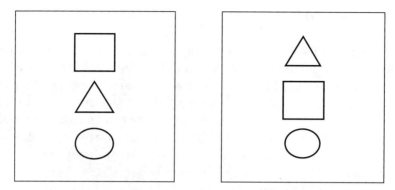

Figure 1.2
Geometric shapes.

example, the sentence in (8) is true if the facts are as depicted in the left box of figure 1.2, and it is false if the facts are as depicted in the right box of figure 1.2.

(8) The square is above the triangle.

In general, the conditions under which a sentence is true are called the sentence's **truth conditions**. So we can say that the truth conditions for the sentence in (8) are met in in the left box of figure 1.2 and are not met in the right box of figure 1.2. This may seem obvious to you, but that is because you are a speaker of English. Compare what you know about the English example sentence above to what you know about the Q'eqchi' sentence in (9):

(9) Li oxxukuut wan rub'el li kaaxukuut.

If you don't speak Q'eqchi', you don't know the meaning of that sentence, so you couldn't say if it is true or false in either of the two situations depicted in figure 1.2. This illustrates a tight connection between knowing the meaning of a sentence and knowing its truth conditions. With the English example sentence in (8), you know its meaning and hence you know its truth conditions; in the Q'eqchi' example sentence in (9), you don't know the meaning, and you don't know its truth conditions.[2]

While truth conditions might not be the first thing that comes to mind when you think of meaning, focusing on truth conditions in working out a grammar of the kind described in section 1.2 turns out to be extremely productive. Our goal will therefore be to develop syntactic and semantic rules that reflect our knowledge of the truth conditions of sentences of the language.

To get a sense of the advantage of focusing on truth conditions, think about the data that we need to collect to develop our grammar and to test its predictions. If you asked several English speakers to describe the meaning of the sentence *The square is above the triangle*, you'd likely get a range of unwieldy answers. On the other hand, if you asked several English speakers if the sentence is true when the facts are as depicted in the left box of figure 1.2, you would get the same answer across speakers, and it will be clear: *Yes*.

In working with this idea of truth conditions, it is important to keep in mind the difference between <u>knowing the truth conditions of a sentence</u> and <u>knowing whether or not a sentence is true</u>. Consider the following example:

(10) The Empire State Building is on fire.

I don't know whether or not (10) is true. What I'm missing are facts about the world. If I went over to the Empire State Building, I could ascertain whether (10) is true or not. In so doing, I would <u>not</u> be learning more English. Rather, I would be using my knowledge of the truth conditions, and depending on whether those conditions are met or not, I would determine whether the sentence is true or not.

TRUE and FALSE are called **truth values**. We have just been discussing the idea that the truth value of a sentence is determined by its truth conditions plus whatever facts obtain in the world. The following formula summarizes this idea:

(11) truth conditions + facts about the world → truth value.

This formula applies to sentences since sentences have truth conditions and truth values. When we confront nonsentential expressions with facts in the world, we don't get a truth value; rather, we get different types of entities. Here are some examples. *Dilma Rousseff* is a linguistic expression—it has phonological properties and syntactic properties. And there is some nonlinguistic entity, namely an **individual**, that that expression stands for. That individual is the woman who was elected president of Brazil in 2011. The noun *horse* stands for not one entity, but a **set** of entities—the set of all horses. The preposition *above* stands for a **relation** between entities. The square bears that relation to the triangle in the situation depicted in the left box in figure 1.2. And the triangle bears that relation to the circle but not to the square. The noun *brother* stands for a different relation: Orville Wright bore that relation to Wilbur Wright.

The entities that expressions stand for—a woman, a set of horses, a relation—these are called **extensions**. The extension of an expression is determined by its meaning along with facts about the world. To a considerable degree, the truth value of a sentence is determined by both the extensions of the words in that sentence and the syntax of the sentence. We will use that idea as a starting point for our study of the semantics of English. For much of this course, we will be developing semantic rules that will take us from word extensions, via syntactic structure, to truth values for sentences. We will judge our progress in terms of how closely the system we develop tracks the intuitions speakers have about the truth of a sentence in different situations. In (11) above, we offered a formula describing a path from facts to truth values. We can now elaborate that path making reference to extensions:

(12) word meanings + facts about the world → extensions.
       extensions + syntax → truth value.

Unlike (11) above, (12) makes no reference to truth conditions, but the paths laid out in (11) and (12) are related. A sentence has truth conditions that determine whether or not it is true:

• When the truth conditions are met, the extensions of the words along with the syntax yield an assignment of TRUE.

• When the truth conditions are not met, the extensions of the words along with the syntax yield an assignment of FALSE.

Exercise (1.6)

[A] Describe how the world would be if the nouns *doctor* and *woman* had the same extension.

[B] Suppose the world was as you described in [A] and so the nouns *doctor* and *woman* had the same extension. For each pair of sentences below, decide whether under those circumstances, it would be possible for one sentence in the pair to be true and the other false. If it's possible, describe a situation in which one of the sentences is true and the other false. If it's not possible, write "must be same truth value."

(i) A woman bought Arash's apartment. A doctor bought Arash's apartment.

(ii) Every woman in Arash's neighborhood owns a car. Every doctor in Arash's neighborhood owns a car.

(iii) The woman who bought Arash's car lives in Monsey. The doctor who bought Arash's car lives in Monsey.

(iv) Arash lives above the woman who bought Amaya's car. The doctor who bought Amaya's car lives above Arash.

(v) Some doctor liked the president's speech. Some woman didn't like the president's speech.

[C] Is it possible for two sentences of English to have the same truth value but different truth conditions? If so, provide an example.

[D] Is it possible for two sentences of English to have the same truth conditions but different truth values? If so, provide an example.

Exercise (1.7)

Above we asserted that sentences can be true or false; they have truth conditions. While this is the case for many sentences, such as the examples used in the text, it is not the case for all sentences. Attempt to provide one or more examples of grammatical sentences whose form indicates that they are not capable of being true or false—in other words, sentences for which it makes no sense to ask if they are true or false. <u>Note</u>: We're looking for sentences that cannot be true or false—not sentences whose truth value we cannot know because we lack the relevant facts.

Exercise (1.8)

Reconsider the Q'eqchi' sentence provided in (9), repeated below, and figure 1.2, also reproduced here. It turns out that the truth conditions of (9) are met in the left box of figure 1.2, and they are not met in the right box of figure 1.2. The sentence in (13) below has the opposite truth conditions.

(9) Li oxxukuut wan rub'el li kaaxukuut.

(13) Li kaaxukuut wan rub'el li oxxukuut.

[A] The truth conditions of (13) are met in the right box of figure 1.2 but not in left box of figure 1.2. Come up with a hypothesis about the meanings of the words making up those sentences. In particular, you should

(i) Make a list of the words used in the Q'eqchi' sentences. Next to each word, provide its English translation according to your hypothesis.

(ii) Based on your translations, provide the extensions for the words *kaaxukuut* and *oxxukuut*.

[B] Hypothesize about the meanings of the morphemes making up the words *kaaxukuut* and *oxxukuut*.

Up to this point, we've established that semantic rules need to take syntactic structure as input and that they need to be capable of producing meanings out of combinations of other

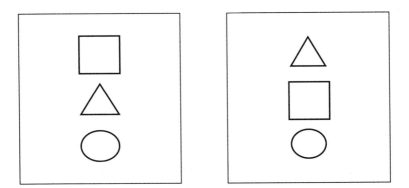

Figure 1.2
Geometric shapes.

meanings. These ideas are summarized in the second line of the formula in (12) above. But what do such rules look like? Logicians have addressed this question in some detail, as we will see in the next chapter, where we will look at how logicians define and interpret symbolic languages.

Key Ideas

• A grammar generates a set of sentences paired with meanings.

• In developing a grammar, we focus on meaning-related notions: truth conditions, truth values, and extensions.

• Truth conditions, together with whatever facts obtain in the world, determine the truth value of a sentence.

• The meaning of a word, together with whatever facts obtain in the world, determine its extension.

• A goal of semantic theory is to develop semantic rules that will take us from word extensions, via syntactic structure, to truth values for sentences.

• We will judge our progress in terms of how closely the system we develop tracks the intuitions speakers have about the truth of a sentence in different situations.

New Terminology

• truth conditions

• truth values

• extensions

• individual

• set

• relation

1.4 Entailment and Synonymy

Consider the following pair of sentences:

(14) On July 11, Nadir clumsily assembled a metal bookcase.

(15) Nadir assembled a bookcase on July 11.

There are various possible situations in which (14) would be true. It may be that Nadir assembled the bookcase at home, at his friend's house, or in a store. He might have done so while listening to music or while talking to a friend. But no matter what situation makes (14) true, it will also make (15) true. In this case we say that (14) **entails** (15). The reverse does not hold. There are situations that would make (15) true that would not make

(14) true—for example, if Nadir assembled a wooden bookcase on July 11 and that was all he assembled. In other words, (15) does not entail (14). Compare that to the following pair of sentences:

(16) Nadir sold a car to Gadarine.

(17) Gadarine bought a car from Nadir.

It is not possible for there to be a situation in which (16) is true and (17) is false. And it is not possible for there to be a situation in which (17) is true and (16) is false. In other words, (16) and (17) entail each other. In this case, we say that they are **synonymous**.

Entailment and synonymy are relations that hold between sentences by virtue of their truth conditions. They therefore offer another source of data to test the grammars we will be constructing. Speakers have the intuition that (14) entails (15). If our grammar accurately captures our intuitions, then for any situation where the grammar assigns TRUE to (14), it will also assign TRUE to (15). And if the grammar doesn't do that, it will need to be revised.

Exercise (1.9)

[A] For each pair of sentences in (18)–(20) below, try to find a situation in which the first member of the pair is true and the second false, and then try to find a situation in which the second is true and the first false. In some cases, this won't be possible because of entailment relations holding between the two sentences. Report your results using the symbol '⊨' to mean "entails," as follows:

(i) If (a) entails (b), write '(a) ⊨ (b)'. If (a) doesn't entail (b), describe a situation that makes (a) true and (b) false.

(ii) If (b) entails (a), write '(b) ⊨ (a)'. If (b) doesn't entail (a), describe a situation that makes (b) true and (a) false.

(18) a. Nadir is older than Gadarine.
      b. Gadarine is younger than Nadir.

(19) a. Jeremy lives in Düsseldorf.
      b. Akna lives in Düsseldorf.

(20) a. Amaya owns a submarine.
      b. Amaya owns a yellow submarine.

[B] There is something not quite right about saying that (21)a below entails (21)b. Say what the problem is and offer a way to describe the intuitive semantic relationship that holds between the two sentences:

(21) a. Arash ate a burrito that was very hot.
      b. Arash ate something that was very spicy.

New Terminology

- synonymy
- entailment

Applications

- A grammar that assigns truth conditions to sentences can be tested against speaker intuitions about entailment.

- To show that one sentence does <u>not</u> entail another, you need to describe a situation in which the first is true and the second is false.

✪ Important Practice and Looking Ahead ✪

Assessing the truth value of a sentence in a given situation, detecting entailment relations, and producing unambiguous paraphrase are skills that a semanticist needs, and they all take practice. The examples in the text above are fairly straightforward. But other examples can be tricky. The exercises below give you a taste of the challenges. Examples like the ones used in these exercises will be of central importance in the chapters ahead.

Exercise (1.10)

There are two situations depicted in figure 1.3: s_1 and s_2. The circles in those diagrams are touching triangles. Choose the situation in which it is true that *exactly one triangle is touching every circle.*

Exercise (1.11)

In which, if any, of the two situations, s_1 and s_2, depicted in figure 1.3 is the following sentence true? *At least one triangle is touching no circle.*

Exercise (1.12)

There are two situations depicted in figure 1.4: s_3 and s_4. In which situation is the following sentence true? *Between one and three triangles are touching every square, but only one triangle is touching every circle.*

Exercise (1.13)

In which, if any, of the two situations, s_3 and s_4, depicted in figure 1.4, is the following sentence true? *At least one triangle is touching no circle.*

Figure 1.3
Geometric shapes.

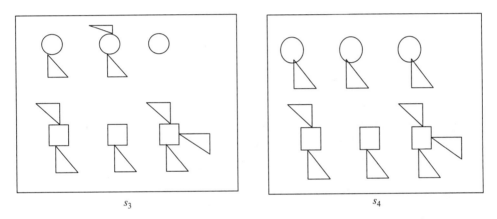

Figure 1.4
Geometric shapes.

Exercise (1.14)

In the diagram in figure 1.5, there are three squares, a line, and a circle. The diagram depicts a situation in which the following is true: *Every square is above the line.*

[A] If possible, draw a diagram depicting a situation in which (i) below is true and (ii) below is false. If it is not possible, write: '(i) ⊨ (ii)'.

(i) It is not the case that every square is above the line.

(ii) Every square is such that it is not above the line.

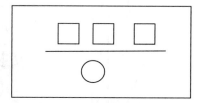

Figure 1.5
Geometric shapes.

[B] If possible, draw a diagram depicting a situation in which (ii) above is true and (i) above is false. If it is not possible, write: '(ii) ⊨ (i)'.

Exercise (1.15)

Figure 1.6 has two circles and two triangles. The diagram depicts a situation in which the following is true: *A circle is touching two triangles.*

[A] Draw a diagram depicting a situation in which (i) below is true and (ii) below is false. If it is not possible, write: '(i) ⊨ (ii)'.

(i) There is exactly one triangle such that it is touching every circle.

(ii) For every circle, there is exactly one triangle that is touching it.

[B] Draw a diagram depicting a situation in which (ii) above is true and (i) above is false. If it is not possible, write: '(ii) ⊨ (i)'. You can use one of the diagrams $s_1\_s_4$ from previous exercises, if it fits the requirements.

Exercise (1.16)

After doing exercise (1.5) and exercise (1.10) through exercise (1.15), reflect on the following questions. Ideally, this should be done after pooling answers by the entire class.

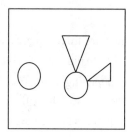

Figure 1.6
Geometric shapes.

[A] Which of the following sentences is ambiguous?

Exactly one triangle is touching every circle.
At least one triangle is touching no circle.
Every square is not above the line.
Every passenger was not examined.

[B] For some of the sentences in [A] that are ambiguous, there is an entailment relation between the readings of the sentences. For which sentences is there an entailment relation between the two readings? (Note: This logical fact is relevant in experimental and acquisition contexts where it is often the case that one can get evidence that a sentence is true but one can't get evidence that a sentence is false. In those settings, it is difficult to find evidence for an ambiguity when one reading entails the other.)

1.5 Set Theory

Semantic rules are often written using the language of elementary set theory. We already saw above that the extension of the noun *horse* is the set of all horses. It will be helpful, therefore, to say a few words about sets before we dive into semantics.

A set has **members**. Copán is a member of the set of all cities in Honduras. The number 5 is a member of the set of numbers greater than 2. There is no constraint on what can be a member of a set. And elements of a set do not have to have anything in common. There is a set whose members are the sun, the number 5, and all the stars in the Milky Way. The members of a set are also called **elements** of the set.

The word *class* is sometimes used synonymously with *set*, although within modern set theory these terms are not synonymous.

A set is completely defined by its members. That means that if you remove an element from a set, you've got a different set. And if you add an element, again you have a different set. In this respect, sets are different from groups of people. We might say that the committee that passed resolution A is the same committee that passed resolution B, regardless of the fact that the composition of the committee changed between resolutions. Or Jack might say his family lived in Paterson in 1990 and in Jefferson in 1995, even though the family grew between 1990 and 1995. It's regarded as the same family, but the set that is comprised of the members of his family in 1990 is a different set from the one that is comprised of the members of his family in 1995.

The symbol '$\in$' is used to mean "is a member of." So, if E is the set of all even numbers, (22) below is true and (23) is false.

(22) $4 \in E$ (true). E is the set of all even numbers.

(23) $5 \in E$ (false).

The symbol '$\notin$' is used to mean "is not a member of." So, if E is the set of all even numbers, (24) below is false and (25) is true.

(24) $4 \notin E$ (false). E is the set of all even numbers.

(25) $5 \notin E$ (true).

There are several ways to describe a set. One way is to list the elements. For that we can use **list notation** in which the elements are enclosed in curly brackets: {3, 5, 7}. Since a set is completely defined by its members, it doesn't matter how they are ordered in the list: {3, 5, 7} = {5, 7, 3}. This is intuitive. Whether we list the names of the students in our class in alphabetical order or in reverse alphabetical order, it is the same set of students that we've listed.

Generally lowercase letters from the beginning of the alphabet are used to name non-sets, and uppercase letters from the beginning of the alphabet are used to name sets:

(26) B = {a, b, d, m}   K = {a, d}   C = {d}.

Notice that the set C in (26) consists of just one element. That is called a **singleton set**. This is one place where the meaning of the technical term *set* diverges from the colloquial meaning of the word *set*.

A set can have many elements. In fact, there are sets that have an infinite number of elements. When sets are large, it becomes unwieldy or impossible to name the set using list notation. In that case, we make use of another option known as **predicate notation**, also sometimes referred to as **definition by condition**. This option, which is enclosed in curly brackets, uses a letter from the end of the alphabet as a variable, and after a colon, states the condition on which membership in the set depends. Here is an example:

(27) $\{x : x$ lives in Banjul}.

The expression in (27) names the set of all individuals who live in Banjul. The notation is read as: "the set of all x, such that x lives in Banjul." The following statement is true:

(28) $d \in \{x : x$ lives in Banjul} if and only if d lives in Banjul.

And similarly, the following statements are all true:

(29) $c \in \{y :$ Rihanna knows $y\}$ if and only if Rihanna knows c.

(30) $a \in \{x :$ Akna is taller than $x\}$ if and only if Akna is taller than a.

(31) $5 \in \{z : 1 + z = 9\}$ if and only if $1 + 5 = 9$.

(32) $b \in \{x :$ Amaya likes x and x is short} if and only if Amaya likes b and b is short.

Notice that the statements in (28)–(32) all use the expression *if and only if*. That expression is common in definitions and is often abbreviated as *iff*. *If and only if* is stronger than *if* by itself. Here's an example to show that. Suppose Natchaya gets angry easily. One of the things that ticks her off is when people leave the garage door open. On our way home, I might say: *If the garage door is open, Natchaya will be angry.* If we come home to find

Natchaya in a rage and the garage door closed, we might try to figure out what has angered her this time. We would not necessarily conclude that my statement on the way home was false. On the other hand, we would conclude that I had been mistaken if I had said: *If the garage door is open and only if the garage door is open will Natchaya be angry.*

A single set can be the result of combining two sets. There are two standard ways of combining sets: **union** and **intersection**. The union of two sets is the result of combining all the members of both sets. The symbol for union is '∪'. Here are two examples:

(33) $(\{a, b, c\} \cup \{1, 2\}) = \{a,b,c,1,2\}$.

(34) $(\{x : x \text{ lives in Banjul}\} \cup \{y : y \text{ lives in Perth}\}) = \{z : z \text{ lives in Banjul or Perth}\}$.

The intersection of two sets contains just those elements that the two sets have in common. The symbol for intersection is '∩'. Here are two examples:

(35) $(\{a, b, c\} \cap \{b, c, d\}) = \{b,c\}$.

(36) $(\{x : x \text{ rides a bike}\} \cap \{y : y \text{ lives in Perth}\}) = \{z : z \text{ rides a bike and lives in Perth}\}$.

Consider now, the following pairs of sets:

(37) a. $\{a, b, c\}$.
　　 b. $\{a, b, c, d, e\}$.

(38) a. $\{x : x \text{ lives in Washington, DC}\}$.
　　 b. $\{x : x \text{ lives in the United States}\}$.

In both cases, the elements in the first set are also elements in the second set. For example, $a \in \{a,b,c\}$ and $a \in \{a, b, c, d, e\}$, and anyone who lives in Washington, DC, also lives in the United States. When sets are related in this way, we say the first is a subset of the second. The symbol '⊆' is used to name the **subset relation**. It's defined in (39), and thus the statements in (40) are true:

(39) For any sets A and B, $A \subseteq B$ *iff* every element of A is also an element of B.

(40) $\{a, b, c\} \subseteq \{a, b, c, d, e\}$.

(41) $\{x : x \text{ lives in Washington, DC}\} \subseteq \{x : x \text{ lives in the United States}\}$.

Exercise (1.17)

[A] Fill in the blank below in a way that doesn't use any set theory notation. That is, use only colloquial English.

$c \in \{y : y \text{ is hungry or } y \text{ is tired}\}$ *iff* _____.

[B] Use predicate notation to name the set of numbers that are greater than 2 and less than 69.

[C] Which of the following statements is true and which is false?

(i) $c \in \{a,b,c\}$.

(ii) $d \notin \{a,b,c\}$.

(iii) If $a \in \{z : z$ is a city and z is in Mexico$\}$, then $a \in \{z : z$ is a city$\}$.

(iv) $b \in \{z : z$ is a square and z has exactly three sides$\}$.

(v) $c \subseteq \{a,b,c\}$.

(vi) $\{c\} \subseteq \{a,b,c\}$.

(vii) $\{a,b,c,d\} \subseteq \{a,b,c\}$.

(viii) $\{a,b,c\} \subseteq \{a,b,c\}$.

(ix) $\{y : y$ rides a bike and lives in Perth$\} \subseteq \{z : z$ lives in Perth$\}$.

[D] What are the elements of the following set? ($\{1, 2, 3, 4\} \cap \{n : n$ is a number greater than 2$\}$)

Exercise (1.18)

Assume that the set A is the extension of the noun *astronaut* and the set D is the extension of the noun *doctor*.

[A] Fill in the blanks below in a way that doesn't use any set theory notation. That is, use only colloquial English.

$b \in (A \cap D)$ *iff* _____.

$d \in (A \cup D)$ *iff* _____.

[B] Suppose that the truth conditions are met for the sentence *There are exactly two astronauts who are doctors*. What does that tell you about the set $(A \cap D)$? What about the set $(A \cup D)$?

New Terminology

- member
- element
- list notation
- singleton set
- predicate notation
- intersection
- union

1.6 Lexicons

Throughout much of the course, we will be studying how meanings of expressions of various sizes are combined to form meanings of larger expressions. But to get the ball rolling, our grammar will have to include word meanings, and we'll need a way to make reference to the meaning of a particular word. To make this precise, we'll introduce a formal device that works like a dictionary—namely, a **lexicon**—and then we'll introduce notation corresponding to "finding a meaning in the dictionary" and "adding words to a dictionary."

Let's begin by reflecting a bit on how dictionaries commonly work. Below are a few entries from an online dictionary of English:

red adjective \'red\ : having the color of blood
read verb \'rēd\ : to look at and understand the meaning of letters, words, symbols, etc
reed noun \'rēd\ : a tall, thin grass that grows in wet areas

Each word, identified by its spelling, syntactic category and pronunciation, is paired with a description of its meaning. In the simplest case, then, a dictionary is a <u>set</u> of entries, each entry being a <u>pair</u> of an expression and a meaning description.

Table 1.1 provides some entries from a Q'eqchi'-English dictionary.[3]

Once again, the dictionary is a set of pairs, each pair consisting of a word that is defined and its definition. In this case, the defined words are Q'eqchi', and the definitions are expressions of English. To look a word up in a dictionary is to find the item that is paired with that word in an entry in the dictionary. In table 1.1, *sulul* is paired with *mud*, so according to that dictionary *sulul* means mud.

To formalize these ideas, we introduce the mathematical term **ordered pair**. An ordered pair $\langle a, b \rangle$ consists of two elements: a is the first element of the pair, and b is the second. The pair $\langle a, b \rangle$ is distinct from the pair $\langle b, a \rangle$. This contrasts with sets where order plays no role. Recall that $\{3, 5, 7\} = \{5, 7, 3\}$.

Let *QE* be the set of ordered pairs whose first element is a Q'eqchi' word from table 1.1 and whose second element is the English expression in the adjacent column. The following statements are true:

$\langle sulul, \text{mud} \rangle \in QE.$ $\langle palaw, \text{sea} \rangle \in QE.$

$\langle sulul, \text{sea} \rangle \notin QE.$ $\langle \text{mud}, sulul \rangle \notin QE.$

Table 1.1
Q'eqchi'-English dictionary.

ch'och'	land	choxa	sky	pek	stone or rock
ch'ina ha'	spring	ha'	water	po	moon
ch'och'	soil	k'iche'	forest	saq'e	sun
chahim	star	nima'	river or stream	sulul	mud
che'	wood	ochoch pek	cave	tzuul	mountain or hill
chi re ha'	shore	palaw	sea		

To look a word up in the dictionary is to locate that word and then to check what it is paired with. The following statement introduces the notation '$F(...)$', which corresponds to that activity:

$F(...)$ notation

If F is a set of pairs and α is a first element of exactly one of the pairs in F, then $F(\alpha)$ is the second element of the pair in F whose first element is α.

Here are a couple of true statements:

$QE(sulul) =$ mud.

$QE(palaw) =$ sea.

Above, we looked at some entries from an online dictionary of English. If we let *Dict* name the set of pairs of words and definitions in that dictionary, then the following is true:

$Dict(reed) =$ a tall, thin grass that grows in wet areas.

It follows from the '$F(...)$' notation that if $F(x) = y$, then $\langle x,y \rangle \in F$.

Exercise (1.19)

[A] Using table 1.1, fill in the blanks below so that the resulting statement is true:

(i) $QE(ha') = $ _____ .

(ii) $QE(choxa) = $ _____ .

(iii) $QE($_____$) = $ moon.

[B] If α and β were words defined in the online dictionary above, under what circumstances would the following be true? $Dict(\alpha) = Dict(\beta)$.

Exercise (1.20)

[A] Let $G = \{\langle a, \square \rangle, \langle b, \Diamond \rangle, \langle c, O \rangle, \langle d, \nabla \rangle, \langle e, \Delta \rangle\}$.

Assume the facts depicted in figure 1.7. For each of the statements below, create a true statement by inserting in the blank an expression of the form '$G(\alpha)$' where α is a, b, c, d, or e and G is the set of pairs defined above.

(i) $G(a)$ is directly above _____ .

(ii) $G(a)$ is right next to _____ .

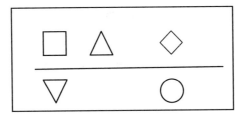

Figure 1.7
Geometric shapes.

(iii) $G(b)$ is directly above _____.

[B] Let R be a set of pairs defined as follows:

$R = \{\langle a, 1\rangle, \langle b, 2\rangle, \langle P, \{1,2,3\}\rangle, \langle B, \{2,3,4\}\rangle\}$.

Fill in the blanks below so that the resulting statements are true.

(i) $R(a) =$ _____.

(ii) $R(b) =$ _____.

(iii) $R(B) =$ _____.

Which of the following statements, if any, are true?

(i) $R(a) \in R(P)$.

(ii) $R(a) \in R(B)$.

(iii) $R(b) \in R(P)$.

(iv) $R(b) \in R(B)$.

The definition of $F(...)$ notation requires α to be the first element of exactly one of the pairs in F. This notation is based on ideas about mathematical **functions**. A definition follows.

A **function** is a set of pairs. The first elements of those pairs form the domain of the function, and every element in the domain is the first element of exactly one pair in the set of pairs.

With this definition in mind, we can think of a restaurant menu as a function whose domain is the set of all dishes served. The function assigns to each dish the price of that dish.

Exercise (1.21)

The Q'eqchi'-English dictionary in table 1.1 is not a function. Why not?

✪ Important Practice and Looking Ahead ✪

Below you will find an exercise giving you further practice with functions. The exercise gives you a glimpse of how we can use set theory to write the extension of a relation, a topic that will be central in chapter 2 and beyond.

Exercise (1.22)

Suppose K is a set of pairs whose first elements are all people and where each person is paired with the set of people who know that person. We can write this as

$K = \{\ \langle x, Y \rangle : x$ is a person and Y is the set of all the people that know $x\}$.

[A] Explain how K fits the definition above for *function*.

[B] What is the domain of K?

[C] Write a sentence in colloquial English that says what the following set-theoretical statement says: Gadarine $\in K$(Nadir).

So far we have considered two kinds of dictionaries. In the first, words are paired with descriptions of their meanings. In the second, words in one language are paired with words from another language. Given the goals of the course, our focus will be on a lexicon in which an expression of the language is paired with an extension. For example, the name *Dilma Rousseff* would be paired with the woman who was elected president of Brazil in 2011 and the noun *horse* would be paired with the set of all horses.

During one's life, especially the earlier part, one constructs a mental lexicon that grows with time. Entries are added to create a new, expanded lexicon. To formalize that idea, we'll introduce a notation, '$M+ \langle ..., ... \rangle$', for adding a new pair to a set of pairs:

$M+ \langle ..., ... \rangle$ notation

If M is a set of pairs that does not include a pair whose first element is α, then $M + \langle \alpha, \beta \rangle$ is a set that consists of the pairs in M plus the pair $\langle \alpha, \beta \rangle$.

So now the following statement is true: $\{\ \langle 1,2 \rangle, \langle 3,4 \rangle, \langle 5,6 \rangle \ \} + \langle 7,8 \rangle = \{\ \langle 1,2 \rangle, \langle 3,4 \rangle, \langle 5,6 \rangle, \langle 7,8 \rangle \ \}$.

As another example, consider the Q'eqchi' word *ak'ach*, which is not defined in the Q'eqchi'-English dictionary entries in table 1.1, repeated below.

Since *ak'ach* is not an element of one of the pairs in QE, the expression '$QE(ak'ach)$' is **undefined**. It turns out that *ak'ach* means *turkey*. We can add that word to our dictionary,

Table 1.1
Q'eqchi'-English dictionary

ch'och'	land	choxa	sky	pek	stone or rock
ch'ina ha'	spring	ha'	water	po	moon
ch'och'	soil	k'iche'	forest	saq'e	sun
chahim	star	nima'	river or stream	sulul	mud
che'	wood	ochoch pek	cave	tzuul	mountain or hill
chi re ha'	shore	palaw	sea		

to create a new, expanded dictionary. We refer to the expanded dictionary as: $QE+ \langle ak'ach,$ turkey$\rangle$. And the following are true statements:

$QE+ \langle ak'ach,$ turkey$\rangle$ $(ak'ach)=$ turkey.

$QE+ \langle ak'ach,$ turkey$\rangle$ $(sulul)=$ mud.

The second statement says that the definition of *sulul* in the expanded dictionary is mud, just as it was before the expansion. This process of expansion can be repeated. If we discover that the word *mes* means cat, we can add this to get an even larger dictionary in which the following are true:

$QE+ \langle ak'ach,$ turkey$\rangle + \langle mes,$ cat$\rangle$ $(mes)=$ cat.

$QE+ \langle ak'ach,$ turkey$\rangle + \langle mes,$ cat$\rangle$ $(ak'ach)=$ turkey.

$QE+ \langle ak'ach,$ turkey$\rangle + \langle mes,$ cat$\rangle$ $(sulul)=$ mud.

These statements give the meanings of the words *mes*, *ak'ach*, and *sulul* in the expanded dictionary.

✪ Important Practice and Looking Ahead ✪

Below you will find an exercise giving you practice with M+ $\langle..., ... \rangle$ notation. This notation will be crucial in chapter 2, when we introduce semantic rules for quantifier expressions.

Exercise (1.23)

[A] S is a set of pairs whose first elements are: a, b, c, P. The pairings are as follows: a is paired with Abraham Lincoln (the sixteenth president of the United States), b is paired with the novelist Charlotte Brontë, c is paired with Marie Curie (the co-discoverer of radium), and P is paired with the set of all US presidents. The pairing with P can also be described this way:

$\langle P, \{x : x$ is a U.S. president$\}\rangle \in S$.

Which of the following are true statements?

(i) $S(a) \in S(P)$.

(ii) $S(b) \in S(P)$.

(iii) $S(c) \in S(P)$.

Now we add the pair whose first element is d and whose second element is Dwight David Eisenhower (the thirty-fourth president of the United States). Which of the following is a true statement?

(iv) $S+ \langle d, \text{Eisenhower} \rangle (a) \in S(P)$.

(v) $S+ \langle d, \text{Eisenhower} \rangle (c) \in S(P)$.

(vi) $S+ \langle d, \text{Eisenhower} \rangle (b) \in S(P)$.

(vii) $S+ \langle d, \text{Eisenhower} \rangle (d) \in S(P)$.

[B] Let $T = \{\langle 1, \$ \rangle, \langle 2, \# \rangle\}$.

(i) Use list notation to name the set $T+ \langle 3, @ \rangle$.

(ii) Use list notation to name the set $T+ \langle 3, @ \rangle + \langle 4, \% \rangle$.

(iii) Put a single symbol in each blank below to make the statement true. If the expression to the left of the equal sign is undefined, then just write 'undefined' in the blank.

a. $T(3) = $ _____ .

b. $T+ \langle 3, @ \rangle (3) = $ _____ .

c. $T+ \langle 3, @ \rangle + \langle 4, \% \rangle (3) = $ _____ .

Here's a question that is addressed in research on bilingualism: Does a bilingual person have two mental dictionaries to recognize the words in each language, or a single combined dictionary? We can extend our plus notation to allow us a simple specification of what a combined dictionary is:

[$M + N$] notation

Let M and N be two sets of pairs.

If M and N have no first elements in common, then [$M+N$] is defined.

If [$M+N$] is defined, then it consists of all the pairs in M along with all the pairs in N.

According to this definition, if

$H = \{ \langle a, 1 \rangle, \langle b, 2 \rangle, \langle d, 0 \rangle \}$, and

$J = \{ \langle c, 9 \rangle , \langle d, 12 \rangle \}$,

then $[H+J]$ is not defined. That's because they have a first element, d, in common. On the other hand, if

$R = \{ \langle a, 1 \rangle , \langle b, 2 \rangle , \langle P, \{1,2,3\} \rangle , \langle B, \{2,3,4\} \rangle \}$,

and

$C = \{ \langle c, 9 \rangle , \langle d, 0 \rangle \}$,

then $[R+C]$ is defined, and

$[R+C] = \{ \langle a, 1 \rangle , \langle b, 2 \rangle , \langle P, \{1,2,3\} \rangle , \langle B, \{2,3,4\} \rangle , \langle c, 9 \rangle , \langle d, 0 \rangle \}$.

It follows from the definition that if $[M+N]$ is defined, then $[M+N] = (M \cup N)$, where '$\cup$' stands for set-union, as defined in section 1.5. The square brackets will often be left off where no ambiguity exists, so we'll just write '$M+N$'.

So now, if *Eng* is the mental lexicon of a monolingual speaker of English and *Aram* is the mental lexicon of a monolingual speaker of Aramaic, then [*Eng+Aram*] could be the combined lexicon possessed by a bilingual speaker of English and Aramaic.

Exercise (1.24)

[A] Which one of the following expressions is undefined (*QE* is the dictionary in table 1.1)

(i) [Eng+*QE*](*sulul*)

(ii) *QE*(*sulul*)

(iii) *Eng*(*sulul*)

(iv) [Eng+*QE*]+ ⟨*jun*, one⟩ (*sulul*)

[B] *S* is a set of pairs whose first elements are *a*, *b*, *c*, *P*; *a* is paired with Abraham Lincoln (the sixteenth president of the United States), *b* is paired with the novelist Charlotte Brontë, *c* is paired with Marie Curie (the co-discoverer of radium), and *P* is paired with the set of all U.S. presidents.

D is a set of pairs whose first elements are 1, 2, 3, *A*; 1 is paired with the physicist Albert Einstein, 2 is paired with *S*(*b*), 3 is paired with *S*(*c*) and *A* is paired with the set of all scientists. Which of the following is true?

(i) [*S+D*](1) ∈ [*S+D*](*P*).

(ii) [*S+D*](*c*) ∈ [*S+D*](*A*).

(iii) [*S+D*](3) ∈ [*S+D*](*A*).

(iv) [*S+D*](*b*) = [*S+D*](2).

Key Ideas

- In some dictionaries, a word is paired with a description of its meaning(s).
- In some dictionaries, a word is paired with a word from another language.
- In this class, we'll focus on a lexicon in which an expression of the language is paired with an extension.
  - To "look up a word" we select a pair in the lexicon in which the word we're after is the first element and we identify the second element of the pair.
  - A lexicon can be augmented by adding pairs to it.
  - Two lexicons can be combined by pooling the pairs in them.

Definitions

F(...) notation

If F is a set of pairs and α is a first element of exactly one of the pairs in F, then $F(\alpha)$ is the second element of the pair in F whose first element is α.

M+ ⟨..., ... ⟩ notation

If M is a set of pairs that does not include a pair whose first element is α, then $M+\langle\alpha, \beta\rangle$ is a set that consists of the pairs in M plus the pair $\langle\alpha, \beta\rangle$.

[M+N] notation

Let M and N be two sets of pairs.

If M and N have no first elements in common, then $[M+N]$ is defined.

If $[M+N]$ is defined, then it consists of all the pairs in M along with all the pairs in N.

New Terminology

- lexicon
- ordered pair
- undefined
- function

Further Reading

Carnie, Andrew. *Constituent Structure*. Oxford: Oxford University Press, 2010.

Jacobson, Pauline. "Constituent Structure." In *Concise Encyclopedia of Syntactic Theories*, edited by E. K. Brown and J. E. Miller, 54–68. Oxford: Pergamon, 1996.

Partee, Barbara H., Alice ter Meulen, and Robert E. Wall. *Mathematical Methods in Linguistics*. Studies in Linguistics and Philosophy, Vol. 30. Dordrecht: Kluwer Academic, 1993.

The Stanford Encyclopedia of Philosophy. https://plato.stanford.edu. See especially the following entries: Ambiguity (by Adam Sennet); Compositionality (by Zoltán Gendler Szabó); Early Development of Set Theory (by José Ferreirós); Set Theory (by Joan Bagaria); Truth (by Michael Glanzberg); Truth Values (by Yaroslav Shramko and Heinrich Wansing).

2   Symbolic Logic

In this chapter, we will introduce a symbolic logic language, which we call *SL*. We'll be using symbolic logic in subsequent chapters as part of our grammar of English.

SL did not come into being the way a natural language would. It was designed from scratch. In designing such a language, one has to figure out how to describe all the sentences of the language and to say what the interpretation is for each one. This is a difficult task, and, in fact, it took a very long time for logicians to find a way do that kind of thing. To appreciate what has been achieved, it often helps to pause and understand what problem is being solved. This is especially the case with **variables** to be discussed in section 2.3.

Foreign language courses often begin by teaching individual words and some basic rules for combining them. Formal language learning begins the same way, even if the rules themselves are formulated differently. Once you learn the rules and practice applying them to several examples, you start to get an intuition about what a grammatical sentence looks like and what it says. While it takes some work in the beginning, this can be a rewarding experience. Seeing an entire language come to life in this way leads one to reflect on how natural languages are defined and learned. Indeed, such reflections led to the birth of **generative grammar**.[1]

2.1   Atomic Sentences and Their Parts

The simplest sentences of SL are called **atomic sentences**. Like the atoms of the physical universe, they themselves have smaller parts. These parts are of two kinds.

One kind is an **individual constant**. It resembles a proper name of English. A lexicon for this language pairs each individual constant with an individual. We will use proper names of English as individual constants of SL, as well as small letters in the beginning of the alphabet.

Another kind of symbol used to make an atomic sentence is a **predicate**. An atomic sentence can be formed by combining individual constants with a predicate. Predicates are divided into classes, depending on the number of individual constants that they combine with. A **one-place predicate** combines with a single individual constant to make an atomic sentence; a **two-place predicate** combines with two individual constants to make an atomic sentence. A lexicon for this language pairs each one-place predicate with a set, and each two-place predicate with a relation. Whether an atomic sentence is true or false is determined by these sets and relations, along with whatever the individual constants in the sentence stand for.

We will use capitalized words of English as our predicate symbols. In an atomic sentence containing a one-place predicate, the predicate precedes the individual constant, which is enclosed in parentheses. Suppose we have a lexicon L according to which 'Clever' stands for the set of clever individuals, and 'Agatha' stands for Agatha. Then 'Clever(Agatha)' is a sentence in SL that corresponds to the English sentence *Agatha is clever*. Likewise, if according to L, 'Happy' stands for the set of all happy individuals, and 'Frank' stands for Frank, then 'Happy(Frank)' is a sentence that corresponds to *Frank is happy*.

In an atomic sentence containing a two-place predicate, the predicate is followed by two individual constants, each enclosed in parentheses. If we have a lexicon according to which 'Likes' stands for the liking relation, then 'Likes(Mary)(Sue)' is a sentence in SL corresponding to the English sentence *Sue likes Mary*, and 'Likes(Sue)(Mary)' corresponds to *Mary likes Sue*. While English generally uses subject-verb-object order (SVO), SL is more of a verb-object-subject (VOS) language.

As mentioned, the interpretation of a symbol of SL is determined by a lexicon. The same sentence may be true relative to one lexicon and false relative to another. Suppose that Alan is clever but that he is not tall, and suppose we have two different lexicons, L and K. According to lexicon L, 'Clever' stands for the set of clever individuals, and 'Alan' stands for Alan. 'Clever(Alan)' is true relative to lexicon L. According to lexicon K, 'Clever' stands for the set of tall individuals, and 'Alan' stands for Alan. 'Clever(Alan)' is false relative to lexicon K. This role of the lexicon influences how we write semantic rules and how we talk about translation. Since the lexicon determines the meanings of vocabulary items, our rules for interpreting phrases of SL will all be stated relative to a choice of a lexicon.

Turning to translation, observe that the word *palaw* is judged to be a good Q'eqchi' translation for *sea* because those two words have the same extension. Likewise, 'Clever' is a good translation for the English word *clever* relative to lexicon L but not relative to lexicon K. That's because the interpretation of 'Clever' relative to L is the same as the extension of the English word *clever*, while the interpretation of 'Clever' relative to K is not the same as the extension of the English word *clever*. As a result of this difference, 'Clever(Alan)' is a good translation for the English sentence *Alan is clever* relative to lexicon L but not relative to lexicon K. In our discussion below we will refer to various lexicons for SL, but among them there is one that will be of particular interest. That is the lexicon that assigns to the symbols of SL the same extension as the corresponding word of English. So for example, it will assign to 'Clever' the set of clever individuals, and to 'Agatha' the individual called *Agatha*. We refer to that particular lexicon as L.

Exercise (2.1)

Describe how the world would have to be for (i) below to be true. Do the same for (ii) The symbol '$\varnothing$' stands for a set that is empty. In other words, it has no elements.

(i) $(L(\text{Lawyer}) \cap L(\text{Doctor})) = \varnothing$.

(ii) $(L(\text{Lawyer}) \cup L(\text{Doctor})) = \varnothing$.

Before continuing, we should clarify a typographical aspect of the presentation so far. There is an abundance of single quotation marks (' ') and italics in the text above. This has to do with the **use-mention distinction**. To understand what that is about, consider the two English sentences below:

(1) Tegucigalpa is the capital of Honduras.

(2) *Tegucigalpa* starts with a consonant.

The sentence in (1) is about a city. The sentence in (2) is about a word. Correspondingly, the subject of (1) stands for the city and the subject of (2) stands for a word. The word *Tegucigalpa* is <u>used</u> in (1). The word *Tegucigalpa* is <u>mentioned</u> in (2) and this is indicated in (2) with italics. In this text, we use single quotation marks to indicate that a symbol or phrase of SL is mentioned, and we use italics to indicate that a word or phrase of a natural language, usually English, is mentioned. Generally, when you see the mention-quotation marks or mention-italics, you can read them as: "the phrase/word/symbol_____." The sentence in (2) is synonymous with (3). By contrast, the sentence in (1) is not synonymous with (4).

(3) The word *Tegucigalpa* starts with a consonant.

(4) The word *Tegucigalpa* is the capital of Honduras.

Exercise (2.2)

One of the words in the sentence in (i) below is mentioned and not used. Rewrite the sentence using italics (or underlining if handwritten) to indicate that a word is mentioned.

(i) Even even has an even number of letters.

There are two correct answers to this exercise, related to two different ways to pronounce the sentence. You need to provide only one answer.

We direct our attention now to the interpretation of the simplest atomic sentences of SL. Assuming lexicon L according to which 'Clever' stands for the set of clever individuals, and 'Agatha' stands for Agatha, it should follow from our rules that

(5) 'Clever(Agatha)' is true with respect to L iff Agatha is clever.

This tells us what the truth conditions are for the whole sentence 'Clever(Agatha)' but it doesn't do so in terms of the meanings assigned to 'Clever' and to 'Agatha'. That's not good if we want to arrive at a general rule that will apply to any atomic sentence formed from a one-place predicate and an individual constant. We'd like to have a statement that is like (5) but with the part to the right of *iff* populated with L(Clever) and L(Agatha), the meanings of 'Clever' and 'Agatha' with respect to the lexicon L. As noted above, L(Clever) is the set of clever people, so we'd like to replace the statement *Agatha is clever* with a statement about sets. The following fact from set theory will be helpful:

(6) Agatha is clever iff Agatha is a member of the set of clever individuals.

Given the equivalence in (6), we can replace *Agatha is clever* in (5) with the equivalent set theoretic statement to get

(7) 'Clever(Agatha)' is true with respect to L iff Agatha is a member of the set of clever individuals.

Given what was said earlier about the lexicon L, we have the following equations:

(8) a. L(Agatha) = Agatha.
    b. L(Clever) = the set of clever individuals.

Given the equivalences in (8), we can replace *Agatha* and *the set of clever individuals* in (7) with the equivalent expressions that use L to get

(9) 'Clever(Agatha)' is true with respect to L iff L(Agatha) is a member of L(Clever).

And using our set-theory symbol '$\in$' we have

(10) 'Clever(Agatha)' is true with respect to L iff L(Agatha) $\in$ L(Clever).

As desired, we've arrived at a statement of the truth conditions of 'Clever(Agatha)' that makes reference to the meanings of 'Clever' and of 'Agatha'.

In moving from (5) through to (10), there were several places where we replaced one expression with an equivalent one in a larger context, leaving everything else the same. This type of inference will be important going forward so we'll introduce an explicit rule for it. The rule, called REPLACE, makes use of the Greek letters 'ϕ' (phi) and 'ψ' (psi):

REPLACE [Rule of Inference]

If two statements φ and ψ are logically equivalent (φ iff ψ), then from a statement including φ, infer the statement that results from replacing φ with ψ.

If two expressions E_1 and E_2 stand for the same entity, then from a statement that includes E_1, infer the statement that results from replacing E_1 with E_2.

The first part of this rule of inference was used, for example, in going from (5) to (7) above. The second part was used twice in going from (7) to (9). As a result of our inferences, we arrived at (10), which is, once again,

(10) 'Clever(Agatha)' is true with respect to L iff L(Agatha) ∈ L(Clever).

This statement achieves what we wanted: a statement of the truth conditions of 'Clever(Agatha)' in terms of the meanings of its parts.

Having worked out how a particular sentence of this kind is interpreted, we can now state a general rule that will apply no matter what the predicate or individual constant is. In order to state such a rule, we'll use the Greek letter 'π' (pi) to stand for any predicate, the Greek letter 'α' (alpha) to stand for any individual constant, and we'll use 'M' to stand for any lexicon of the language. Generalizing from (10), we want our rules to say that

(11) 'π(α)' is true with respect to M iff M(α) ∈ M(π).

This will work when the one-place predicate is simple. But, as we'll see in a moment, there will be cases where we have complex one-place predicates. To allow for this possibility, we'll get to (11) in two steps. First, we introduce the double-bracket notation.

DOUBLE-BRACKET NOTATION

$[\![φ]\!]^M$ stands for the interpretation of the expression φ with respect to the lexicon M.

Next, we introduce a basic vocabulary rule that tells us how to interpret the vocabulary items of SL.

VOCABULARY [Semantic Rule]

If α is an individual constant, then $[\![α]\!]^M = M$(α).

If π is a simple predicate, then $[\![π]\!]^M = M$(π).

And now we can formulate our rule for atomic sentences formed with one-place predicates.

ATOMIC-1 [Semantic Rule]

If π is a one place predicate, then
'$\pi(\alpha)$' is true with respect to M iff $[\![\alpha]\!]^M \in [\![\pi]\!]^M$.

Let's test our rules by applying them to a new sentence. Above, we said that if according to L, 'Happy' stands for the set of all happy individuals, and 'Frank' stands for Frank, then 'Happy(Frank)' is a sentence in SL that corresponds to the English sentence *Frank is happy*. Let's see how our rules capture that. First we will apply the rule ATOMIC-1, by taking the predicate π to be 'Happy' and the individual constant α to be 'Frank'; the lexicon will be L. That gives us

(12) 'Happy(Frank)' is true with respect to L iff $[\![\text{Frank}]\!]^L \in [\![\text{Happy}]\!]^L$.

Next, we apply VOCABULARY and the inference rule REPLACE introduced above to get

(13) 'Happy(Frank)' is true with respect to L iff $L(\text{Frank}) \in L(\text{Happy})$.

Since $L(\text{Frank}) = \text{Frank}$ and $L(\text{Happy}) = $ the set of all happy individuals, by our inference rule REPLACE we get from (13) to

(14) 'Happy(Frank)' is true with respect to L iff Frank is a member of the set of all happy individuals.

From set theory we have

(15) Frank is a member of the set of all happy individuals iff Frank is happy.

And so we can use REPLACE to get from (14) and (15) to

(16) 'Happy(Frank)' is true with respect to L iff Frank is happy.

This is the desired result. Relative to the lexicon L, 'Happy(Frank)' is a good translation of the sentence *Frank is happy*. Our rules work as intended.

ATOMIC-1 will apply to any sentence formed from <u>any</u> one-place predicate and <u>any</u> individual constant because it is stated in terms of **metavariables**, π and α. Syntacticians use 'VP' and 'NP' as metavariables over verb phrases and noun phrases. Phonologists use 'V' and 'C' as metavariables over vowels and consonants. By replacing the metavariables with actual expressions, you get an instance of a rule. This is called **instantiation**. Here's a precise definition:

INSTANTIATE **[Rule of Inference]**

From a rule stated in terms of metavariables, infer the result of substituting the metavariables with object language expressions of the right kind—taking care to substitute all occurrences of a given variable with the same expression.

This rule uses the phrase *object language*. **Object language** is the language being studied, while **metalanguage** is the language in which the theory is stated. In this chapter, the object language is SL. In most of the rest of this textbook, the object language is English. 'VP' is part of the syntactician's metalanguage. 'C' is part of the phonologist's metalanguage.

Like REPLACE, INSTANTIATE is not a rule of the grammar of SL. It is a general logical principle that allows us to deduce facts about the grammar. The reasoning behind this rule of inference is very similar to the reasoning we employ in applying laws. Here's an illustration. Suppose there is a law that says:

(17) If a person owns a dog, that person has to get a license for the dog in the state where that person resides.

That's a general rule. Suppose now that Toto and Yala are both dogs. The statements below are instantiations of the general rule in (17).

(18) If Dorothy owns Toto, then Dorothy has to get a license for Toto in the state where Dorothy resides.

(19) If Natchaya owns Yala, then Natchaya has to get a license for Yala in the state where Natchaya resides.

In (18), we instantiated with Dorothy/Toto and in (19) with Natchaya/Yala. In contrast to (18) and (19), (20) and (21) below would be incorrect instantiations:

(20) If Dorothy owns Toto, then Dorothy has to get a license for Yala in the state where Dorothy resides.

(21) If Dorothy owns Toto, then Toto has to get a license for Dorothy in the state where Toto reside.

The error in (20) is that we first used *Toto* for the dog and then used *Yala* after that. In fact, the intention of the lawmaker is for the law to apply to the same dog throughout. It's this intuition that is captured in INSTANTIATE when the rule says: "substitute all occurrences of a given variable with the same expression."

The error in (21) appears after the comma: we used *Toto* to instantiate a person, when *Toto* refers to a dog; we used *Dorothy* to instantiate a dog, when *Dorothy* refers to a person. The law distinguishes people and dogs and the instantiations must respect that. It's this intuition that is captured in INSTANTIATE when the rule says to substitute meta-variables "with expressions of the <u>right kind</u>."

Finally, suppose it's the case that Natchaya resides in the state of Rhode Island. In that case, we can perform a replacement inference on (19) to get

(22) If Natchaya owns Yala, then Natchaya has to get a license for Yala in Rhode Island.

As just illustrated, these inferencing rules are not rules of grammar. They are general logical principles that allow us to deduce facts about the grammar. We've just illustrated a use of INSTANTIATE in daily life. A common use of the rule REPLACE comes in editing. Suppose Natchaya plans to write a news report that includes the statement

If the weather is good, the White Sox will be beaten by the Tigers.

Natchaya's friend, Baboloki, doesn't like the use of the passive (*be beaten by*), so he recommends that Natchaya change her statement to

If the weather is good, the Tigers will beat the White Sox.

Baboloki assumes that *the Tigers will beat the White Sox* is equivalent to *the White Sox will be beaten by the Tigers*, and so he replaces one statement with the other. Notice that the remainder of the initial statement, *if the weather is good*, is repeated untouched.

Exercise (2.3)

[A] Suppose that Alan is a poor doctor, Betty is a wealthy doctor, and Cathy is not wealthy and is not a doctor. Which of the following is true with respect to the lexicon L?

(i) Wealthy(Alan)

(ii) Doctor(Betty)

(iii) Wealthy(Betty)

(iv) Doctor(Alan)

(v) Doctor(Cathy)

(vi) Wealthy(Cathy)

[B] Following the steps used in (12)–(16) above to interpret 'Happy(Frank)', write out the steps for determining the truth conditions for 'Wealthy(Betty)' with respect to the lexicon L. Label each step with the name(s) of the rule(s) used in getting to that step from the previous one. The first step should be labeled 'ATOMIC-1'.

[C] The line below is the result of an incorrect application of the inference rule INSTANTIATE to the semantic rule ATOMIC-1. What has gone wrong?

'Doctor(Betty)' is true with respect to K iff $[\![\text{Betty}]\!]^L \in [\![\text{Doctor}]\!]^L$.

We now move on to sentences formed with two-place predicates, and for that we need a new semantic rule. A standard way to proceed is to have a rule that tells you when a sentence like 'Likes(Mary)(Sue)' is true, in terms of the meanings assigned to 'Likes', 'Sue', and 'Mary'. But for our purposes, it will be advantageous to do this compositionally, in two steps. First, we form a one-place predicate out of a two-place predicate and an individual constant, 'Likes(Mary)'. We'll need a new semantic rule for that combination. We'll call that rule ATOMIC-2 because it will tell us how two-place predicates figure in the interpretation of atomic sentences. Once that is done, we'll be able to get a meaning for the one-place predicate 'Likes(Mary)', and we can use it along with ATOMIC-1 to interpret the sequence 'Likes(Mary)(Sue)'.

To figure out what ATOMIC-2 should look like, we'll have to work backward, first from what we want an atomic sentence to mean and then what we'll want the complex one-place predicate to mean. Earlier we said that relative to the lexicon L, 'Likes(Mary)(Sue)' corresponds to the English sentence *Sue likes Mary*. More precisely,

(23) 'Likes(Mary)(Sue)' is true with respect to L iff Sue likes Mary.

Now, if we are assuming that 'Likes(Mary)' is a one-place predicate, then we can apply ATOMIC-1 to 'Likes(Mary)(Sue)' instantiating π with 'Likes(Mary)'. Doing that, we get

(24) 'Likes(Mary)(Sue)' is true with respect to L iff $[\![\text{Sue}]\!]^L \in [\![\text{Likes(Mary)}]\!]^L$.

To connect the statements in (23) and (24), we need this observation:

(25) Sue likes Mary iff Sue is a member of the set of individuals who like Mary.

Using REPLACE with (23) and (25), we get

(26) 'Likes(Mary)(Sue)' is true with respect to L iff Sue is a member of the set of individuals who like Mary.

And now from (24), (26), and the fact that $[\![\text{Sue}]\!]^L$ is Sue, we deduce that

(27) $[\![\text{Likes(Mary)}]\!]^L =$ the set of individuals who like Mary.

Our next goal is to figure out how to get the result in (27) using the individual Mary and the meaning of 'Likes'. Suppose we interpret 'Likes' as follows:

(28) $[\![\text{Likes}]\!]^L = \{\, \langle x, Y \rangle : Y$ is the set of individuals who like $x\}$.

According to (28), $[\![\text{Likes}]\!]^L$ picks out a set of pairs, in which each first element is paired with one and only one second element. Comparing (27) and (28), we can see that we arrive at the interpretation of 'Likes(Mary)' by finding the second element of the pair whose first element is Mary. This means we can use $F(\dots)$ notation (see the end of chapter 1 for the definition) to formulate the rule ATOMIC-2:

ATOMIC-2 [Semantic Rule]

If π is a two place predicate, then $[\![\pi(\alpha)]\!]^M = [\![\pi]\!]^M ([\![\alpha]\!]^M)$.

Using ATOMIC-2 and the meaning in (28), we get (27). $[\![\text{Likes}]\!]^L$ is a set of pairs, and $[\![\text{Likes}]\!]^L([\![\text{Mary}]\!]^L)$ gives us the second element of the pair in $[\![\text{Likes}]\!]^L$ whose first element is Mary. Looking back at (28), that second element will be the set of individuals who like Mary, just as (27) requires.

In general, if π is a two-place predicate, then for any lexicon M, $M(\pi)$ is a set of pairs, $\langle x, Y \rangle$, where Y is a set of entities. The lexicon L will assign the set of pairs in which each x is paired with the set Y of individuals who bear the 'π-relation' to x. For example,

(29) $L(\text{Knows}) = \{ \langle x, Y \rangle : Y$ is the set of individuals who know $x\}$.

(30) $L(\text{Above}) = \{ \langle x, Y \rangle : Y$ is the set of entities that are above $x\}$.

We now amend our vocabulary rule so that it makes the connection between the kind of predicate that π is and its meaning:

VOCABULARY [Semantic Rule]

If α is an individual constant, then $[\![\alpha]\!]^M = M(\alpha)$, and $M(\alpha)$ is an entity.

If π is a simple one-place predicate, then $[\![\pi]\!]^M = M(\pi)$, and $M(\pi)$ is a set of entities.

If π is a two-place predicate, then $[\![\pi]\!]^M = M(\pi)$, and $M(\pi)$ is a set of pairs; the first element of each pair is an entity, and the second is a set of entities.

Let's test our rules using the lexicon L and the sentence 'Knows(Jack)(Jill)'. We begin by instantiating ATOMIC-1:

(31) 'Knows(Jack)(Jill)' is true with respect to L iff $[\![\text{Jill}]\!]^L \in [\![\text{Knows(Jack)}]\!]^L$.

By applying VOCABULARY, $[\![\textit{Jill}]\!]^L = L(\text{Jill})$, and $L(\text{Jill}) = \text{Jill}$, so REPLACING we get

(32) 'Knows(Jack)(Jill)' is true with respect to L iff Jill $\in [\![\text{Knows(Jack)}]\!]^L$.

Next, instantiating ATOMIC-2, we have

(33) $[\![\text{Knows(Jack)}]\!]^L = [\![\text{Knows}]\!]^L ([\![\text{Jack}]\!]^L)$.

By the $F(\dots)$ notation,

(34) $[\![\text{Knows}]\!]^L ([\![\text{Jack}]\!]^L)$ is the second element of the pair in $[\![\text{Knows}]\!]^L$ whose first element is $[\![\text{Jack}]\!]^L$.

From (29) and the fact that $[\![\text{Jack}]\!]^L$ is Jack, we have

(35) the second element of the pair in $[\![\text{Knows}]\!]^L$ whose first element is $[\![\text{Jack}]\!]^L$ = the set of individuals who know Jack.

Using predicate-notation from set-theory, we can rewrite (35) as

(36) the second element of the pair in $[\![\text{Knows}]\!]^L$ whose first element is $[\![\text{Jack}]\!]^L = \{z : z$ knows Jack$\}$.

Using REPLACE a few times, as well as (32)–(34) and (36), we have

(37) $[\![\text{Knows}]\!]^L ([\![\text{Jack}]\!]^L) = \{z : z$ knows Jack$\}$.

(38) $[\![\text{Knows(Jack)}]\!]^L = \{z : z$ knows Jack$\}$.

(39) 'Knows(Jack)(Jill)' is true with respect to L iff Jill $\in \{z : z$ knows Jack$\}$.

And now by set theory, we derive the intended truth conditions:

(40) 'Knows(Jack)(Jill)' is true with respect to L iff Jill knows Jack.

Let's try another example. Suppose we have a lexicon G and that according to G, 'Dave' stands for the diamond in figure 2.1, 'Cyrus' stands for the circle, and 'Above' picks out the above relation. Formally, we have

(41) $G(\text{Dave}) = \Diamond$.
$G(\text{Cyrus}) = \bigcirc$.
$G(\text{Above}) = \{ \langle x, Y \rangle : Y$ is the set of entities that are above $x\}$.

Using our ATOMIC-2 rule, VOCABULARY, and our inference rules, we have

(42) $[\![\text{Above(Cyrus)}]\!]^G = \{z : z$ is above $G(\text{Cyrus})\}$.

(43) $[\![\text{Above(Dave)}]\!]^G = \{z : z$ is above $G(\text{Dave})\}$.

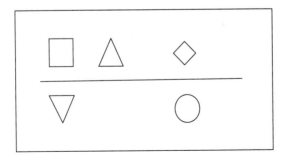

Figure 2.1
Geometric shapes with Dave the diamond and Cyrus the circle.

Using ATOMIC-1, we have

(44) 'Above(Cyrus)(Dave)' is true with respect to G iff $[\![\text{Dave}]\!]^G \in [\![\text{Above(Cyrus)}]\!]^G$.

(45) 'Above(Dave)(Cyrus)' is true with respect to G iff $[\![\text{Cyrus}]\!]^G \in [\![\text{Above(Dave)}]\!]^G$.

Using the VOCABULARY rule, set theory, our inference rules, and (42)–(45), we have

(46) 'Above(Cyrus)(Dave)' is true with respect to G iff G(Dave) is above G(Cyrus).

(47) 'Above(Dave)(Cyrus)' is true with respect to G iff G(Cyrus) is above G(Dave).

Given (41), by using REPLACE, we get

(48) 'Above(Cyrus)(Dave)' is true with respect to G iff in figure 2.1, the diamond is above the circle.

(49) 'Above(Dave)(Cyrus)' is true with respect to G iff in figure 2.1, the circle is above the diamond.

And now, given the facts in figure 2.1, it follows that

(50) 'Above(Cyrus)(Dave)' is true with respect to G,

and

'Above(Dave)(Cyrus)' is false with respect to G.

'Above(Cyrus)(Dave)' and 'Above(Dave)(Cyrus)' use all the same symbols but they are put together differently. The fact that we found a situation in which one is true and the other false means they have different truth conditions. This difference has to be due to the syntactic difference between them. We now have a model for how syntax can play a role in determining truth conditions.

Exercise (2.4)

[A] In this exercise, we assume a lexicon J and use italicized lowercase letters from the alphabet to represent individuals. Here are some facts about lexicon J:

J(Painted) = { $\langle a, \{c,d\}\rangle$, $\langle b, \{a, d\}\rangle$, $\langle c, \{a,b\}\rangle$ }.

J(Meretricious) = $\{a, d\}$.

J(Alan) = a.

J(Betty) = b.

J(Carl) = c.

J(Dallas) = d.

J(Waterloo) = w.

Using the semantic rules developed so far, find a set or an individual that is equivalent to each of the expressions in (i)–(iii) below (use the letters *a*, *b*, *c*, *d* and set theoretic notation for your answers).

(i) $[\![\text{Alan}]\!]^{J}$

(ii) $[\![\text{Painted}]\!]^{J}$

(iii) $[\![\text{Painted(Alan)}]\!]^{J}$.

[B] Find a complex one-place predicate that, when inserted in the blank, will make the following statement true:

$[\![\quad]\!]^{J} = [\![\text{Meretricious}]\!]^{J}$.

[C] Is the statement 'Painted(Betty)(Carl)' true or false with respect to the lexicon *J*?

[D] Let 'From' be a two-place predicate. Suggest an interpretation with respect to the lexicon *J* of the predicate 'From' so that all three of the following come out true with respect to *J*:

'From(Dallas)(Alan)';

'From(Waterloo)(Betty)';

'From(Waterloo)(Carl)'.

Since you are supplying an interpretation for a two-place predicate, your answer should be a set of pairs, and the second element of each pair should be a set of individuals. Your answer should be in list notation. There are many possible correct answers. Write your answer as an equation, with $[\![\textit{From}]\!]^{J}$ to the left of the equal sign and your set to the right.

Key Ideas

In this section, we've introduced a piece of new notation, three semantic rules, and two rules of inference:

Double-Bracket Notation

$[\![\phi]\!]^{M}$ stands for: the interpretation of the expression ϕ with respect to the lexicon *M*.

Vocabulary [Semantic Rule]

If α is an individual constant, then $[\![\alpha]\!]^{M} = M(\alpha)$, and $M(\alpha)$ is an entity.

If π is a simple one-place predicate, then $[\![\pi]\!]^{M} = M(\pi)$, and $M(\pi)$ is a set of entities.

If π is a two-place predicate, then $[\![\pi]\!]^{M} = M(\pi)$, and $M(\pi)$ is a set of pairs; the first element of each pair is an entity and the second is a set of entities.

ATOMIC-1 [Semantic Rule]

If π is a one place predicate, then '$\pi(\alpha)$' is true with respect to M iff $[\![\alpha]\!]^M \in [\![\pi]\!]^M$.

ATOMIC-2 [Semantic Rule]

If π is a two place predicate, then: $[\![\pi(\alpha)]\!]^M = [\![\pi]\!]^M ([\![\alpha]\!]^M)$.

REPLACE [Rule of Inference]

If two statements ϕ and ψ are logically equivalent (ϕ iff ψ), then from a statement including ϕ, infer the statement that results from replacing ϕ with ψ.

If two expressions E_1 and E_2 stand for the same entity, then from a statement that includes E_1, infer the statement that results from replacing E_1 with E_2.

INSTANTIATE [Rule of Inference]

From a rule stated in terms of metavariables, infer the result of substituting the metavariables with object language expressions of the right kind—taking care to substitute all occurrences of a given variable with the same expression.

- INSTANTIATE allows us to use ATOMIC-1 to arrive at statements such as

(51) 'Bored(Natchaya)' is true with respect to L iff $[\![\text{Natchaya}]\!]^L \in [\![\text{Bored}]\!]^L$.

- INSTANTIATE allows us to use ATOMIC-2 to arrive at statements such as

(52) $[\![\text{From(Boston)}]\!]^L = [\![\text{From}]\!]^L ([\![\text{Boston}]\!]^L)$.

- And REPLACE allows us to use VOCABULARY and facts from the lexicon to go from (51) and (52) to (53) and (54), respectively.

(53) 'Bored(Natchaya)' is true with respect to L iff Natchaya is bored.

(54) $[\![\text{From(Boston)}]\!]^L = \{y : y \text{ is from Boston}\}$.

The lexical facts needed for (54) are that $L(\text{Boston})$ is Boston and that

$L(\text{From}) = \{\langle x, Y \rangle : Y \text{ is the set of entities that are from } x\}$.

New Terminology

- atomic sentences
- individual constant
- one-place predicate
- two-place predicate
- instantiate
- metavariables
- object language

2.2 Connectives

In the previous section, we introduced a syntax and semantics for atomic sentences such as 'Clever(Agatha)' and 'Likes(Sue)(Mary)'. In this section, we introduce a syntax and semantics for **compound sentences**. A compound sentence has one or more smaller sentences as one of its parts. One way to form a compound sentence is to combine two sentences with the connective '&', pronounced as *and*, and to enclose them in parentheses. Here are some examples:

(55) a. (Clever(Alan) & Kind(Carl)).
     b. (Likes(Sue)(Mary) & Clever(Alan)).
     c. ((Clever(Alan) & Kind(Carl)) & Bored(Donald)).

In order to spell out the syntax and semantics of compound sentences, we'll need metavariables over sentences. We'll use 'ϕ' and 'ψ'. So here's a general statement of the syntactic rule for '&':

(56) If ϕ and ψ are sentences, then '(ϕ & ψ)' is a sentence.

And here is the semantic rule that interprets sentences formed in this way:

AND [Semantic Rule]

'(ϕ & ψ)' is true with respect to M iff
ϕ is true with respect to M and ψ is true with respect to M.

Let's use this rule to calculate the truth conditions of the sentence '(Clever(Agatha) & Happy(Frank))' relative to the lexicon L. First we instantiate the AND rule:

(57) '(Clever(Agatha) & Happy(Frank))' is true with respect to L iff 'Clever(Agatha)' is true with respect to L and 'Happy(Frank)' is true with respect to L.

The following statements come from our discussion in section 2.1 of the truth conditions of 'Clever(Agatha)' and 'Happy(Frank)' relative to lexicon L:

(58) 'Happy(Frank)' is true with respect to L iff Frank is happy.

(59) 'Clever(Agatha)' is true with respect to L iff Agatha is clever.

So now we can use REPLACE twice in (57) to get

(60) '(Clever(Agatha) & Happy(Frank))' is true with respect to L iff Agatha is clever and Frank is happy.

Assuming lexicon L, we deduce from this calculation that '(Clever(Agatha) & Happy(Frank))' has the same truth conditions as the English sentence *Agatha is clever and Frank is happy*. In general, sentences formed with '&' correspond to those using conjunctions such as *and* in English.

To see another example, look again at the lexicon G from (41) ($\Diamond$ and $\bigcirc$ are the shapes in figure 2.1).

(41) G(Dave) = $\Diamond$.
 G(Cyrus) = $\bigcirc$.
 G(Above) = { $\langle x, Y \rangle$: Y is the set of entities that are above x}.

Relative to G, the sentence 'Above(Cyrus)(Dave) & Above(Dave)(Cyrus)' has the same truth conditions as the English sentence *The diamond in figure 2.1 is above the circle in figure 2.1, and the circle is above the diamond.* That English sentence is false, because the circle is not above the diamond. Likewise, the symbolic logic sentence '(Above(Cyrus)(Dave) & Above(Dave)(Cyrus))' is false relative to G given the facts depicted in figure 2.1. In general, as the rule AND states, for a conjunction to be true, <u>both</u> conjuncts have to be true.

✪ Important Practice and Looking Ahead ✪

Exercise (2.5) below is about whether a given expression of SL corresponds to a given expression of English. Such questions will be vital in the next chapter and the chapters thereafter, which propose rules of translation. Some of the data in this exercise exemplify a phenomenon known as *narrative progression*, which will be discussed in the next chapter and will serve as an important diagnostic in chapter 4. This exercise gives you the opportunity to develop your intuitions beforehand.

Exercise (2.5)

We just saw that '(Clever(Agatha) & Happy(Frank))' has the same truth conditions relative to L as *Agatha is clever, and Frank is happy* and therefore corresponds to that English sentence. Similarly '(Above(Cyrus)(Dave) & Above(Dave)(Cyrus))' has

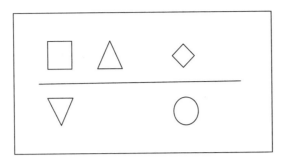

Figure 2.1
Geometric shapes with Dave the diamond and Cyrus the circle.

the same truth conditions relative to *G* as the English sentence *The diamond in figure 2.1 is above the circle in figure 2.1, and the circle is above the diamond.* The task of this exercise is to think about whether the connective '&' always corresponds to the English word *and*. To do so, consider the English sentences below. For each pair in (i)–(iv), say whether there are any differences in the truth conditions of (a) versus (b). If you find differences, say what they are. Based on your answers, do you think '&' is a good translation of *and*? Justify your answer, making sure to discuss the AND rule.

(i) a. They got married and had a baby.
    b. They had a baby and got married.

(ii) a. Justin plays the trumpet. Ava plays the sax.
    b. Justin plays the trumpet and Ava plays the sax.

(iii) a. Akna fell. Amaya pushed her.
    b. Akna fell and Amaya pushed her.

(iv) a. Lev had a good meal last night. He had lamb.
    b. Lev had a good meal last night, and he had lamb.

A second way to form a compound sentence is to put the symbol '¬' in front of a sentence in parentheses. The symbol '¬' is pronounced *it is not the case that* or sometimes just *not*. Here are some examples:

(61) a. ¬(Clever(Alan)).
    b. ¬(Likes(Sue)(Mary)).
    c. ¬((Clever(Alan) & Kind(Cyrus))).
    d. ¬(((Clever(Alan) & Kind(Carl)) & Bored(Dina))).

The rule for interpreting sentences formed with '¬' is called NOT.

> **NOT [Semantic Rule]**
>
> '¬(φ)' is true with respect to *M* iff it is not the case that 'φ' is true with respect to *M*.

Let's use this rule to calculate the truth conditions of the sentence '¬(Clever(Alan))' relative to the lexicon *L*. First we instantiate the NOT rule:

(62) '¬(Clever(Alan))' is true with respect to *L* iff it is not the case that 'Clever(Alan)' is true with respect to *L*.

And now given that

(63) 'Clever(Alan)' is true with respect to *L* iff Alan is clever,

by using REPLACE, we get

(64) '¬(Clever(Alan))' is true with respect to *L* iff it is not the case that Alan is clever.

From (64) we conclude that with respect to lexicon *L*, '¬(Clever(Alan))' is a good translation of the English sentence *Alan is not clever*.

Exercise (2.6)

[A] Provide a sentence of SL that with respect to lexicon *L* is a good translation of the English sentence in (i) below. Do the same for (ii). Form your SL sentences using just parentheses and the symbols: '¬', '&', 'Sam', 'George', 'Boston', 'From', 'Love'.

(i) George is not from Boston.

(ii) Sam loves himself, but Sam doesn't love George.

[B] In the situation depicted in figure 2.1, the sentence 'Above(Dave)(Cyrus)' is false with respect to the lexicon *G*, while 'Above(Cyrus)(Dave)' is true with respect to the lexicon *G*. Which of the following sentences of SL are true with respect to the lexicon *G*, in the situation depicted in figure 2.1?

(i) ¬(Above(Dave)(Cyrus)).

(ii) ¬(Above(Cyrus)(Dave)).

(iii) (Above(Dave)(Cyrus) & Above(Cyrus)(Dave)).

(iv) ¬((Above(Dave)(Cyrus) & Above(Cyrus)(Dave))).

(v) (¬(Above(Dave)(Cyrus)) & Above(Cyrus)(Dave)).

Key Ideas

In this section, we introduced two semantic rules.

> **AND [Semantic Rule]**
>
> '(ϕ & ψ)' is true with respect to *M* iff
> 'ϕ' is true with respect to *M* and 'ψ' is true with respect to *M*.

> **NOT [Semantic Rule]**
>
> '¬(ϕ)' is true with respect to *M* iff it is not the case that 'ϕ' is true with respect to *M*

Instantiating these rules leads to statements about conjunctions and negations, such as

(65) '(Clever(Agatha) & Happy(Frank))' is true with respect to *L* iff 'Clever(Agatha)' is true with respect to *L* and 'Happy(Frank)' is true with respect to *L*.

(66) '¬(Clever(Alan))' is true with respect to *L* iff it is not the case that 'Clever(Alan)' is true with respect to *L*.

The statements above contain atomic sentences following *iff*. This allows us to apply our rules for atomic sentences and then our rules of inference. Using facts from the lexicon, we can then go from (65) to (67) and from (66) to (68), thus:

(67) '(Clever(Agatha) & Happy(Frank))' is true with respect to *L* iff Agatha is clever and Frank is happy.

(68) '¬(Clever(Alan))' is true with respect to L iff it is not the case that Alan is clever.

New Terminology

- compound sentence
- connective
- negation

2.3 Quantifiers

The English examples below exemplify a kind of statement that we don't yet have in our symbolic language.

(69) a. No girl submitted a story about herself.
     b. Every boy submitted a story about himself.
     c. At least one mother submitted a story about herself.

These sentences are taken from the description of a writing workshop attended by a group
of mothers and children. The sentences report on stories the instructor received at the end
of the first week. Each statement reports on a **quantity**. The first says that the number of
girls who submitted stories about themselves was zero. The second says that 100 percent
of the boys submitted stories about themselves. And the last one says that the number of
mothers who submitted stories about themselves was greater than zero. These are quantificational statements. To include such statements in our symbolic language, SL, we need
to add new symbols, along with their syntax and semantics. To get an idea of what needs
to be added, we should consider some differences between the quantificational statements
above and the sentence below:

(70) Nadir submitted a story about himself.

The subject of (70), *Nadir*, is a name. Like individual constants in the symbolic language,
names refer to particular individuals. By contrast, the subjects of the quantificational
statements don't work semantically the way that names do. There is no individual that
is referred to by *no girl* or by *every boy*. *At least one mother* could be <u>about</u> a particular
individual, but it can't be used to <u>refer</u> to that individual: as it moves from sentence to sentence, it isn't fixed to one person. To see that, think about the sentence *At least one person
sang, and at least one person danced*. It doesn't require the same person to have sung and
to have danced. Compare that with *Nadir sang, and Nadir danced*. To accomplish our task
we're going to need expressions called **quantifiers** whose semantics gives rise to truth
conditions that depend on facts about several objects at once.

Another important difference between the statements in (69) and (70) is the interpretation of the pronouns *himself* and *herself*. In (70), the pronoun *himself* intuitively refers to
Nadir. It's a story about Nadir that's being described. By contrast, the pronoun *herself*
in (69)a doesn't refer to anyone in particular. In a sense, its reference varies according
to which girl is under consideration. Suppose Nicole and Rebecca were among the girls.
Then the sentence says that Nicole didn't submit a story about Nicole, and it says that
Rebecca didn't submit a story about Rebecca. For each girl whom we consider, we temporarily treat the pronoun as a name for that girl. The same type of procedure works
for the other examples. If Henry and Brett are among the boys, then (69)b tells us that
Henry submitted a story about Henry and that Brett submitted a story about Brett. The
pronouns are functioning somewhat like temporary names, referring to different entities
as the interpretation proceeds.

To accomplish our task of adding quantificational statements to the symbolic language,
we will need to have special symbols that work like temporary names. These symbols will
be called **variables**, and they will be lower-case letters from near the end of the alphabet:
x, y, z. The semantic rule that interprets them will work in tandem with the quantifiers.
Each time the quantifier considers a new object, we'll add a variable to the lexicon with
that object as its meaning. We'll use the $M+ \langle \ldots, \ldots \rangle$ notation to do that. For example, if

we have a lexicon L and an object o, we can enlarge the lexicon to: $L+ \langle x,o \rangle$. Recall from chapter 1, that $L+ \langle x,o \rangle$ is a lexicon according to which 'x' stands for the object o; otherwise $L+ \langle x,o \rangle$ is just like L. What lies ahead, then, is the introduction of new quantifier symbols as well as variables. Along with these new symbols, we'll need syntactic rules to tell us how to form sentences with them and semantic rules that guide us to an interpretation of quantificational sentences.

Variables have the same syntax as individual constants. They can therefore combine with one- and two-place predicates to form **formulas** as well as complex one-place predicates:

(71) a. Clever(x)
      b. Likes(Sue)(y)
      c. (Clever(z) & Happy(Frank))
      d. From(x)

Because the expressions in a.–c. have variables in them, they are called *formulas* and not *sentences. formula* is a general term. Among the formulas, those with no variables are sentences. So 'Happy(Frank)' is a sentence and therefore a formula. We'll briefly return to this distinction below. Now that we have variables in our language SL, the metavariable 'α' can be instantiated with individual constants as well as with variables. That means our two ATOMIC rules apply to 'Clever(x)' and 'Likes(z)', respectively. Since variables are meant to function like temporary names, they are not assigned a value by any of the initial lexicons that we consider. In other words, L does not by itself assign a meaning to 'x'; it's only when we form $L+ \langle x,o \rangle$ that we get a lexicon that assigns a meaning to 'x'. Some pronouns in natural language work like that. The pronoun *she*, for example, can be used to refer to a particular individual, but it is not listed in the dictionary paired with that individual. Each time *she* is used, it serves temporarily like a name. In a moment, we'll see the mechanics for how quantifiers expand a lexicon. Once the lexicon is expanded, it can perform the task of assigning an interpretation to the variable. The following rule states that precisely. It makes use of double-bracket notation, in which $[\![\phi]\!]^M$ stands for the interpretation of the expression 'ϕ' with respect to the lexicon M.

VARIABLE [Semantic Rule]

If the variable u is the first member of a pair in M, then $[\![u]\!]^M = M(u)$.

'u' here is a metavariable over variables. It can be instantiated by 'x', or 'y' or 'z'. 'M' is a metavariable over lexicons, it could be instantiated by $L+ \langle y,o \rangle$. How this all works should become clear once we introduce quantifiers, since variables work in tandem with them.

2.3.1   Existential Quantifier

The first type of quantifier we'll consider is formed using the symbol '∃', a backwards letter *E*. This quantifier, called the **existential quantifier**, enters formulas via the following syntactic rule:

(72)   If φ and ψ are formulas and *u* is a variable, then '[∃*u* : φ] (ψ)' is a formula.

Here are some formulas produced by that rule:

(73)   a. [∃*x*: Person(*x*)](Clever(*x*)).
      b. [∃*y*: Horse(*y*)](Likes(Sue)(*y*)).
      c. [∃*z*: Person(*z*)]((Clever(*z*) & Happy(Frank))).

Next we formulate a semantic rule for existentially quantified formulas called EXIST.

EXIST [Semantic Rule]

'[∃*u*: φ] (ψ)' is true with respect to *M* iff

for some entity *o* such that 'φ' is true with respect to *M*+ ⟨*u,o*⟩ , 'ψ' is true with respect to *M*+ ⟨*u,o*⟩ .

Let's use that rule to see what truth conditions we get when we interpret the formula below relative to the lexicon *L*.

    '[∃*x*: Person(*x*)](Clever(*x*))'.

First we instantiate the rule EXIST, using '*x*' for '*u*', 'Person(*x*)' for 'φ', 'Clever(*x*)' for 'ψ', and *L* for '*M*':

(74)   '[∃*x*: Person(*x*)](Clever(*x*))' is true with respect to *L* iff
      for some entity *o* such that 'Person(*x*)' is true with respect to *L*+ ⟨*x,o*⟩ , 'Clever(*x*)' is true with respect to *L*+ ⟨*x,o*⟩ .

It is <u>very</u> important here to carefully follow the rule INSTANTIATE, making sure to replace <u>every</u> instance of '*u*', 'φ', and 'ψ' with the corresponding expression. Notice that '*u*' occurs in the rule EXIST in <u>three</u> places and that it was instantiated in three places in (74); similarly for 'φ' and 'ψ'.

The last part of (74) says:

(75)   'Clever(*x*)' is true with respect to *L*+ ⟨*x,o*⟩ .

The rule ATOMIC-1, repeated below, applies to the statement in (75).

ATOMIC-1 [Semantic Rule]

If π is a one place predicate, then 'π(α)' is true with respect to *M* iff $[\![\alpha]\!]^M \in [\![\pi]\!]^M$.

If we instantiate Atomic-1 using 'Clever' for π, 'x' for α, and $L+\langle x,o\rangle$ for 'M', then from (75) we get

(76) 'Clever(x)' is true with respect to $L+\langle x,o\rangle$ iff $[\![x]\!]^{L+\langle x,o\rangle} \in [\![\text{Clever}]\!]^{L+\langle x,o\rangle}$.

Our Vocabulary rule and our new Variable rule let us simplify the right-hand side to

(77) 'Clever(x)' is true with respect to $L+\langle x,o\rangle$ iff $L+\langle x,o\rangle\,(x) \in L+\langle x,o\rangle$ (Clever).

By the definition of the plus notation (see section 1.6 of the previous chapter), we get

(78) a. $L+\langle x,o\rangle\,(x)=o$.
　　b. $L+\langle x,o\rangle$ (Clever) $=L$(Clever) .

So now we can use Replace to get

(79) 'Clever(x)' is true with respect to $L+\langle x, o\rangle$ iff $o \in L$(Clever).

And now, (79) allows for a replacement in (74) as follows:

(80) '[$\exists x$: Person(x)](Clever(x))' is true with respect to L iff
　　for some entity o such that 'Person(x)' is true with respect to L+$\langle x,o\rangle$, $o \in L$(Clever).

Next, using the fact that L(Clever)$=$the set of all clever individuals, by Replace and set theory notation, we get

(81) $o \in L$(Clever) iff o is clever.

And then we Replace in (80) to get

(82) '[$\exists x$: Person(x)](Clever(x))' is true with respect to L iff
　　for some entity o such that 'Person(x)' is true with respect to L+$\langle x,o\rangle$, o is clever.

By the same kind of reasoning as used with 'Clever(x)', we can conclude that

(83) 'Person(x)' is true with respect to $L+\langle x,o\rangle$ iff o is a person.

And then we Replace in (82) to get

(84) '[$\exists x$: Person(x)](Clever(x))' is true with respect to L iff
　　for some entity o such that o is a person, o is clever.

(84) tells us what the truth conditions are for '[$\exists x$: Person(x)](Clever(x))' relative to L. Given these truth conditions, we might translate that SL formula, relative to L, as *Some person is clever* or simply as *Someone is clever*. Similarly, *Some horse likes Sue* would translate relative to L as

[$\exists y$: Horse(y)](Likes(Sue)(y)).

And '([$\exists z$: Person(z)](Clever(z)) & Happy(Frank))' would translate as *Some person is clever, and Frank is happy*. In general, formulas of the form '[$\exists u$:ϕ](ψ)' are said to represent existential quantification because they entail that something exists.

In (72), we introduced a syntactic rule for producing quantificational formulas. That rule is reproduced below along with two other syntactic rules that have been introduced only informally so far.

(85) If φ and ψ are formulas and u is a variable, then '[∃u: φ] (ψ)' is a formula.

(86) If π is a one-place predicate and α is an individual constant or a variable, then 'π(α)' is a formula.

(87) If π is a two-place predicate and α is an individual constant or a variable, then 'π(α)' is a one-place predicate.

Two properties of this syntax are worth highlighting. First, notice that the rule in (85) is **recursive**. It uses formulas as input and it produces formulas. As a result of this property, SL has formulas with multiple quantifiers. The following example shows why. Instantiating 'u' in (85) with 'x', 'φ' with 'Square(x)', and 'ψ' with 'Above(x)(y)', we get

[∃x: Square(x)](Above(x)(y)).

If we now instantiate 'u' in (85) with 'y', 'φ' with 'Round(y)', and 'ψ' with the recently formed formula '[∃x: Square(x)](Above(x)(y))', we get

[∃y: Round(y)]([∃x: Square(x)](Above(x)(y))).

Exercise (2.7) is designed to take you through the steps of determining what the meaning of that formula is. Before moving to that exercise, however, we'd like to highlight the difference between the syntax of quantifier formulas in SL and their translations in English. Consider *Some dog barked* and its SL translation relative to L of '[∃z: Dog(z)] (Barked(z))'. English makes use of three expressions, a determiner (*some*), a noun (*dog*) and a verb (*barked*), where SL uses two formulas, a variable and a special quantifier symbol. Moreover, whereas a **determiner phrase** (DP) like *some dog* can appear pretty much wherever a name can, the square-bracketed quantifiers are more restricted. The following formulas are not **well formed**, meaning they don't conform to SL syntax. We indicate that with an asterisk:

(88) *Knows(Amaya)([∃x: Dog(x)]).

(89) *Knows([∃x: Dog(x)])(Amaya).

The rules in (86) and (87) call specifically for an individual constant or variable to combine with a one- or two-place predicate. The closest we can get to (88) and (89) are

[∃x: Dog(x)] (Knows(Amaya)(x)).

[∃x: Dog(x)] (Knows(x)(Amaya)).

Those turn out to be good translations relative to L of *some dog knows Amaya* and *Amaya knows some dog*, respectively. This difference between the two languages, SL and

English, is related to the fact that in English *some dog* is a constituent, a DP, formed on its own. By contrast, bracketed expressions such as '[∃x: Dog(x)]' are not in fact formed on their own by the syntax. Nevertheless, we will informally refer to bracketed expressions such '[∃x: Dog(x)]' as quantifiers.

Exercise (2.7)

[A] Let k be some entity. For each of the two formulas below, say what conditions must be met in order for them to be true with respect to $L+ \langle z, k \rangle$. Your answer should not make reference to SL. For (ii) provide <u>all the steps</u> in your calculation of the truth conditions using the rules of SL. As a reminder, L(Above)= { $\langle x,Y \rangle$: Y is the set of entities that are above x}.

(i) Broken(z)

(ii) Above(z)(Alan)

[B] Provide the result of applying just the rule EXIST to the formula '[∃y: Round(y)] (Broken(y))' using the lexicon L. Provide an English translation for that formula.

[C] Calculate the truth conditions for the formula '[∃z: Broken(z)](Above(z)(Alan))' relative to lexicon L. Your calculation in [A] should be helpful. For this exercise, <u>do not turn in the intermediate steps in your calculation—just the final line</u>. That should be a statement that looks like (84).

[D] Calculate the truth conditions for the formula '[∃z: Broken(z)](Above(z)(y))' with respect to $L+ \langle y, k \rangle$ (you don't need to turn in the calculation—but it's necessary to do the calculation to understand what's going on). Study your results. On the basis of your results, state how to correctly fill in the blank below:

For any entity o', '[∃z: Broken(z)](Above(z)(y))' is true with respect to $L+ \langle y,o' \rangle$ *iff* _____ .
    <u>Your answer should not make reference to elements of SL.</u>

[E] Provide the result of applying the rule EXIST to the following formula using the lexicon L:

[∃y: Round(y)]([∃z: Broken(z)](Above(z)(y))).

[F] Study your results in [B], [D], and [E]. Think about what conditions must be met in order for the formula in [E] to be true with respect to L. Provide an English translation.

[G] Provide an SL translation relative to L for *Some porpoise is round and soft*.

[H] Provide an English translation relative to L for '[∃z: Red(z) & Balloon(z)] (Popped(z))'. To arrive at a translation, think through a few of the steps in the calculation of the truth conditions assigned to that formula.

2.3.2 Universal Quantifier

The next type of quantifier we'll consider, called a **universal quantifier**, is formed using the symbol '$\forall$', an upside down A. It gets introduced into a formula via the following syntactic rule:

(90) If ϕ and ψ are formulas and u is a variable, then '$[\forall u{:}\ \phi]\ (\psi)$' is a formula.

Here are some formulas produced by that rule:

(91) a. $[\forall x{:}\ \text{Person}(x)](\text{Clever}(x))$.
      b. $[\forall y{:}\ \text{Horse}(y)](\text{Likes}(\text{Sue})(y))$.
      c. $[\forall z{:}\ \text{Person}(z)]((\text{Clever}(z)\ \&\ \text{Happy}(\text{Frank})))$.

Next we formulate a semantic rule for universally quantified formulas:

UNIVERSAL **[Semantic Rule]**

'$[\forall u{:}\ \phi]\ (\psi)$' is true with respect to M iff

for every object o such that 'ϕ' is true with respect to $M{+}\ \langle u,o \rangle$, 'ψ' is also true with respect to $M{+}\ \langle u,o \rangle$.

Let's instantiate the universal rule with '$\text{Pig}(x)$' for ϕ, '$\text{Happy}(x)$' for ψ, 'x' for u, and L for M:

(92) '$[\forall x{:}\ \text{Pig}(x)]\ (\text{Happy}(x))$' is true with respect to L iff
      for every object o such that '$\text{Pig}(x)$' is true with respect to $L{+}\ \langle x,o \rangle$, '$\text{Happy}(x)$' is also true with respect to $L{+}\ \langle x,o \rangle$.

By a calculation similar to the one done for '$\text{Clever}(x)$' in (77)–(80), we get

(93) '$\text{Pig}(x)$' is true with respect to $L{+}\ \langle x,o \rangle$ iff $o \in L(\text{Pig})$.
      '$\text{Happy}(x)$' is true with respect to $L{+}\ \langle x,o \rangle$ iff $o \in L(\text{Happy})$.

Using set theory, the way L is defined, and REPLACE, we get

(94) '$\text{Pig}(x)$' is true with respect to $L{+}\ \langle x,o \rangle$ iff o is a pig.
      '$\text{Happy}(x)$' is true with respect to $L{+}\ \langle x,o \rangle$ iff o is happy.

From (92), (94) and REPLACE, we get

(95) '$[\forall x{:}\ \text{Pig}\ x]\ (\text{Happy}(x))$' is true with respect to L iff
      for every object o such that o is a pig, o is happy.

And so, with respect to L, an adequate English translation for '$[\forall x{:}\ \text{Pig}(x)]\ (\text{Happy}(x))$' would be *Every pig is happy*. Similarly, *Every horse likes Sue* can be translated as

$[\forall y{:}\ \text{Horse}(y)](\text{Likes}(\text{Sue})(y))$.

And '([∀z: Person(z)](Clever(z)) & Happy(Frank)))' can be translated as *Every person is clever, and Frank is happy.*

Exercise (2.8)

As observed at the outset of this section, the symbol '∀' is an upside down letter *A*. The reason for this is that '∀x' is often read "for all *x*." This suggests that the determiner *all* corresponds to '∀' in the same way as the determiner *every* does. Do you think this is the case? To answer this question, think about whether *Every dog barked* has the same truth conditions as *All dogs barked.* After answering this question, think about whether there are other determiners in English that correspond to '∀'.

Exercise (2.9)

Provide an SL translation relative to *L* of the sentence *Every pig is happy and healthy.*

Exercise (2.10)

Provide an SL translation relative to *L* of the sentence *Jack likes all pigs.*

Exercise (2.11)

Assuming lexicon *L*, calculate the truth conditions for the formula below and submit just the final line of your calculation. It should have the same form as (95).

[∀x: Giraffe(x)] (Knows(Jack)(x)).

Exercise (2.12)

[A] Let *k* be some entity. Calculate the truth conditions for the formula '[∀x: Giraffe x] (Know(y)(x))' with respect to *L*+ ⟨y, k⟩ (you don't need to turn in the calculation—but it's necessary to do the calculation to understand what's going on). Study your results. On the basis of your results, state how to correctly fill in the blank below. Your answer should not make reference to elements of SL.

For any entity *o'*, '[∀x: Giraffe(x)](Know(y)(x))' is true with respect to *L*+ ⟨y,o'⟩ *iff* _____.

[B] Provide an English translation for

(i) [∀x: Giraffe(x)](Know(x)(x)).

(ii) [∃y: Lion(y)] ([∀x: Giraffe(x)] (Know(y)(x))).

(iii) $[\forall x: \text{Giraffe}(x)] ([\exists y: \text{Lion}(y)] (\text{Know}(y)(x)))$.

    If you are unsure about (ii) and (iii), review exercise (2.7), part [F].

✪ Important Practice and Looking Ahead ✪

The following exercise concerns the ambiguity that results from the combination of a quantifier and a negation. It builds on exercise (1.5) in the previous chapter and provides useful preparation for chapter 3.

Exercise (2.13)

Recall from the previous chapter that the sentence *every passenger was not examined* is ambiguous. The two readings can be paraphrased as

(i) Every passenger is such that it is not the case that (s)he was examined.

(ii) It is not the case that every passenger is such that (s)he was examined.

    Produce an SL translation relative to L of each of the paraphrases in (i) and (ii). In creating your formulas, make use of the one-place predicate 'Examined' with the following extension:

$L(\text{Examined}) = \{x : x \text{ was examined}\}$.

Exercise (2.14)

The rule for forming universal formulas is, once again:

(90) If ϕ and ψ are formulas and u is a variable, then '$[\forall u: \phi] (\psi)$' is a formula.

    In the examples looked at so far, 'ϕ' was instantiated with an atomic formula. But the rule allows ϕ to be any sort of formula including one that contains a quantifier. Using the syntactic rule for existential formulas, we can produce

(i) $[\exists x: \text{Book}(x)](\text{Own}(x)(z))$.

    And now using (i) to instantiate ϕ in (90) we can produce this formula:

(ii) $[\forall z: [\exists x: \text{Book}(x)](\text{Own}(x)(z))](\text{Left}(z))$.

[A] Let k be some entity. Say what conditions must be met in order for (i) to be true with respect to $L+ \langle z, k \rangle$.

[B] Provide an English translation with respect to L for the formula in (ii).

[C] Provide an SL translation with respect to L for the English sentence in (iii) below. Translate *student*, *solved*, and *problem* in the usual way but translate *was included in our survey* with the ad hoc predicate IncludedInSurvey, where *L*(IncludedInSurvey) is the set of individuals included in our survey.

(iii) A student [who solved every problem] was included in our survey.

2.3.3 Free Variables, Undefinedness, and Wellformedness

We began our discussion of quantifiers by introducing variables—that is, special symbols that are meant to work like temporary names. A lexicon such as *L* assigns meanings to individual constants, one- and two- place predicates, and nothing else. In particular, it does not assign meanings to variables. However, in the course of applying the semantic rules for quantifiers, variables are added to the lexicon using the plus notation.

M+ ⟨... , ...⟩ notation

If *M* is a set of pairs that does not include a pair whose first element is α, then **M+ ⟨α, β⟩** is a set that consists of the pairs in *M* plus the pair ⟨α, β⟩ .

Recall our definition of *F*(...) notation, as well:

F(...) notation

If *F* is a set of pairs and α is a first element of exactly one of the pairs in *F*, then **F(α)** is the second element of the pair in *F* whose first element is α.

Since variables are not in *L*, there is no pair in *L* whose first element is '*x*', so *L*(*x*) is not defined. It is undefined for the same reason that it makes no sense to look up the definition of the Q'eqchi' word *palaw* in an English dictionary: there is no pair in that dictionary whose first element is *palaw*. Given that *L*(*x*) is not defined, the following statement couldn't possibly be true:

(96) *L*(*x*) ∈ *L*(Person).

And so given our rules ATOMIC-1, VARIABLE, and VOCABULARY, 'Person(*x*)' could never be true with respect to *L*. We might go even further and say that if *L*(*x*) is not defined, then the statement in (96) isn't defined either, and so 'Person(*x*)' shouldn't be true or false with respect to *L*. Likewise, 'Clever(*x*)' is not defined relative to *L*.

But now we have a puzzle. A person can be a perfectly competent speaker of English and not know the meanings of words of Q'eqchi'. That's because English grammar doesn't assign meanings to words of Q'eqchi'. And because it doesn't assign meanings to Q'eqchi' words, it also doesn't assign meanings to sentences that are half English and half Q'eqchi'. If a part of a sentence does not get assigned a meaning, then the sentence itself can't get assigned a meaning. But we just said that 'Person(x)' doesn't have an interpretation relative to L, so how is it that '[∃x: Person(x)](Clever(x))', which contains 'Person(x)', <u>does</u> in fact have an interpretation relative to L? The answer lies in the semantic rule EXIST. It changes the lexicon so that 'Person(x)' and 'Clever(x)' get interpreted not relative to L but relative to a lexicon that does in fact include 'x'. In that case, we say that the variable 'x' is **bound**. Similarly, '[∀x: Pig(x)] (Happy(x))' has perfectly well-defined truth conditions with respect to L due to the semantic rule UNIVERSAL, which ensures that the variable 'x' is bound in that formula.

A variable that is not bound is called a **free variable**. We began this chapter by talking about how to form sentences of SL. Technically, a sentence is a formula that contains no free variables. With that definition in mind, consider the formula '[∀x: Pig(x)](Happy(z))'. Note that the quantifier is '[∀x: Pig(x)]' but the formula attached to it contains 'z'. That 'z' is free. The formula is syntactically well formed. We might say it is grammatical. However, it contains the free variable 'z', and because of that, '[∀x: Pig(x)](Happy(z))' is undefined with respect to L, for the same reason that 'Person(x)' is undefined. It is a formula but not a sentence in the technical sense.

Variables are like names in one way, and unlike them in another. On the one hand, they refer to entities, just as names do. On the other hand, they don't have a fixed reference the way names do. Variables are like pronouns in some ways, but unlike them in others. On the one hand, variables refer to entities but they are not permanently tied to a given entity, just like pronouns. On the other hand, free variables don't have meanings, and so the formulas containing them aren't defined relative to L. They work only if there are quantifiers to bind them. Pronouns are different. They can occur in sentences without quantifiers.

✪ Important Practice and Looking Ahead ✪

The next exercise introduces the question of how **free pronouns** get interpreted. We will return to this question in the next chapter.

Exercise (2.15)

Arnold gets on a crowded city bus and finds himself standing next to a man and a woman engaged in conversation. The man says: "She once suggested a solution that was almost exactly the solution for which Norman Baldy is so famous." The woman reacts with shock. This arouses Arnold's interest. He's curious to know the meaning of the man's utterance but he doesn't know who *she* refers to or who Norman Baldy is. He takes out his phone and uses it to discover who Norman Baldy is. His phone is of no use to discover who *she* refers to. This discrepancy is due to the fact that pronouns and names work differently—they get their referents in different ways.

The pronoun *herself* in *No girl submitted a story about herself* is a **bound pronoun**. Above we discussed how *herself* is interpreted (see the discussion of (69) above). The pronoun *she* in the utterance that Arnold overheard on the bus is a **free pronoun**. Its interpretation makes use of information gleaned form the discourse.

[A] Try to state a general rule for how a participant in a conversation comes to know what the referent of a free pronoun is. Say, in terms of your rule, why Arnold can't use his phone to discover who *she* refers to.

[B] The sentence in (a) below has a reading in which the pronoun *she* is free and another reading in which the pronoun is bound.

(a) No woman in Arash's building got the studio she had asked for.

(i) Provide two unambiguous paraphrases for (a) that isolate the two readings. Your paraphrase for the free pronoun reading will necessarily contain its own free pronoun.

(ii) Describe a speech context in which (a) is used on the free pronoun reading. Explain how the free pronoun is interpreted, making reference to the rule you offered in [A].

[C] The sentence in (b) below has a reading in which the pronoun *him* is used to refer to Phil, and another reading in which *him* is used to refer to Stanley. Does the rule you offered in [A] predict that (b) is ambiguous? If not, discuss how it might be modified to cover this case.

(b) Phil tickled Stanley, and Liz poked him.

Exercise (2.16)

For each of the following formulas, determine whether or not it is well formed. For those that are well formed, determine whether or not they are defined with respect to L. Provide your answer in the form of two lists: [1] well-formed and defined formulas and [2] well-formed, but undefined formulas. Use the roman numerals provided to name the formulas. Formulas that are not well formed will not appear on either of your lists.

(i) Attacked(Fido)(Jack)

(ii) Attacked(Jack)(Fido)

(iii) Jack(Attacked)(Fido)

(iv) Attacked(Fido)(x)

(v) [$\forall x$: Dog](Barked(x))

(vi) Barked([$\exists z$: Dog(z)])

(vii) [∀x: Dog(z)](Barked(x))

(viii) Knows(Jack)([∃z: Dog(z)])

(ix) [∀x: Dog(x)](Barked)

(x) [∃z: Dog(z)](Knows(x)(z))

The relevant syntactic rules are, once again:

- If ϕ and ψ are formulas and u is a variable, then '[∃u: ϕ] (ψ)' is a formula.
- If ϕ and ψ are formulas and u is a variable, then '[∀u: ϕ] (ψ)' is a formula.
- If π is a one-place predicate and α is an individual constant or a variable, then 'π(α)' is a formula.
- If π is a two-place predicate and α is an individual constant or a variable, then 'π(α)' is a one-place predicate.

2.3.4 More Quantifiers

We can now extend our language by adding the quantifier words No and THE:

No [Semantic Rule]

'[No u: ϕ] (ψ)' is true with respect to M iff

there is no object o such that 'ϕ' is true with respect to M+ ⟨u,o⟩ and 'ψ' is also true with respect to M+ ⟨u,o⟩ .

THE [Semantic Rule]

'[The u: ϕ] (ψ)' is true with respect to M iff

there is exactly one object o such that 'ϕ' is true with respect to M+ ⟨u,o⟩ and there is exactly one object o such that 'ϕ' and 'ψ' are both true with respect to M+ ⟨u,o⟩ .

The intuition behind the wording of the last rule, THE, can be appreciated by reconsidering figure 2.1.

It's true that <u>the square</u> is on the left side of the figure, and it's true that <u>the diamond</u> is on the right side. It would be odd or false to say that the triangle is on the left side because there are two triangles. When we use a singular definite like *the triangle* and we say *the triangle is on the left*, we're saying that there is exactly one triangle and it is on the left.

We now have several quantifiers. And once a quantifier is added to a formula, we get a new formula, which can then be combined with yet another quantifier to give us SL sentences such as

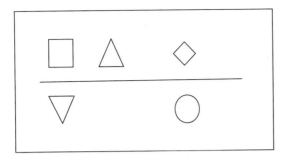

Figure 2.1
Geometric shapes with Dave the diamond and Cyrus the circle.

[No y: Student(y)] ([$\exists x$: Car(x)] (Bought(x)(y))).

Relative to lexicon L, that sentence is true if and only if for no student y, is there a car x such that y bought x. It could be translated as *No student bought a car.*

In some of the following exercises you are asked to translate between English and SL. In each case, assume that SL is interpreted relative to lexicon L.

Exercise (2.17)

[A] Provide an SL translation for (i)–(iv) below. Each translation should include a quantifier.

(i) Every pig grunted.

(ii) Mary met some gardener.

(iii) No frog danced.

(iv) All teachers know Sue.

[B] Use the semantic rules to calculate the truth conditions relative to lexicon L for

[No x: (Grey(x) & Pig(x))] (Sings(x)).

Hand in <u>only</u> the last line of your calculation.

[C] Provide an SL translation for *Some black horse liked Mary.*

[D] Provide English translations for

(i) [$\forall x$: Circle(x)] ([$\exists y$: Square(y)] (Touch(y)(x))).

(ii) [$\forall x$: (Circle(x) & Brown(x))] ([$\exists y$: Square(y)] (Touch(x)(y))).

(iii) [$\forall x$: Circle(x)] ([$\exists y$: (Square(y) & Brown(y))] (Touch(y)(x))).

(iv) [$\forall x$: Circle(x)] ([$\exists y$: (Square(y) & Brown(y))] (Touch(x)(y))).

Exercise (2.18)

[A] Suppose we have a quantifier forming symbol 'Ex1'. Provide a syntactic rule that will allow us to generate the sentence '[Ex1 y: Pig(y)] (Happy(y))'. Provide a new semantic rule that, along with our existing semantic rules, guarantees that

'[Ex1 y: Pig(y)] (Happy(y))' is true with respect to L iff there is exactly one object o such that o is a pig and o is happy.

[B] Making use of 'Ex1' from the previous task, provide SL translations for (i) and (ii) below.

(i) There is exactly one triangle such that it is touching every circle.

(ii) For every circle, there is exactly one triangle that is touching it.

Note: The sentences in (i) and (ii) are unambiguous paraphrases of the ambiguous sentence *Exactly one triangle is touching every circle*. This ambiguity was observed in exercise (1.10) in the previous chapter. Your two SL translations are now themselves unambiguous paraphrases of that ambiguous sentence of English. Symbolic languages are quite often used as tools to discover and display ambiguities of natural language.

Exercise (2.19)

In section 2.3.1, we calculated the conditions under which a simple formula with an existential quantifier was true. On the basis of that calculation, we determined that the formula could be translated into English using *some*. English has several determiners that are used to assert the existence of some entity, and they are not all semantically equivalent. Compare the following three sentences: *Some dog barked; at least one dog barked; a dog barked*.

Which if any of these three is the best translation for '[$\exists x$: Dog(x)](Barked(x))'? Is there one that requires a different quantifier? If you think so, present your intuitions by describing situations in which the formula and the English sentence differ in truth value. Having done that, propose a new SL quantifier that could be used to translate the sentence you've chosen. As in exercise (2.18), provide a semantic rule for your newly proposed quantifier.

2.4 Predicate Conjunction

Consider the English sentence

(97) Every coin is round and flat.

The SL sentence in (98) below is an adequate translation of (97) relative to lexicon L.

(98) [$\forall x$: Coin(x)]((Round(x) & Flat(x))).

In the English sentence the predicates *round* and *flat* have an *and* between them, while in the SL sentence, '&' combines two formulas, not two predicates. '(Round & Flat)' is not well formed! This represents a syntactic difference between the languages, but it doesn't render SL less expressive. Assuming lexicon *L*, (97) and (98) say the same thing—they just say it differently. For most purposes, that is all that matters to a logician creating a symbolic language. Moreover, if one tried to extend the language so that predicates could be conjoined, it would complicate the language in a way that would interfere with the logician's goals.

Recall, however, that our goal is to understand how natural language works, and since natural language often has constructions in which two or more predicates are directly combined, it will be useful to explore how to connect predicates directly in SL. For this we'll need a new symbol to stand for predicate conjunction, as well as a semantic rule for interpreting phrases formed with that connective.

The meaning of a one-place predicate is a set. This holds for simple one-place predicates like 'Round' and for complex one-place predicates like 'From(Boston)'. Just as '&' puts together two formulas to get a new formula, predicate conjunction combines two one-place predicates to get a new one-place predicate. Semantically that means combining two set-denoting expressions to get a new set-denoting expression. Thus, we want a connective whose interpretation will be an operation taking two sets to form a new one. Two obvious choices are union and intersection, introduced in chapter 1, section 1.5. To decide between them, we should think about what predicate conjunction means. If something is round, it's in the set of round things. If something is flat, it's in the set of flat things. If something is round and flat, it's in both sets; in other words, predicate conjunction is interpreted as intersection. We'll be using the symbol '⊓' to combine one-place predicates. Here, then, are the syntactic and semantic rules:

(99) If π_1 is a one-place predicate and π_2 is a one-place predicate, then $(\pi_1 \sqcap \pi_2)$ is a one-place predicate.

PREDCON [Semantic Rule]

$$[\![(\pi_1 \sqcap \pi_2)]\!]^M = ([\![\pi_1]\!]^M \cap [\![\pi_2]\!]^M).$$

Let us emphasize that '⊓' is a symbol of SL. It connects predicates. '∩' is a symbol of set-theory—it connects two sets denoting expressions. So '(Dog ⊓ Cat)' is well formed, but '(Dog ∩ Cat)' is not well formed.

Below is a calculation of the truth conditions of an SL sentence in which predicates are conjoined.

(100) (Young $\sqcap$ Happy)(Jack) is true with respect to L

      iff $[\![\text{Jack}]\!]^L \in [\![(\text{Young} \sqcap \text{Happy})]\!]^L$ ATOMIC-1

      iff Jack $\in [\![(\text{Young} \sqcap \text{Happy})]\!]^L$ VOCABULARY, REPLACE

      iff Jack $\in ([\![\text{Young}]\!]^L \cap [\![\text{Happy}]\!]^L)$ PREDCON, REPLACE

         $[\![\text{Young}]\!]^L = \{x : x \text{ is young}\}$ VOCABULARY

         $[\![\text{Happy}]\!]^L = \{x : x \text{ is happy}\}$ VOCABULARY

         $([\![\text{Young}]\!]^L \cap [\![\text{Happy}]\!]^L) = (\{x : x \text{ is young}\} \cap \{x : x \text{ is happy}\})$ REPLACE

         $([\![\text{Young}]\!]^L \cap [\![\text{Happy}]\!]^L) = \{x : x \text{ is young and happy}\}$ set theory

      iff Jack $\in \{x : x \text{ is young and happy}\}$ REPLACE

      iff Jack is young and happy.   set theory, REPLACE

      '(Young $\sqcap$ Happy)(Jack)' is true with respect to L iff Jack is young and happy.   REPLACE

✪ Important Practice and Looking Ahead ✪

The purpose of the next exercise is to prove an equivalence involving predicate conjunction and formula conjunction. This equivalence will come in handy in the chapters that follow.

Exercise (2.20)

Prove that for any lexicon M, if (i) below is true with respect to M, then (ii) below is true with respect to M, and if (ii) below is true with respect to M then so is (i). Do that by using our semantic rules to arrive at the truth conditions for (i) and (ii) and then explaining why there could not be a situation in which one of the sentences is true and the other false.

(i) (Clever $\sqcap$ Tall)(a).

(ii) (Clever(a) & Tall(a)).

The equivalence that you were asked to demonstrate in exercise (2.20) is a specific instance of a generalization that refers to **conjunction equivalence** and is stated in (101).

(101) For any one-place predicates, π_1 and π_2, and individual constant or variable α and lexicon M, '($\pi_1 \sqcap \pi_2$)(α)' is defined with respect to M if and only if '($\pi_1(\alpha)$ & $\pi_2(\alpha)$)' is defined with respect to M. When defined, '($\pi_1 \sqcap \pi_2$)(α)' is true with respect to M if and only if '($\pi_1(\alpha)$ & $\pi_2(\alpha)$)' is true with respect to M.

On the basis of conjunction equivalence, we can determine, for example, that the formulas in (i) are logically equivalent and so are the formulas in (ii):

(i) [$\exists x$: Pig(x)]((Happy(x) & Healthy(x))).   [$\exists x$: Pig(x)]((Happy $\sqcap$ Healthy)(x)).

(ii) [$\forall z$: (Young(z) & Pig(z))](Happy(z)).   [$\forall z$: (Young $\sqcap$ Pig)(z)](Happy(z)).

Exercise (2.21)

[A] Assume lexicon L. Provide English translations for the following sentences of SL. Make your translations colloquial, if possible.

(i) $[\forall x: (\text{Round} \sqcap \text{Coin})(x)](\text{Silver}(x))$.

(ii) $[\exists x: (\text{Boy} \sqcap \text{From}(\text{Texas}))(x)]\ (\text{Danced}(x))$.

(iii) $(\text{Danced} \sqcap \text{Sang})(\text{Jack})$.

(iv) $[\text{No } x: \text{Candidate}(x)]\ ([\forall y: (\text{Current} \sqcap \text{Issue})(y)]\ (\text{Know}(y)(x)))$.

(v) $[\exists x: (\text{Black} \sqcap \text{Horse})(x)]\ (\text{Liked}(\text{Mary})(x))$.

[B] We began our discussion of quantifiers with the following sentences of English:

(69) a. No girl submitted a story about herself.
     b. Every boy submitted a story about himself.
     c. At least one mother submitted a story about herself.

Provide a sentence of SL that with respect to lexicon L would be a good translation for (69)b. The pronoun *himself* will correspond to a variable in your translation. Make sure the variable is bound by a quantifier. Translate *about* as the two-place predicate 'About'. As much as possible, aim for a sentence of SL that groups together expressions in way that the corresponding English expressions are grouped. For example, *story about himself* forms a constituent, so if possible have 'Story' and 'About' in a unit to the exclusion of 'Submitted'.

Exercise (2.22)

[A] SL includes a two-place predicate 'In', a one-place predicate 'Dog', and an individual constant 'Alaska'. Using those three symbols and any others from SL, write an expression of SL that is assigned, as its meaning relative to L, the set of dogs in Alaska.

[B] Explain why neither of the expressions in (i) and (ii) below would work as an answer to [A].

(i) Dog(In(Alaska)).

(ii) In(Alaska)(Dog).

[C] Use your answer in [A] to write a sentence that says that Fido is a dog in Alaska.

[D] What's wrong with the following? (In(Alaska)(Fido) $\sqcap$ Dog).

Exercise (2.23)

In the next chapter, we'll have reason to consider a formula of SL with the following form:

$[\forall x: \text{Problem}(x)]([\exists y: (\text{Student} \sqcap \text{Solved}(x))(y)](\text{IncludedInSurvey}(y)))$.

The formula is about a survey that was taken. L(IncludedInSurvey) is the set of individuals included in the survey. So for example, 'IncludedInSurvey(Jack)' would translate relative to L as *Jack was included in the survey*. Provide an English translation for the formula above.

2.5 The Rules of SL

Metavariables

α   variables and individual constants

π   one-place and two-place predicates

φ, ψ   sentences / formulas

u   variables

M   lexicons

Notation

$[\![\phi]\!]^M$ stands for the interpretation of the expression 'φ' with respect to the lexicon *M*.

Vocabulary

• Individual constants are proper names of English and lowercase letters from the beginning of the alphabet.

• Variables are lowercase letters from the end of the alphabet.

• Simple one-place predicates are capitalized words of English including intransitive verbs nouns and adjectives.

• Two-place predicates are capitalized words of English including prepositions, transitive verbs and relational nouns and adjectives.

Syntactic Rules

1. If π is a one-place predicate, and α is an individual constant or a variable, then 'π(α)' is a formula.

2. If π is a two-place predicate and α is an individual constant or a variable, then 'π(α)' is a one-place predicate.

3. If π_1 is a one-place predicate and π_2 is a one-place predicate, then '$(\pi_1 \sqcap \pi_2)$' is a one-place predicate.

4. If φ is a formula, then '¬(φ)' is a formula.

5. If φ and ψ are formulas, then '(φ & ψ)' is a formula.

6. If φ and ψ are formulas and u is a variable, then '[∃u: φ] (ψ)', '[∀u: φ] (ψ)', '[No u: φ] (ψ)', and '[The u: φ] (ψ)' are formulas.

Semantic Rules

Interpreting vocabulary items

If α is an individual constant, then $[\![α]\!]^M = M(α)$ and $M(α)$ is an entity.

If π is a simple one-place predicate, then $[\![π]\!]^M = M(π)$ and $M(π)$ is a set of entities.

If π is a simple two-place predicate, then $[\![π]\!]^M = M(π)$ and $M(π)$ is a set of pairs, each of which has an entity as the first element and a set of entities as the second element.

If the variable u is the first member of a pair in M, then $[\![u]\!]^M = M(u)$.

Interpreting constituents

[atomic-1]   If π is a one-place predicate, then 'π(α)' is true with respect to M iff $[\![α]\!]^M ∈ [\![π]\!]^M$.

[atomic-2]   If π is a two-place predicate, then $[\![π(α)]\!]^M = [\![π]\!]^M ([\![α]\!]^M)$.

[and]   '(φ & ψ)' is true with respect to M iff 'φ' is true with respect to M and 'ψ' is true with respect to M.

[predcon] $[\![(π_1 ⊓ π_2)]\!]^M = ([\![π_1]\!]^M ∩ [\![π_2]\!]^M)$.

[not]   '¬(φ)' is true with respect to M iff it is not the case that: 'φ' is true with respect to M

[exist]   '[∃u: φ] (ψ)' is true with respect to M iff
for some object o such that 'φ' is true with respect to M+ $⟨u,o⟩$, 'ψ' is also true with respect to M+ $⟨u,o⟩$.

[universal]   '[∀u: φ] (ψ)' is true with respect to M iff
for every object o such that 'φ' is true with respect to M+ $⟨u,o⟩$, 'ψ' is also true with respect to M+ $⟨u,o⟩$.

[no]   '[No u: φ] (ψ)' is true with respect to M iff
there is no object o such that 'φ' is true with respect to M+ $⟨u,o⟩$ and 'ψ' is also true with respect to M+ $⟨u,o⟩$.

[the]   '[The u: φ] (ψ)' is true with respect to M iff
there is exactly one object o such that 'φ' is true with respect to M+ $⟨u,o⟩$, and there is exactly one object o such that 'φ' and 'ψ' are both true with respect to M+ $⟨u,o⟩$.

In addition to the rules above, we've introduced two rules of inference. They are repeated below. These rules are not part of SL; they only guide us in reasoning logically about the rules in SL. In the same way, traffic laws or laws of physics don't include logical principles; rather, logical principles are used to apply those laws to specific situations.

REPLACE [Rule of Inference]

If two statements ϕ and ψ are logically equivalent (ϕ iff ψ), then from a statement including ϕ, infer the statement that results from replacing ϕ with ψ.

If two expressions E_1 and E_2 stand for the same entity, then from a statement that includes E_1, infer the statement that results from replacing E_1 with E_2.

INSTANTIATE [Rule of Inference]

From a rule stated in terms of metavariables, infer the result of substituting the metavariables with expressions of the right kind—taking care to substitute all occurrences of a given variable with the same expression.

New Terminology

- quantifiers
- variables, free variables
- formulas
- determiner phrase (DP)
- existential quantifier
- universal quantifier
- predicate conjunction
- symbolic logic

2.6 Truth Values, Truth Conditions, Extensions, Languages, Grammars

SL is a system of rules that defines an infinite set of expressions (vocabulary and syntax) and that specifies how truth values are assigned to sentences and how extensions are assigned to complex predicates in terms of the extensions of individual constants and simple predicates (semantic rules). Once a particular lexicon is chosen, every well-formed sentence of SL gets assigned a truth value. Let's illustrate these ideas with two examples discussed earlier. Exercise (2.4) included the statements

J(Meretricious) = $\{a, d\}$,

and

J(Alan) = a.

J(Carl) = c.

J(Dallas) = d.

With the choice of lexicon J, the extension of 'Meretricious' is $\{a,d\}$, the extension of 'Carl' is c, and the extension of 'Dallas' is d. Given the rules of SL, 'Meretricious(Carl)' and 'Meretricious(Dallas)' are both well formed and are both assigned truth values: TRUE for 'Meretricious(Dallas)'and FALSE for 'Meretricious(Carl)'. Next we consider the well-formed formula 'Clever(Agatha)', and this time we choose the lexicon L. To determine the truth value of 'Clever(Agatha)' with this choice of lexicon, we again need to first determine extensions. Recall how L is defined. It is the lexicon that assigns to the symbols of SL the same extension as the corresponding word of English. Given this definition, L(Clever), the extension of 'Clever' is the set of individuals who are clever. If Agatha is clever, she's in the extension of 'Clever' and otherwise she isn't. Given the rules of SL, 'Clever(Agatha)' is well formed and is assigned a truth value. Which one? Well, that depends on the facts: If Agatha is in fact clever, then she is in the extension of 'Clever', and then 'Clever(Agatha)' is assigned TRUE. If Agatha is not clever, then she is not in the extension of 'Clever', and then 'Clever(Agatha)' is assigned FALSE. Using 'SL+L' to refer to the result of choosing the lexicon L and applying the rules of SL, we can summarize our findings as

(102) 'Clever(Agatha)' is assigned TRUE by SL+L *iff* Agatha is clever.

What we have in (102) are the truth conditions that are associated with a formula of SL. SL+L is a kind of grammar. It generates well-formed expressions, and it assigns meanings to all of them: extensions to individual constants and predicates, and truth values to formulas. And the resulting pairings of expressions and meanings form a kind of language. Let's revisit our statements from chapter 1 about facts and meanings in connection with this language:

(103) truth conditions + facts about the world → truth value.

(104) word meanings + facts about the world → extensions.

       extensions + syntax → truth value.

If we want to know if the formula 'Clever(Agatha)' in the language of SL+L is true or not, then following (103), we confront the truth conditions given in (102) with the relevant facts about Agatha. And substituting 'symbol' for 'word' in (104) yields a good description of how the grammar SL+L works.

In subsequent chapters, we will use the term *SL* loosely, referring sometimes to the grammar SL+*L* and sometimes to the language described by that grammar. This is not unlike the way *English* and other language names are used.

Exercise (2.24)

Up to now, we've been ignoring lexical ambiguity and this simplification will continue in subsequent chapters. This simplification allows us to define L as the lexicon that assigns to the symbols of SL <u>the same extension</u> as the corresponding word of English. Explain what goes wrong when lexical ambiguity is acknowledged. Think, for example, about what counts as an SL translation with respect to L of *The soup is hot*. Suggest a method for dealing with this problem.

Further Reading

Stanford Encyclopedia of Philosophy, The. https://plato.stanford.edu. See especially the following entries: Descriptions (by Peter Ludlow); Generalized Quantifiers (by Dag Westerståhl); Negation (by Laurence Horn and Heinrich Wansing).

Txurruka, Isabella. "The Natural Language Conjunction *and.*" *Linguistics and Philosophy* 26 (2003): 255–85.

3   Sentences and Determiner Phrases

Beginning with this chapter, we will develop rules for assigning truth values to English sentences. After setting up the outlines of the approach we will take, we'll focus on **determiner phrases** (DPs), including quantifiers and pronouns; sentential conjunction; negation; and various modifiers, including prepositional phrases (PPs), adjectives, adverbs, and relative clauses.

3.1 Syntax

Our aim is a grammar that assigns truth values to natural language sentences based on the extensions of the parts of the sentence. For this to work, one needs to know what the parts of the sentences are and how they are combined. So we first need to fix ideas about syntax.[1] We will be adopting the view that the grammar of a natural language generates phrase structures, representable as trees, and that movement transformations can apply to these to create new phrase structures. We also take for granted some means by which morphemes are combined into words; for example, *see* + Past becomes *saw*.

We'll be adopting the idea that sentential subjects are generated within a **verb phrase** (VP), giving us structures like the one shown in figure 3.1. The VP there is the basis for a sentence. It can be extended with various functional categories. For example, there can be a negation above the VP, as shown in figure 3.2. As suggested by the captions of figure 3.1 and figure 3.2, these trees are called **base structures**, and they will be the input to rules of interpretation. Base structures are also input to further syntactic and morphological rules that produce **surface structures**.

In this chapter, our base structures will be VPs and NegPs (as in figure 3.2). In later chapters, the functional structure above the VP will grow as we learn about new phenomena such as tense and aspect.

When discussing syntactic structures, we employ the following standard terminology. The points connected by lines are called **nodes**. The base structure for *Every giraffe saw Agatha* in figure 3.1 has 7 nodes.

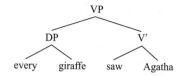

Figure 3.1
Base structure for *Every giraffe saw Agatha.*

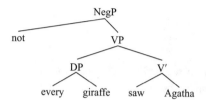

Figure 3.2
Base structure for *Every giraffe didn't see Agatha.*

Figure 3.3
Constituent corresponding to node DP *every giraffe.*

A higher node <u>dominates</u> a lower one. For example, the node labeled VP dominates the nodes DP, V′, *every*, *giraffe*, *saw*, and *Agatha*. Among the nodes that VP dominates, there are two, DP and V′, that are immediately below it. In that case, we say that DP and V′ are the **daughters** of VP. Likewise, the daughters of DP are *every* and *giraffe* and the daughters of V′ are *saw* and *Agatha*. A node that has two or more daughters is a **branching node**. To every node α, there is a **constituent** that corresponds to node α. It consists of α and all the nodes that α dominates. The constituent that corresponds to the node DP is shown in figure 3.3. *every* is a determiner and the 'D' in the node label 'DP' stands for "determiner". The constituent that corresponds to the node VP is the entire base structure depicted in figure 3.1.

Exercise (3.1)

This exercise pertains to the base structure in figure 3.2.

[A] List the branching nodes in that structure.

[B] What are the daughters of the node labeled VP?

[C] What is the constituent that corresponds to the node DP?

3.2 Direct and Indirect Interpretation

There are two different ways of assigning truth values to sentences of natural language. The first way is called **direct interpretation**. By this method, extensions are assigned to words of the language, and then semantic rules govern how those extensions are combined. Direct interpretation is often executed using the same techniques as those we used in the previous chapter to interpret symbolic logic (SL). There is another method called **indirect interpretation**. By this method, a natural language such as English is translated into a symbolic language, and then the sentences of the symbolic language are assigned truth values. For example, if the symbolic language that is chosen is SL, then to interpret the sentence *Bruce sang* we first apply rules of translation that get us to the formula 'Sang(Bruce)'. Then the semantic rules of SL assign a truth value to 'Sang(Bruce)', and we count that value as the truth value for *Bruce sang*. Figure 3.4 illustrates this process. The method is called "indirect interpretation" because the truth values are assigned to sentences of natural language indirectly, via an intermediate translation language. In this textbook, we will be doing indirect interpretation.

Simple sentences like *Bruce sang* are useful to illustrate what indirect interpretation is. But the potential advantages of doing indirect interpretation rather than direct interpretation are realized only once we start to analyze more complex sentences. So for now, you should understand how truth values get assigned to sentences of English in the indirect method, without necessarily seeing why one would choose this method.

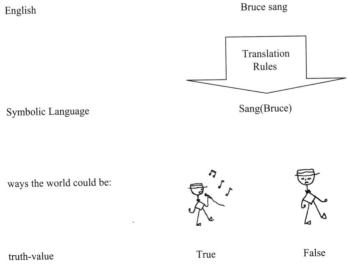

Figure 3.4
Indirect interpretation.

Above we said that 'Sang(Bruce)' might serve as the translation for *Bruce sang* according to the indirect approach. In SL there is an arbitrary connection between the form of a predicate or individual constant and its meaning. One lexicon may assign to 'Sang' the set of all individuals who sang, and another lexicon might assign it the set of all rabbits. This degree of freedom is not useful for the purpose of assigning truth values to natural language sentences. When we translate *sang*, we want to be sure that the translation picks out the singers and not the rabbits. Likewise, when we translate *Bruce,* we want the translation to be a constant that gets assigned Bruce and not Aurélie. To guarantee these results, we insist that in the two-step process of assigning truth values to natural language sentences, formulas of SL are interpreted with respect to L, the lexicon that assigns to predicates and constants the extensions of the corresponding English words. And we'll adopt the following as our first rule of translation:

(1) LEXICON

A symbol of SL is a translation for an English word if the extension of the SL symbol relative to L is the same as the extension of the English word.

EXAMPLE: 'Dog' is a translation for the English word *dog*.

Since the rules of translation are part of the system that assigns meanings, we must make sure that those rules are sensitive to syntax, for the reasons emphasized in chapter 1. That means we will be translating not strings of words, but rather syntactic structures such as those in figure 3.5.

In figure 3.5, underneath each of the trees is an adequate SL translation with respect to L. By comparing the translations and the syntactic structures, we arrive at the following generalization: For any node in the tree, its translation results from taking the translations of its daughters and concatenating them with parentheses around one of the translations. We'll codify this generalization in our second rule of translation, which we'll call MERGE. The MERGE rule will make use of a format designed to make translation rules concise. We'll introduce this format in steps beginning with the MERGE rule itself:

(2) MERGE $\{\alpha, \beta\} \leadsto \alpha'(\beta')$

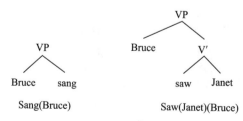

Figure 3.5
Syntactic structures and their translations.

This rule says: A node whose daughters are α and β has a potential translation of the form α′(β′), where α′ is a potential translation of α and β′ is a potential translation of β. Let's apply this rule to the top node of the tree in figure 3.5 on the left. Its daughters are *Bruce* and *sang* and, by the LEXICON rule in (1), they are translated as 'Bruce' and 'Sang'. The MERGE rule then says that 'Sang(Bruce)' is a potential translation for the top node. The rule allows another potential translation, one that is undesirable, a fact we'll return to in a moment. The rule in (2) above illustrates the following features of our translation format:

• Greek letters from the beginning of the alphabet are used as metavariables ranging over nodes in a syntactic structure.

• A primed symbol stands for a potential translation for what the corresponding unprimed symbol stands for.

• We may name a node in the structure by naming the set of its daughters using list notation.

• '↝' connects a node with a potential translation for that node.

A key feature of the rule in (2) is that it doesn't care about the order of the constituents. That allows it to apply to the V′ node in the tree on the right in figure 3.5, to give 'Saw(Janet)' and then again to the top node to give 'Saw(Janet)(Bruce)'. In the first case α (*saw*) is on the left. In the second case, α (*saw Janet*) is on the right.

One way to demonstrate the effect of translation rules is to draw a syntactic structure with labeled nodes and then to provide the translation of each labeled node along with the rule used to arrive at that translation. When doing this, we'll usually restrict attention to branching nodes, as shown in the example in figure 3.6

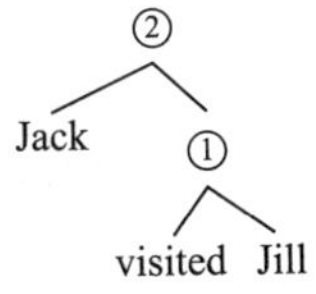

① ↝ Visited(Jill)   MERGE

② ↝ Visited(Jill)(Jack)   MERGE

Figure 3.6
Application of MERGE.

Exercise (3.2)

According to the MERGE rule there is more than one potential translation for *Bruce sang*. One translation is 'Sang(Bruce)' What is the other one?

We now address the problem of undesirable translations. MERGE gives rise to the translations listed in figure 3.6, but it also says, for example, that a potential translation of node ② is 'Jill(Visited)' and a potential translation of node ① is 'Jill(Visited)(Jack)'. These are not what we want. We might revise our translation rules to avoid these results, but if we did, we would be duplicating work already done by SL. The syntactic rules of SL already rule out those formulas. All we need to do is impose the requirement that a translation be well-formed:

(3) WELLFORMEDNESS FILTER   Any potential translation of an expression of English that is a well-formed expression of SL is a translation of that expression.

Given this set-up, 'Jill(Visited)' and 'Visited(Jill)' are both <u>potential</u> translations for the node labeled ② above, but only 'Visited(Jill)' is a translation for that node. When we assess the predictions of our evolving grammar, we'll only pay attention to those potential translations that contribute to well-formed formulas.

Summarizing now, we distinguish between **translations** and **potential translations**. A potential translation is one that is produced by our rules of translation. Among the potential translations, there are some that are well-formed expressions of SL. These are the translations. This arrangement allows us to capitalize on the work done by the syntactic rules of SL.

The translation rules LEXICON and MERGE along with SL now determine the truth values for all simple transitive and intransitive clauses. The translation rules get us from *Jack visited Jill* to the SL formula 'Visited(Jill)(Jack)', and the semantic rules of SL along with lexicon *L* tell us that that formula is true if and only if Jack visited Jill. Using the same words, but different syntax, we build the sentence *Jill visited Jack*, which leads to a different formula, one that is true if and only if Jill visited Jack. The conditions under which the first English sentence comes out to be true are different from the conditions under which the second comes out to be true. This difference is the result of using different syntax. We now have an account of how syntax influences meaning.

Our grammar now consists of a syntactic component that generates base structures and a translation component that include rules of translation, the WELLFORMEDNESS FILTER, SL, and the lexicon *L*. Together these assign meanings (extensions and truth values) to base structures.

Exercise (3.3)

Provide the meaning that our grammar assigns to *visited Jack*. List all the rules that play a role in arriving at the meaning. Your list will include rules of translation that get to a translation for *visited Jack* and semantic rules of SL that get to the meaning of that translation. (Semantic rules of SL are summarized in section 2.5, toward the end of chapter 2.)

✪ Important Practice and Looking Ahead ✪

Exercise (3.4) provides practice with LEXICON, MERGE, and the WELLFORMEDNESS FILTER. The exercise leads to an outstanding issue with prepositional phrases (PPs), which will come up again later in the chapter and will motivate developments in the next chapter.

Exercise (3.4)

[A] For (i) and (ii) below, demonstrate what translation is assigned using the method illustrated in figure 3.6 with numbered or labeled trees and translations for each node.

(i) Amaya danced

(ii) in Cuba.

[B] Our rules produce a potential translation for the expression *house in Cuba* (see figure 3.7). But that translation doesn't pass the WELLFORMEDNESS FILTER in (3). Explain what goes wrong and suggest a new rule of translation that will solve the problem. You'll want a rule of translation that, along with our other rules, gives *house in Cuba* a translation that, according to the semantic rules of SL, has as its extension the set of houses that are in Cuba.

Figure 3.7
Syntactic structure for *house in Cuba*.

In the grammar we are developing, there is a tight connection between syntactic categories and semantic categories, where "semantic category" means kinds of extensions. Names are assigned individuals, intransitive verbs have sets of entities as extensions, and so on. In table 3.1, we list the correspondences between syntactic and semantic categories of

Table 3.1
Correspondence between syntactic and semantic categories

Syntactic category of English	Syntactic category of SL	Semantic category
Name	Individual constant	Entity
Intransitive verb, adjective, noun, noun phrase	One-place predicate	Set of entities
Transitive verb, preposition	Two-place predicate	Sets of pairs whose first element is an entity and whose second element is a set of entities
Sentence (VP)	Formula	Truth value

English for the kinds of expressions studied so far. As we develop our grammar, we'll chart our progress by extending the list. Just as meanings are assigned to expressions of English indirectly, so the correspondence between syntactic and semantic categories of English is captured indirectly. This is reflected in the middle column in which you find the SL intermediaries between a syntactic category of English and its corresponding semantic category.

3.3 Quantificational Determiner Phrases

We turn now to the interpretation of sentences with quantificational DPs, such as:

(4) Some person liked every dish.

This sentence is ambiguous. Its readings are captured in the paraphrases below:

(5) a. Every dish was such that there was some person who liked it.
   b. There was some person such that that person liked every dish.

The fact that the sentence has several readings means that there is a mechanism that associates the sentence *Some person liked every dish* with different translations. But there is a puzzle as to how this could be, for as demonstrated in the previous section, translations are associated by rule with syntactic structures, and the sentence *Some person liked every dish* has only one base structure, the one pictured in figure 3.8.

To solve this puzzle, we'll adopt the hypothesis according to which, prior to interpretation, base structures may be subject to syntactic manipulation. That manipulation is characterized by the rules in (6)–(7) below. The details of the rules and the motivation for them will be explained as we go along:

(6) QUANTIFIER INDEXING Quantificational determiners are indexed with a variable.

(7) QUANTIFIER RAISING (QR) If a node has an indexed daughter, then the constituent corresponding to that node can be adjoined to a node that dominates it, with a copy of the index inserted in the position formerly occupied by the adjoined constituent.

Applying QUANTIFIER INDEXING to both DPs in the tree in figure 3.8 leads to the result shown in figure 3.9.

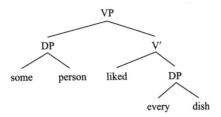

Figure 3.8
Base structure for *Some person liked every dish.*

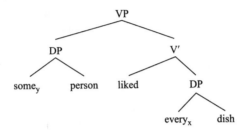

Figure 3.9
QUANTIFIER INDEXING to *some* and *every.*

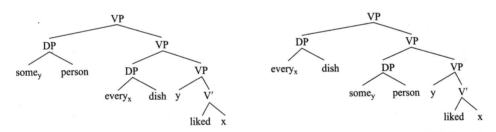

Figure 3.10
Two possible applications of QR.

The rule of QR in (7) is optional, but it is applicable to both the subject and the object in the structure above. The rule doesn't specify exactly which node the moved constituent is adjoined to. This indeterminacy allows multiple applications, and, depending on which nodes are chosen as adjunction sites, the DPs can come in different orders in the resulting structures. In figure 3.10, on the left, QR applied first to *every$_x$ dish* and then *some$_y$ person* was adjoined above it. On the right, QR applied in the opposite order. The interest in these two structures lies in the fact that they differ in the relative order of *some person* and *every dish*, not unlike the two paraphrases in (5) above. Each of these structures is a **logical form** (LF), a name intended to evoke the idea that these structures reflect aspects of the meaning not present in the base structure.

We are now halfway toward an analysis of the ambiguity perceived in *Some person liked every dish*. The task that remains is to provide a rule of translation that can be employed in the trees above. For that we introduce the following new rule of translation:

(8) INDEXEDDAUGHTER $\{\alpha_u, \beta\} \rightsquigarrow [\alpha'u: \beta'(u)]$

(8) says that any node that has two daughters, one of which is indexed with a variable, has a potential translation. That translation is a quantifier whereby the translation of the indexed node gives the quantifier symbol and the translation of the other node is used to fill out the part of the quantifier that follows the colon. Since quantifier symbols are not assigned meanings in SL, the LEXICON rule in (1) is of no use in translating *every* and *some*. Hence, we need a special rule that assigns them a translation:

(9) SPECIFICVOCAB   *every, all* $\rightsquigarrow \forall$
   a, at least one, some $\rightsquigarrow \exists$
   no $\rightsquigarrow$ No
   the $\rightsquigarrow$ The

Instantiating α as *every*, u as x, and β as *dish*, the rules in (8) and (9) yield the following result:

(10) *every*$_x$ *dish* $\rightsquigarrow [\forall x: \text{Dish}(x)]$.

Instantiating α as *some*, u as y, and β as *person*, the rules in (8) and (9) yield the following result:

(11) *some*$_y$ *person* $\rightsquigarrow [\exists y: \text{Person}(y)]$.

Finally, the variables left by the moved DPs will be translated by the following new rule of translation:

(12) VARIABLE   A variable in an LF is translated as the corresponding variable in SL.

Using MERGE and LEXICON, we now arrive at two translations for *Some person liked every dish*, each one arising from a different LF:

(13) $[\forall x: \text{Dish}(x)] ([\exists y: \text{Person}(y)] (\text{Liked}(x)(y)))$

(14) $[\exists y: \text{Person}(y)] ([\forall x: \text{Dish}(x)] (\text{Liked}(x)(y)))$

The two translations now associated with the sentence *Some person liked every dish* correspond to the paraphrases in (5), so we have achieved our goal. Let's review the steps in the analysis in detail, starting with the base structure, as demonstrated in figure 3.11.

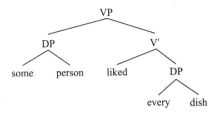

Figure 3.11
Base structure of *Some person liked every dish.*

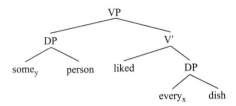

Figure 3.12
QUANTIFIER INDEXING to *some* and *every.*

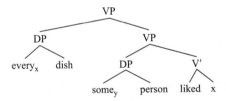

Figure 3.13
every$_x$ *dish* adjoined to VP node in figure 3.12.

First, we apply the rule of QUANTIFIER INDEXING to both determiners (see figure 3.12). Next we turn to the rule of QR:

(7) QUANTIFIER RAISING (QR) If a node has an indexed daughter, then the constituent corresponding to that node can be adjoined to a node that dominates it, with a copy of the index inserted in the position formerly occupied by the adjoined constituent.

In the structure in figure 3.13, the lower DP is a node that has an indexed daughter, so the constituent corresponding to that node, *every*$_x$ *dish*, can be adjoined to a node that dominates it. That gives us license to adjoin *every*$_x$ *dish* to the VP node. Technically that means making a new VP node, one of whose daughters is the old VP node and the other is the adjoined DP, as in figure 3.13.

In figure 3.13, the lower DP is a node that has an indexed daughter, so the constituent corresponding to that node, *some*$_y$ *person*, can be adjoined to a node that dominates it.

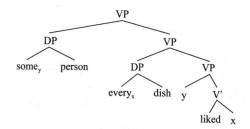

Figure 3.14
some$_y$ person adjoined to the higher VP node in figure 3.13.

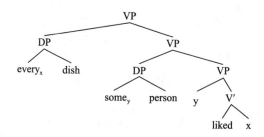

Figure 3.15
some$_y$ person adjoined to the lower VP node in figure 3.13.

One option is to adjoin *some$_y$ person* to the higher VP node, giving us the result shown in figure 3.14.

Looking back at figure 3.13, we can see that another QR option is to adjoin *some$_y$ person* to the lower VP node. Technically that means making a new copy of that node, one of whose daughters is the old lower VP and the other is the adjoined DP, giving us the result shown in figure 3.15.

In figures 3.13–3.15, we implemented three choices for where to adjoin *some$_x$ person* and *every$_y$ dish*. There are other options allowed by QR. These other choices lead either to a structure that doesn't receive any translation or to a structure whose translation we already get from figures 3.14 and 3.15.

We now have two distinct LFs for the sentence *Some person liked every dish*. Let's now translate the LF in figure 3.14. We will want to say what the translation is for each node in the LF without getting confused about which VP or DP we're talking about. Therefore, since the node <u>labels</u> don't matter for interpretation, we'll replace them with numbers, as in figure 3.16.

Our account of the ambiguity perceived in *Some person liked every dish* started with the idea that it is a structural ambiguity. A base structure is mapped to an LF via zero or more applications of QUANTIFIER INDEXING and QR. A resulting LF is then assigned an SL translation, and the translation is assigned a truth value. A given base structure may be

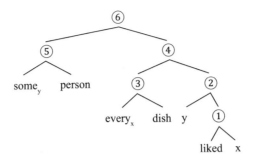

some ~ ∃, *every* ~ ∀	SPECIAL VOCAB
person ~ Person, *dish* ~ Dish, *liked* ~ Liked	LEXICON
y ~ y, x ~ x	VARIABLE
① ~ Liked(x)	MERGE
② ~ Liked(x)(y)	MERGE
③ ~ [∀x: Dish(x)]	INDEXEDDAUGHTER
④ ~ [∀x: Dish(x)](Liked(x)(y))	MERGE
⑤ ~ [∃y: Person(y)]	INDEXEDDAUGHTER
⑥ ~ [∃y: Person(y)] ([∀x: Dish(x)](Liked(x)(y)))	MERGE

Figure 3.16
Applying rules of translation to the LF in figure 3.14.

mapped to several LFs, and these LFs may have translations that can differ in truth value. In that case, the expression is ambiguous in the sense defined in chapter 1. It can be true on one reading and false on the other.

Our grammar now consists of syntactic rules, rules of translation, and SL. The new syntactic rules and rules of translation introduced in this chapter so far are listed in table 3.2.

With wider coverage of English, we can now extend our list of correspondences between syntactic and semantic categories to that shown in table 3.3.

Exercise (3.5)

Draw a base structure for the sentence *No computer crashed*. Provide an LF for that sentence that is assigned a translation by our rules. For each <u>branching</u> node in your LF, state what its translation is and what rule assigns that translation.

Table 3.2
Rules introduced in this chapter so far

	(a) Syntactic Rules
QUANTIFIER INDEXING	Quantificational determiners are indexed with a variable.
QUANTIFIER RAISING (QR)	If a node has an indexed daughter, then the constituent corresponding to that node can be adjoined to a node that dominates it, with a copy of the index inserted in the position formerly occupied by the adjoined constituent.
	(b) Rules of Translation
LEXICON	A symbol of SL is a translation for an English word if the extension of the SL symbol relative to L is the same as the extension of the English word.
SPECIFICVOCAB	a, at least one, some $\rightsquigarrow \exists$, every, all $\rightsquigarrow \forall$
	no $\rightsquigarrow$ No, the $\rightsquigarrow$ The
VARIABLE	A variable in an LF is translated as the corresponding variable in SL.
MERGE	$\{\alpha, \beta\} \rightsquigarrow \alpha'(\beta')$
INDEXEDDAUGHTER	$\{\alpha_u, \beta\} \rightsquigarrow [\alpha'u: \beta'(u)]$
WELLFORMEDNESS FILTER	Any potential translation of an expression of English that is well-formed is a translation of that expression.

Table 3.3
Correspondence between syntactic and semantic categories

Syntactic category of English	Syntactic category of SL	Semantic category (extension)
Name	Individual constant	Entity
Intransitive verb, adjective, noun, NP	One-place predicate	Set of entities
Transitive verb, preposition	Two-place predicate	Sets of pairs whose first element is an entity and whose second element is a set of entities
Sentence (VP)	Formula	Truth value
Variable	Variable	Entity

Exercise (3.6)

Provide a structure that results from applying QR to the base structure shown in figure 3.17, but that does not receive any translation. Your structure will receive a potential translation but it is excluded as a translation by the WELLFORMEDNESS FILTER.

From now on, we will use the term "LF" to refer to any syntactic structure that is assigned a translation, remembering that to be a translation is to be a <u>well-formed</u> expression of SL. An LF may be just a base structure or it may be the result of applying QR to a base structure.

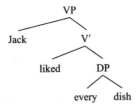

Figure 3.17
Base structure for *Jack liked every dish.*

Exercise (3.7)

[A] Figure 3.18 shows four VPs. VP$_1$ is a base structure for *Jack fell*, and VP$_2$ is an LF for *Jack fell*. VP$_3$ is a base structure for *Some bottle fell* (after QUANTIFIER INDEXING has applied), and VP$_4$ is an LF for *Some bottle fell*. Why can't VP$_3$ itself also be an LF for *Some bottle fell*? In other words, what goes wrong in the translation of VP$_3$ that forces the rule of QR to apply in the case of *Some bottle fell*?

[B] The rule of QR is stated in such a way that it could apply to the same DP multiple times. Draw the structure produced by applying the rule of QR once to *some$_x$ bottle* in VP$_4$ (where QR has already applied). Is the result an LF for *Some bottle fell*? If yes, provide its translation. If not, explain why not.

[C] Is VP$_5$ in figure 3.19 an LF for *Some bottle fell*? If yes, provide its translation. If not, explain why not.

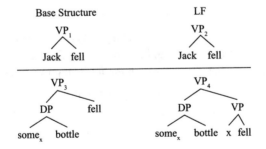

Figure 3.18
Base and LF structures for *Jack fell* and *Some bottle fell.*

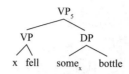

Figure 3.19
LF structure for *Some bottle fell.*

Exercise (3.8)

Above we introduced the rule SPECIFICVOCAB used to translate determiners:

(15) SPECIFICVOCAB   *every, all* ⤳ ∀
        a, at least one, some ⤳ ∃
        no ⤳ No
        the ⤳ The

This list is partial. It does not include *each, any, exactly n, few, several,* and many other quantifiers in English. The list also represents an oversimplification. While it's true that *a, at least one,* and *some* entail existence, the '∃' symbol captures only a small part of their rich semantics. *Every* and *all* can both be said to involve universal quantification of sorts, but they are far from equivalent. Readers are invited to expand and modify the grammar by forming hypotheses about the meanings of various determiners and then augmenting SL and the rules of translation accordingly. If you've done exercise (2.19) in chapter 2, you can make use of those results here.

Exercise (3.9)

The rule of INDEXEDDAUGHTER creates a string that is not an expression of SL. It is part of a well-formed SL formula. It would be possible to change that by replacing the SL syntactic rule for quantified formulas with the following two rules:

• If ϕ is a well-formed formula and u is a variable, then '[∃u: ϕ]', '[∀u: ϕ]', '[No u: ϕ]' and '[The u: ϕ]' are well-formed quantifiers.

• If ω is a well-formed quantifier, and ψ is well-formed formula, then $\omega(\psi)$ is a formula.

If we do that, we can revise table 3.3 by adding the line shown in table 3.4. Is there any reason why we should make this change?

Table 3.4
Hypothetical addition to table 3.3

Syntactic category of English	Syntactic category of SL	Semantic category (extension)
Quantificational DP	Quantifier	None

✪ Thinking Further about Determiner Meaning ✪

The exercise below contemplates a possible modification of our grammar. Although the modification will not be adopted in future chapters, the motivating ideas are interesting and important. They have exerted a powerful influence on the development of linguistic semantics.

Exercise (3.10)

In addition to the WELLFORMEDNESS FILTER, our system of translation consists of the rules LEXICON, MERGE, SPECIFICVOCAB, and VARIABLE, as well as the rule INDEXEDDAUGHTER:

(i) INDEXEDDAUGHTER $\{\alpha_u, \beta\} \rightsquigarrow [\alpha'u: \beta'(u)]$

This exercise contemplates simplifying the system by eliminating the rule of INDEXEDDAUGHTER. Currently, that rule is needed because it is not possible to use MERGE and LEXICON alone to translate the structure in figure 3.20. That is because we have no translation for *every*. SL has no expression whose meaning is the meaning of *every*. However, if 'Every' were an expression of SL whose meaning was that of *every*, we could imagine using MERGE and LEXICON to get

Every bridge collapsed $\rightsquigarrow$ Every(Bridge)(Collapsed).

The purpose of this exercise is to modify SL so that it includes expressions that translate determiners such as *every*, *some*, and *no* along with formulas such as 'Every(Bridge)(Collapsed)' or 'No(Doctor)(Examined(Baboloki))'. By its nature, this change will involve the vocabulary, the syntax, and the semantics of SL. In this exercise, we'll restrict our attention to quantificational DPs in subject position, as in (i) below.

(i) a. Every bridge collapsed.
     b. No doctor examined Baboloki.
     c. Some dog barked.

The kind of formulas we are aiming to include in SL bear a formal resemblance to formulas already in SL formed around two-place predicates. Compare these two, only the second of which is currently well formed:

(ii) Every(Bridge)(Collapsed)
     Knows(Baboloki)(Akna)

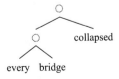

Figure 3.20
Syntactic structure for *every bridge collapsed*.

The formal similarity exhibited in (ii) leads to the idea that if we could treat a determiner semantically as a transitive verb, we might arrive at a meaning of the right kind.

Transitive verbs describe relations that hold between two entities. (iii) below says that the *know* relation holds between the individuals Akna and Baboloki, the extensions of the names *Akna* and *Baboloki*. Pursuing the analogy suggested by (ii), we might say that (iv) describes a relation that holds between two sets, the extensions of *bridge* and *collapsed*.

(iii) Akna knows Baboloki.

(iv) Every bridge collapsed.

So now the question becomes, what relation holds between the sets in (v) below, when and only when (iv) is true?

(v) a. $\{x \mid x$ is a bridge$\}$ *extension of* <u>bridge</u>
     b. $\{y \mid y$ collapsed$\}$ *extension of* <u>collapsed</u>

The answer is **subset**. The set theoretic statement below captures the truth conditions of (iv):

(vi) $\{x \mid x$ is a bridge$\} \subseteq \{y \mid y$ collapsed$\}$

If every element of the set on the left is an element of the set on the right, as '$\subseteq$' requires, then every bridge collapsed. So one can think of (iv) as saying that the subset relation holds between not two entities, but two sets—the set of bridges and the set of collapsed entities. Adopting this way of thinking, we further observe that the truth conditions of (vii) are captured in (viii).

(vii) Some bridge collapsed.

(viii) $(\{x \mid x$ is a bridge$\} \cap \{y \mid y$ collapsed$\}) \neq \varnothing$

So *some* describes a relation that holds between two sets just in case they have elements in common. And one can think of (vii) as saying that the *some* relation holds between the set of bridges and the set of collapsed entities.

[A] With this idea in mind, your task is to modify SL so formulas of the form 'Every$(\pi_1)(\pi_2)$' are well formed and get the right interpretation to serve as translations for English sentences of the form *Every NP verb* or *Every NP verb object*.

[B] When you are all done, supply a proof showing that the sentence in (iv) is assigned TRUE iff (vi) holds.

[C] In your revised SL, L(Every) will be defined. Now add 'Some' and 'No' to the vocabulary of SL. Define L(Some) and L(No).

[D] If 'Ex1' were the translation for *exactly one*, what would L(Ex1) be?

[E] There are many determiners we have not yet considered such as *most*, *at least four*, and *many*. Suggest possible meanings for these, ignoring the fact that they combine with plural noun phrases.

[F] What issues arise when we try to extend the analysis to nonsubject quantificational DPs like in (ix)?

(ix) a. Akna found every book.

    b. Baboloki examined some painting.

    c. Exactly one triangle touches every circle.

3.3.1 Quantifier Jargon

In SL, quantificational formulas have the form

$[Qu : \phi](\psi)$,

where 'Q' could be '∃' or '∀' or 'No' or 'The'. We've been calling the part in square brackets a "quantifier". Now we introduce the terms **restrictor** to refer to the 'ϕ' part and the term **scope** to refer to the remainder, 'ψ'. Applying this terminology, we say that in the formula

$[\exists x: \text{Donkey}(x)](\text{Brayed}(x))$,

the quantifier is '$[\exists x: \text{Donkey}(x)]$', its restrictor is '$\text{Donkey}(x)$', and its scope is '$\text{Brayed}(x)$'.

Consider now one of the translations produced above:

(16) $[\forall x: \text{Dish}(x)] ([\exists y: \text{Person}(y)] (\text{Liked}(x)(y)))$.

(16) contains two quantifiers, each with its own scope. The scope of '$[\exists y: \text{Person}(y)]$' is '$\text{Liked}(x)(y)$', and the scope of '$[\forall x: \text{Dish}(x)]$' is '$[\exists y: \text{Person}(y)] (\text{Liked}(x)(y))$'. Notice that '$[\exists y: \text{Person}(y)]$' is in the scope of '$[\forall x: \text{Dish}(x)]$'. This is described by saying that

'$[\forall x: \text{Dish}(x)]$' **takes scope over** '$[\exists y: \text{Person}(y)]$'.

Another way it's described is by saying that in (16),

'$[\forall x: \text{Dish}(x)]$' has **wide scope**, and '$[\exists y: \text{Person}(y)]$' has **narrow scope**.

The opposite obtains in the other translation for *Some person liked every dish*, repeated in (17) below. In (17), '$[\exists y: \text{Person}(y)]$' takes **wide scope** over '$[\forall x: \text{Dish}(x)]$'.

(17) $[\exists y: \text{Person}(y)] ([\forall x: \text{Dish}(x)] (\text{Liked}(x)(y)))$.

Up to now, we've been discussing terminology used by logicians to describe formulas of a symbolic language. These terms have all been borrowed into linguistics in a way that follows straightforwardly from our translation mechanism. Adopting this jargon, we say that the sentence *Some person liked every dish* is **scopally ambiguous**. It has one reading in which *every dish* has wide scope over *some person* and another reading in which *some person* takes wide scope over *every dish*. And we may say that *every dish* is a quantifier whose restrictor is *dish*.

Exercise (3.11)

[A] The sentence *Gadarine showed exactly one photograph to every contestant* has a reading on which *every contestant* takes scope over *exactly one photograph*. Provide an unambiguous paraphrase of the sentence on that reading.

[B] The sentence *A nurse visited every patient* is scopally ambiguous. One of its readings can be paraphrased as in (i). Characterize the reading paraphrased in (i) using the jargon introduced above.

(i) For every patient, there was a nurse who visited that patient.

[C] Supply a sentence of English in which one quantifier has another quantifier in its restrictor.

Exercise (3.12)

Advertisements use ambiguity in various ways. The simplest is an attention-getting strategy,[2] as in the following ad from Legal Sea Foods:

(i) Jesus fed 5,000 people with a few fish. We do that every day.

Using the jargon introduced above, comment on what is going on in this ad.

3.3.2 Negation and Scope

In chapter 1, we saw that ambiguity can arise when a quantifier occurs in a sentence with negation. Recall the ambiguity in *Every passenger was not examined*. To account for this type of ambiguity, we will need to translate a NegP. Let's begin by adding '¬' to our SPECIFICVOCAB rule:

(18) SPECIFICVOCAB   *every, all* ⤳ ∀
                        a, at least one, some ⤳ ∃
                        no ⤳ No
                        the ⤳ The
                        not ⤳ ¬

To see the effect of this addition, consider the base structure for *Jack didn't sing* and its translation, shown in figure 3.21.

Next we introduce an example sentence in which a quantifier occurs with a negation. This is an excerpt from an online book review:

Personally, I think the book was pretty good. I like that every character didn't survive despite my teardrops that fell on several pages. The reason I like the deaths or should I say the reason I am OK with them is that they added depth to the story.[3]

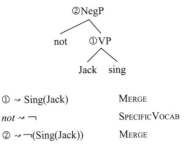

① ∾ Sing(Jack)   MERGE
not ∾ ¬   SPECIFICVOCAB
② ∾ ¬(Sing(Jack))   MERGE

Figure 3.21
Base structure for *Jack didn't sing* and its translation.

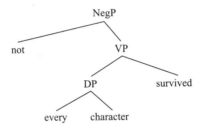

Figure 3.22
Base structure for *Every character didn't survive.*

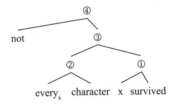

Figure 3.23
LF for *Every character didn't survive.*

It is unclear from this paragraph which reading of *Every character didn't survive* is intended. Did the author intend to convey that no character survived or merely that not all of them survived? The sentence is scopally ambiguous, and we'll now show how the narrow scope negation reading comes about. The base structure for the sentence *Every character didn't survive* is demonstrated in figure 3.22.

If we now index the DP and apply QR, adjoining the DP to VP, we get the result shown in figure 3.23.

Applying our rules of translation, we have for the branching nodes:

① ⤳ Survived(x)   MERGE
② ⤳ [∀x: Character(x)]   INDEXEDDAUGHTER
③ ⤳ [∀x: Character(x)](Survived(x))   MERGE
④ ⤳ ¬([∀x: Character(x)](Survived(x)))   MERGE

Given the translation for ④, we conclude that the LF in figure 3.23 gives rise to the wide
scope negation reading. Raising the subject above negation produces an LF for the narrow
scope negation reading. In section 3.3.1, we defined the **scope of a quantifier**. Here we're
extending that to negation, where the scope of '¬' in a formula of the form '¬(ϕ)' is ϕ.
And as in section 3.3.1, we extend this definition to the corresponding parts of structures
of natural language.

Exercise (3.13)

[A] Draw an LF for the narrow scope negation reading of the sentence *Every character didn't survive*. For each branching node of your LF, specify its translation and
the rule that applies to give that translation. The rules for binary branching nodes are
repeated in table 3.5

[B] Provide the LF for the wide scope negation reading of *Rihanna doesn't like every
poem*. Make sure that the LF you provide gets the right translation. Hand in just the LF.

✪ Thinking about Definite Descriptions ✪

DPs formed with the determiner *the* are sometimes called **definite descriptions**. They
have received a lot of attention in both linguistic and philosophical research. The exercise
below provides a glimpse into this research.

Exercise (3.14)

Let us make the following assumptions:

(i) *the* ⤳ The   SPECIFICVOCAB

(ii) *the* is a quantificational determiner and is subject to the rule of QUANTIFIER
INDEXING

Table 3.5
Current rules of translation applicable at nodes with two daughters

MERGE	$\{\alpha, \beta\} \rightsquigarrow \alpha'(\beta')$
INDEXEDDAUGHTER	$\{\alpha_u, \beta\} \rightsquigarrow [\alpha'u: \beta'(u)]$

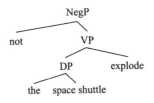

Figure 3.24
Base structure for *The space shuttle didn't explode.*

Along with our other rules of syntax and translation, these two assumptions lead to a grammar in which sentences with definite descriptions are interpreted along the lines proposed by Bertrand Russell, so, we'll refer to the grammar that includes the assumptions in (i) and (ii) as the "Russell Grammar."

The sentence *The space shuttle did not explode* has the base structure represented in figure 3.24, in which the compound noun *space shuttle* is treated as a single word.

[A] Construct two LFs that the Russell Grammar assigns to this sentence. Your LFs should differ by the relative order of *not* and *the space shuttle*. Label your LF in which *not* is higher "LF-not," and label the one in which *the space shuttle* is higher "LF-the."

[B] Describe a situation in which both LFs are assigned TRUE by the Russell Grammar. Call that situation s_1. Assume that

- *space shuttle* ↝ Shuttle
- $L(\text{Shuttle}) = \{z : z \text{ is a partially reusable low Earth orbital spacecraft system}\}$.

To do this, you'll have to apply the rules of translation to get translations for the two LFs you provided in [A]. Then you will have to consult the rules of SL to figure out what situations make each of the translations true (see below for the rule called THE). The only thing you should hand in is a description of s_1.

[C] Describe a situation s_2. In s_2, nothing explodes. Fill out the details of s_2 in such a way that one of your LFs comes out true and the other false.

[D] Now we're going to create a new grammar that captures a different idea about the interpretation of definite descriptions. This idea is attributed to Gottlob Frege, so we'll call it the "Frege Grammar."[4] To get to the Frege Grammar, we adopt the assumption in (i) from above but not the one in (ii):

(i) *the* ↝ The   SPECIFICVOCAB

(ii) the is a quantification determiner and is subject to the rule of QUANTIFIER INDEXING

Next, we modify SL in several steps. First, we remove the following semantic rule from SL:

[THE]   '[The $u : \phi$] (ψ)' is true with respect to M iff there is exactly one object o such that 'ϕ' is true with respect to $M+\langle u,o \rangle$, and there is exactly one object o such that 'ϕ' and 'ψ' are both true with respect to $M+\langle u,o \rangle$.

Next, we amend the syntactic rule for quantifiers so that it makes no mention of 'The':

If ϕ and ψ are formulas and u is a variable, then '$[\exists u: \phi] (\psi)$', '$[\forall u: \phi] (\psi)$', and '$[\text{No } u: \phi] (\psi)$' are formulas.

And then we add the following rule to the syntax of SL:

If π is a one-place predicate, then 'The(π)' is a complex individual constant

All other syntactic rules that mention individual constants now apply to simple and complex ones. This means, for example, that 'Croaked(The(Frog))' is a well-formed formula. Turning to the semantics, we modify our vocabulary rule for individual constants by adding the word 'simple':

If α is a simple individual constant, then $[\![\alpha]\!]^M = M(\alpha)$, and $M(\alpha)$ is an entity.

Finally, we add this rule of semantics:

If $[\![\pi]\!]^M$ is a singleton set, then $[\![\text{The}(\pi)]\!]^M$ is the single element in $[\![\pi]\!]^M$.

If $[\![\pi]\!]^M$ is not a singleton set, then $[\![\text{The}(\pi)]\!]^M$ is not defined.

For example, if Emmett is an elephant, and he is the only elephant that there is, then $L(\text{Elephant}) = \{\text{Emmett}\}$ and $[\![\text{The(Elephant)}]\!]^L = \text{Emmett}$. If Emmett and Ellen are the only elephants there are, then $L(\text{Elephant}) = \{\text{Emmett, Ellen}\}$ and $[\![\text{The(Elephant)}]\!]^L$ is not defined.

Provide an LF and translation for *The space shuttle didn't explode* according to the Frege Grammar.

[E] In tasks [B] and [C], you provided two situations, s_1 and s_2. Say what truth value, if any, is assigned to the LF from [D] in s_1 and in s_2. If no truth value is assigned, write "undefined."

[F] Provide at least one argument that will help us choose one of the two grammars over the other.

Your argument can be based on an intuition about:

(i) *Truth in a situation.* In that case, completely specify the situation and provide a sentence. State your intuition about whether the sentence is true, false or has no truth value in the situation you describe.

(ii) *Entailment.* In that case, describe the entailment that you intuit.

(iii) *Ambiguity.* In that case, describe the ambiguity. Make sure to give unambiguous paraphrases for the two readings and describe a situation in which the ambiguous sentence is true on one reading but not on the other in the situation you described.

After stating your intuition, as in (i)–(iii), say which grammar agrees with your intuition and which disagrees. If it isn't obvious why the grammars make the predictions you claim, supply a brief explanation.

You can base your argument on the sentence *The space shuttle did not explode.* But you can also think about other sentences with more complex definite descriptions.

3.3.3 Constraints on Quantifier Raising

In section 3.3.1 and section 3.3.2, we introduced the term *scopal ambiguity* to describe the ambiguities perceived in the sentences *Some person liked every dish* and *Every character didn't survive.* The term *scopal ambiguity* derives from the observation that the readings of those sentences correspond to formulas of SL that differ in terms of the scopes of quantifiers and of negation. Within the grammar being developed here, the source of these ambiguities is QR, a syntactic rule that manipulates structures, moving constituents from one position to another, higher position. So, according to the grammar being developed here, a scopal ambiguity is a kind of structural ambiguity.

The rule of QR is optional and unconstrained. That means that according to our rules, whenever an English sentence contains two or more quantificational DPs, we should expect any one of the DPs to take scope over the others. There is a body of work showing that scopal ambiguity is less pervasive than this system predicts. In this subsection, we'll take a very brief look at this rich area of active research.

Since QR is a movement operation, any possible constraints on movement operations will translate into constraints on possible readings of sentences containing quantifiers. We'll now work our way toward an illustration of this idea.

The following examples are from *The Forms of Sentences* by Howard Lasnik (the full reference is in the Further Reading section).

(19) John solved this problem.

(20) * John solved.

(21) This problem, John solved.

(22) *This problem, John solved that problem.

(23) Which problem will John solve?

Lasnik explains the pattern of data by assuming that the verb *solve* requires a direct object. That explains the contrast between (19) and (20) (the asterisk indicates unacceptability). In (21), the verb in fact has a direct object, *this problem*, but it has been moved from object position to the front of the sentence. Merely placing *this problem* in front of a grammatical sentence doesn't work, as (22) shows. It has to have been moved there. Turning now to (23), again the verb *solve* appears to have no direct object, yet it is grammatical. This is explained by the idea that *which problem* is generated as the object of *solve* and then is fronted. (23) starts as *John will solve which problem* and then *which problem* is moved to the front. This operation is called **Wh-movement** and it accounts for the sentence initial position of Wh-words in questions. Wh-movement can front phrases from various positions and over long distances, as the following examples show:

(24) a. Musya told her about *which problem* on Saturday night.
    b. Which problem did Musya tell her about on Saturday night?

(25) a. Musya thought *which problem* was too hard for my class.
    b. Which problem did Musya think was too hard for my class?

(26) a. You said that Musya thought that Baboloki had solved *which problem*.
    b. Which problem did you say that Musya thought that Baboloki had solved?

Nevertheless, there are constraints on the phrases Wh-movement can target. Applied to (27) below, Wh-movement would yield (28), which is not acceptable.

(27) A student [who solved *which problem*] was included in our survey.

(28) *Which problem was a student [who solved] included in our survey?

The bracketed portion of (27) is called a **relative clause** (see section 3.5 below for more in-depth coverage of relative clauses). It turns out that it is not possible to perform any movement operation that has the effect of extracting a phrase from inside a relative clause. Now if relative clauses are barriers to movement and if scopal ambiguity arises as the result of the movement operation QR, then it follows that when one of the quantifiers is inside a relative clause and the other is outside, ambiguity should <u>not</u> arise. That prediction is confirmed. Here is an example:

(29) A student [who solved every problem] was included in our survey.

That sentence does <u>not</u> have the reading paraphrased in (30) or (31). (For (30) assume that L(IncludedInSurvey) is the set of individuals included in the survey, as in chapter 2 exercises 2.14 and 2.23)

(30) $[\forall x: \text{Problem}(x)]([\exists y: (\text{Student} \sqcap \text{Solved}(x))(y)](\text{IncludedInSurvey}(y)))$.

(31) For every problem x, there is a student who solved x and that student was included in the survey.

To see that (31) is not a possible reading of (29), notice that (31) could be true if each problem had a different student-solver and no student solved every problem, whereas (29) asserts the existence of a student who solved every problem. The reading in (31) is missing because to get it, we would need to QR *every problem* outside the relative clause. The very fact that the presence of scopal ambiguity is sensitive to constraints on movement is evidence in favor of the hypothesis we've adopted here, according to which scopal ambiguity is a kind of structural ambiguity.

    Another factor limiting the presence of scopal ambiguity has to do with particular lexical items that favor one scope over the other. Take, for example, the SL sentence:

(32) $\neg([\exists x: \text{Cat}(x)](\text{See}(x)(\text{Fido})))$.

This is best translated into English as

(33) Fido didn't see any cat.

(33) uses the word *any* which is called a **negative polarity item** because it likes to be in the scope of negation. If instead of *any* we used *some* we would get

(34) Fido didn't see some cat.

(34) corresponds best to

(35) $[\exists x: \text{Cat}(x)]\ (\neg(\text{See}(x)(\text{Fido})))$.

In general, when *some* is used with a negation, it tends to have wide scope over it. For that reason it is called a **positive polarity item**. (33) and (34) both contain an existential quantifier and a negation. If quantificational DPs could move freely, we'd expect both to be ambiguous. Something about those determiners limits the possible readings. *Each* is another determiner that forms DPs with a preference for wide scope.

Another constraint on scope relations has to do with **ellipsis**. Consider the sentence

(36) A dog chased every cat, and a squirrel did too.

This sentence is formed from (37) below by eliding *chased every cat* and inserting *did*.[5]

(37) A dog chased every cat, and a squirrel chased every cat too.

Since this is a conjunction of two sentences, each of which contains two DPs, theoretically it is ambiguous in four ways because there are two possible scope orderings within each conjunct. However, the sentence in (36), in which ellipsis has been applied, does not have these four readings; it has only two. It can be read with a *dog* and a *squirrel* each taking scope over the direct object or each taking scope under the direct object; mixed readings are not possible. Some form of identity is a prerequisite for ellipsis and apparently that prerequisite includes quantifier scope.

We've just reviewed some syntactic and lexical factors that constrain or limit scopal relations. But even when there are no grammatical constraints on scope, speakers often do not perceive ambiguity. In some cases, hearers automatically settle on a reading in which the quantifier phrase that occurs first in the surface structure is interpreted as having widest scope. In other cases, one reading may be implausible, and hearers will ignore it. These factors, surface order, plausibility, and others push toward a particular disambiguation. And since the disambiguation is automatic, we often don't perceive the ambiguity in the first place.

Exercise (3.15)

[A] The movement operation that produces (21) from (19) is sometimes called **topicalization**. Does the constraint on Wh-movement described above apply to topicalization? Supply an example as evidence for your answer.

[B] The sentence in (i) below contains a negation and two quantificational DPs. In principle, it should have six different readings! Many of those readings are excluded by the constraints described above. Describe one of the excluded readings of (i) with an unambiguous paraphrase in English or in SL of the missing reading.

(i) Aparajita didn't know any actor who had memorized every poem.

Exercise (3.16)

Recall the Legal Sea Foods advertisement in exercise (3.12):

(i) Jesus fed 5,000 people with a few fish. We do that every day.

The ad works because the antecedent sentence receives one interpretation and the pronoun *that* receives a different interpretation of that same sentence. This is unlike what we saw in (36) where the elided material has to be interpreted the same way as the antecedent. How could we explain this difference?

3.4 Prepositional Phrases, Adjectives, and Adverbs

In chapter 1, we identified examples containing modifiers that appeared to be structurally ambiguous. The sentence *Jack discussed a wedding in Boston* has a reading on which the wedding is in Boston and a different reading on which the discussion was in Boston. Given other facts about English syntax, one is led to associate that sentence with structures that differ by the point of attachment of *in Boston*—either inside the NP headed by *wedding* or outside of that NP. And given the presence of those two structures, one arrives at the hypothesis that the two readings of the sentence correspond to the two structures. This conjecture is plausible, but is it correct? We accept that there are two readings and two structures; what we still need to show is that the readings are indeed correlated with the structures.

On both readings, the PP *in Boston* serves as a modifier. In one case, it's a modifier in a noun phrase and in the other it's a verbal modifier. Our current rules of translation are not suited for modification structures. We'll need to add a new rule for that purpose. Ideally it will apply in both cases, and we can use it to test our conjecture. We begin with the structure in which the PP is internal to NP, as in figure 3.25.

After applying QUANTIFIER INDEXING to *a* and QR to a_x *wedding in Boston* we get the result shown in figure 3.26.

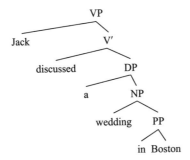

Figure 3.25
Base structure for *Jack discussed a wedding in Boston*.

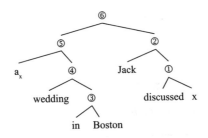

Figure 3.26
LF for *Jack discussed a wedding in Boston*.

For node ③, MERGE will give us 'In(Boston)'. For node ④, MERGE will give us either 'Wedding(In(Boston))' or 'In(Boston)(Wedding)'. Neither of these is well formed. 'Wedding' is a one-place predicate, so it needs to combine with a variable or an individual constant. The same goes for the complex one-place predicate 'In(Boston)'. We need a new rule of translation for this case, namely:

(38) PREDCON $\{\alpha, \beta\} \rightsquigarrow (\alpha' \sqcap \beta')$.

Using that rule along with others already in place, we have the following calculation:

① $\rightsquigarrow$ Discussed(x)		MERGE
② $\rightsquigarrow$ Discussed(x)(Jack)		MERGE
③ $\rightsquigarrow$ In(Boston)		MERGE
④ $\rightsquigarrow$ (Wedding $\sqcap$ In(Boston))		PREDCON
⑤ $\rightsquigarrow$ [$\exists x$: (Wedding $\sqcap$ In(Boston))(x)]		INDEXEDDAUGHTER
⑥ $\rightsquigarrow$ [$\exists x$: (Wedding $\sqcap$ In(Boston))(x)](Discussed(x)(Jack))		MERGE

The translation for node ⑥ says that there is a thing, it's a wedding and it's in Boston, and Jack discussed it. That seems adequate for the NP internal reading. We now add PREDCON to our list of rules of translation (see table 3.6).

Table 3.6
Current rules of translation applicable at nodes with two daughters

MERGE	$\{\alpha, \beta\} \rightsquigarrow \alpha'(\beta')$
INDEXEDDAUGHTER	$\{\alpha_u, \beta\} \rightsquigarrow [\alpha'u: \beta'(u)]$
PREDCON	$\{\alpha, \beta\} \rightsquigarrow (\alpha' \sqcap \beta')$

Exercise (3.17)

Figure 3.27 shows an LF for a sentence of English.

[A] For the nodes ②, ④, ⑤, ⑦, and ⑨, provide the translation and the rule that applies at that node.

[B] Provide the sentence of English for which the structure in figure 3.27 is an LF.

Exercise (3.18)

The following is a formula from an exercise in chapter 2.

[No x : (Grey(x) & Pig(x))] (Sings(x)).

[A] Provide an English translation for that formula.

[B] Provide the formula that our rules of translation assign to the English sentence you provided in [A].

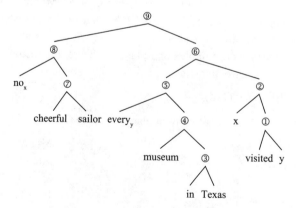

Figure 3.27
LF for a sentence of English.

Exercise (3.19)

Below you'll find formulas from an exercise at the end of chapter 2. Some of the formulas result from applying our current rules of translation to an LF. For those formulas, provide the sentence of English whose LF gets that formula as translation. If a formula below could not be a translation that is produced by our rules, write "not a translation."

(i) $[\forall x: (\text{Round} \sqcap \text{Coin})(x)](\text{Silver}(x))$.

(ii) $[\exists x: (\text{Boy} \sqcap \text{From}(\text{Texas}))(x)]\ (\text{Danced}(x))$.

(iii) $(\text{Danced} \sqcap \text{Sang})(\text{Jack})$.

(iv) $[\text{No } x: \text{Candidate}(x)]\ ([\forall y: (\text{Current} \sqcap \text{Issue})(y)]\ (\text{Knows}(y)(x)))$.

(v) $[\exists x: (\text{Black} \sqcap \text{Horse})(x)]\ (\text{Liked}(\text{Mary})(x))$.

Exercise (3.20)

Provide the translation assigned by our grammar to the example shown in figure 3.28. Translate *of* as a two-place predicate 'Of'.

✪ Important Practice and Looking Ahead ✪

To solve exercise (3.21) below one needs to appeal to a novel LF configuration. This type of configuration will be crucial in the analysis of tense and aspect in chapter 5.

Exercise (3.21)

The sentence *Some bridge in every city collapsed* has a reading according to which every city has at least one collapsed bridge. Provide the LF and translation for the sentence on that reading. The base structure is given in figure 3.29.

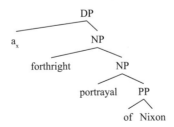

Figure 3.28
Syntactic structure for *a forthright portrayal of Nixon.*

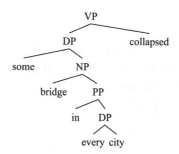

Figure 3.29
Base structure for *Some bridge in every city collapsed.*

We've conjectured that the two readings of *Jack discussed a wedding in Boston* are correlated with the two syntactic structures that differ by the point of attachment of the PP *in Boston*. So far we've seen that with the addition of the rule PREDCON, our grammar indeed associates the NP internal syntax with the reading in which the wedding was in Boston. Now we turn to the other structure, in which *in Boston* is outside the object DP, as in figure 3.30.

After applying QUANTIFIER INDEXING to *a* and QR to a_x *wedding*, we get the result shown in figure 3.31.

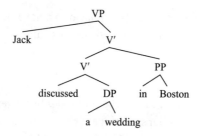

Figure 3.30
Base structure for *Jack discussed a wedding in Boston.*

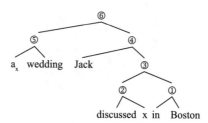

Figure 3.31
LF for *Jack discussed a wedding in Boston.*

Applying our rules of translation we have

① ⤳ In(Boston)	MERGE
② ⤳ Discussed(x)	MERGE
③ ⤳ (Discussed(x) ⊓ In(Boston))	PREDCON
④ ⤳ (Discussed(x) ⊓ In(Boston))(Jack)	MERGE
⑤ ⤳ [∃x: Wedding(x)]	INDEXEDDAUGHTER
⑥ ⤳ [∃x: Wedding(x)]((Discussed(x) ⊓ In(Boston))(Jack))	MERGE

The formula in ⑥ is well-formed. To fix on what it says, we recall an exercise in chapter 2, section 2.4, in which you had to prove an equivalence between '(Clever ⊓ Tall)(a)' and '(Clever(a) & Tall(a))'. By the principle of *conjunction equivalence* introduced there, the formula '(Discussed(x) ⊓ In(Boston))(Jack)' is equivalent to '(Discussed(x)(Jack) & In(Boston) (Jack))', and so the formula in ⑥ is equivalent to

(39) [∃x: Wedding(x)]((Discussed(x)(Jack) & In(Boston)(Jack))).

This result is promising. As required, this translation differs from the previous one in terms of what is located in Boston. In the previous case, the wedding was in Boston, while here nothing is said about the location of the wedding. The success we've had here supports the idea that the semantic relationship between the PP and what it is attached to is the same in the two cases. And it appears to confirm our conjecture that the ambiguity is structural.

Nevertheless, there are several potential problems with this analysis. First, (39) locates Jack in Boston and it says he discussed a wedding, but nothing guarantees that he was in Boston <u>when</u> he discussed the wedding. This is missing from the proposed translation, but it is entailed by the English sentence. There is a related problem that is harder to pin down, which is that the formula locates Jack in Boston when in some sense it should be locating the discussion there. This problem is easier to see when we consider other non-locative modifiers of VP. For example, on an analysis in which the rule of PredCon applies to the V′ node in figure 3.32, *Jack looked toward the door* entails that Jack is toward the door.

The rule of PREDCON was introduced in (38) above as rule of translation applicable when a noun is modified by a PP. As exercises (3.17)–(3.20) show, the rule applies with adjectival modifiers as well. In other words, PREDCON serves quite generally in the interpretation of noun modifiers. Currently we are considering its use when a verbal constituent is modified by a PP. But verbal modification is not limited to PPs. Just as nouns take adjectival modifiers, verbs take adverbial modifiers. If PREDCON is to be of use of with verbs, it should apply in that case as well, and indeed it appears to do so. Assuming that the adverb *quietly* is translated 'Quiet', we translate *Jack sang quietly* as shown in figure 3.33.

But now imagine that Jack is walking in a way that makes a lot of noise—stomping his foot—and at the same time he is singing quietly. By a calculation like the one in figure 3.33, we have

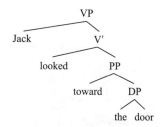

Figure 3.32
Base structure for *Jack looked toward the door.*

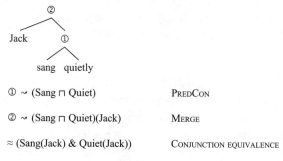

Figure 3.33
Translation of *Jack sang quietly.*

(40) *Jack walked noisily* ⤳ (Walked ⊓ Noisy)(Jack)
                                          ≈ (Walked(Jack) & Noisy(Jack)).

It is a fact of SL, that if '(Sang(Jack) & Quiet(Jack))' is true and '(Walk(Jack) & Noisy(Jack))' is true, then the following formula is also true:

(41) (Sang(Jack) & Noisy(Jack)).

And if (41) is true, then by conjunction equivalence, (42) is also true.

(42) (Sang ⊓ Noisy)(Jack).

But on the proposal under consideration, (42) is the translation of *Jack sang noisily.* We now incorrectly predict that if Jack walked noisily and sang quietly then he sang noisily. Or in more linguistic terms, we incorrectly predict that if both *Jack sang quietly* and *Jack walked noisily* are true, then *Jack sang noisily* is true. This is an undesirable result, and so we are left at this point without an analysis for verbal modification. In the next chapter, we'll work on correcting that. For now we can say that we have only a partial account of how the two structures associated with *Jack discussed a wedding in Boston* could lead to the two readings.

One of the objections to (39) is that it doesn't require Jack to be in Boston when he discusses the wedding, contrary to our intuition about the English sentence. A reasonable response to this objection would be that this intuition has to do with time, and we haven't said anything so far about time. It's plausible that an independent mechanism fixes the time at which the discussing and the being in Boston occur, and it does so in way that makes them simultaneous. Until we discuss tense and time, we can't count this against the proposed analysis. This is a plausible response, and in chapter 5 we will discuss tense. But even without a specific analysis of tense, the objection based on the manner adverbs, *quietly* and *noisily*, still stands. In that case, we chose a situation in which Jack sang quietly and walked noisily at the same time. In such a situation, our analysis incorrectly predicts that Jack sang noisily. Adding in some mechanism that guarantees that the manner adverb and the verb hold at the same time will only solidify the problem.

Exercise (3.22)

[A] Provide an example of your own using different adverbs to make the point made above with the manner adverbs *quietly* and *noisily*. Provide the examples and the situation and spell out the incorrect prediction made by the analysis.

[B] In (40)–(42), we found fault with the proposed analysis by extending it to manner adverbs. But we can make a similar argument when sticking to PP modifiers. Suppose that Jack is on a plane on his way to Bombay and he gets up to go to the bathroom. It is now true that *Jack is flying to Bombay*, and it's true that *Jack is walking to the bathroom*. What incorrect conclusion can we draw from these two sentences given the above analysis? (For the purposes of this exercise, treat *is flying* and *is walking* as simple verbs translated as 'Fly' and 'Walk' respectively. In chapter 5, we will discuss the significance of the *-ing* form).

[C] What happens if we try to make an argument of the kind in [B] using a locative PP like *in Boston*?

✪ Looking Ahead ✪

In the next section, we add new syntactic and semantic rules to SL and a new rule of translation. Although the SL modification is quite important for understanding current semantics literature, future sections of this textbook will not make use of it. Some instructors may choose to skip the next section. For that reason, the new rule of translation proposed here will be omitted from subsequent summaries of the rules of interpretation.

3.5   Relative Clauses

Relative clauses are of two sorts: **restrictive** and **nonrestrictive**. Restrictive relative clauses are ones that are understood to restrict the extension of the NP that they modify. They are not set off from the noun phrases they modify by commas. An example is the relative clause *who Aparajita likes* in the sentence *Every actor who Aparajita likes performs well.* The sentence does not say that all actors perform well; the judgment is restricted to those actors who satisfy the additional condition imposed by the relative clause. If a relative clause is set off by commas, one gets a different, nonrestrictive, reading, as in *Professional athletes, who are paid to train, perform better than most amateurs.* Here the judgment is not understood to be restricted to those professional athletes who are paid to train. The sentence rather expresses two distinct propositions. The main proposition expressed is what you get by just ignoring the relative clause: *Professional athletes perform better than most amateurs.* The secondary proposition expressed is the one obtained by writing the relative clause on its own, replacing the relative pronoun *who* by the rest of the DP in which the clause occurs; in the case above this would yield: *Professional athletes are paid to train.*

In asserting a sentence with a nonrestrictive relative clause, the speaker is usually committed to more than just the joint truth of the primary and secondary claims; generally one expects a connection between the claims. For example, someone who utters the sentence *Professional athletes, who are paid to train, perform better than most amateurs* would generally be thought to communicate the idea that professional athletes perform better than most amateurs *because* they are paid to train. This is a default assumption; it is possible in various contexts to use a nonrestrictive relative clause to make a comment that is not explanatory of the main claim. Suppose that someone has said that every number has magnitude; you might reply: *Zero, which is a number, has no magnitude.* Here the relative clause just provides a compact way to explain how the fact that zero has no magnitude is relevant to the point at issue, but it does not explain why zero has no magnitude.

Exercise (3.23)

The authors of the *Port Royal Logic* (1662; II.5)[6] say that certain uses of adjectives mean the same as certain uses of relative clauses; their example is

Invisible God created the visible world.

They say it means the same as

God, who is invisible, created the world, which is visible.

Since the latter contains nonrestrictive relative clauses, this suggests that adjectives can also be used nonrestrictively. Let's examine this observation in light of the analysis of modifiers in the previous section. Consider the sentence:

The visible world stinks.

Provide the translation assigned by our rules to this sentence. Explain why your translation treats the adjective as restrictive. Describe a situation in which that sentence is true/false on a reading where the adjective is restrictive but would have a different truth value if it were nonrestrictive. Suggest a way to expand our grammar so that it assigns that sentence the nonrestrictive reading.

3.5.1 Syntax of Restrictive Relative Clauses

Relative clauses in English usually take the form of a sentence with a gap in it, where the sentence may be preceded by a complementizer *that* or a relative pronoun such as *who* or *which*. Relative clauses modify nouns or noun phrases. Here are some examples of a noun phrase with a modifying relative clause:

singer who [*Musya likes* __]	*book that* [*I wrote* ____]
author who [*I introduced* __ *to Rihanna*]	*movie* [*I like* ____]
dog that [__ *chased the cat*]	*chair which* [*I sat on* ____]
place that [*I visited* ___ *last summer*]	*place* [*I wrote a story about* ___]

In all of these examples, the gap corresponds to a DP. That is, in each case, we can insert a DP in the gap and get a grammatical sentence:

[*Musya likes <u>Vladimir Vysotskij</u>*]	[*I wrote <u>some book</u>*]
[*I introduced <u>an author</u> to Rihanna*]	[*I like <u>every movie</u>*]
[<u>*Fido*</u> *chased the cat*]	[*I sat on <u>the chair</u>*]
[*I visited <u>Madagascar</u> last summer*]	[*I wrote a story about <u>Madagascar</u>*]

We'll restrict our attention to restrictive relative clauses like the ones above in which the gap corresponds to a DP.

In section 3.3.3 we argued that gaps in Wh-interrogatives are formed by movement of the Wh-phrase. The same type of arguments can be applied to the gaps in relative clauses, using the data in (43)–(47).

(43)   Musya likes Vladimir.

(44)   *Musya likes.

(45)   Vladimir, Musya likes.

(46)   *Vladimir, Musya likes Vladimir.

(47)   Jack met every actor who Sue likes.

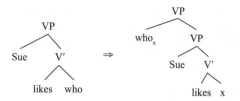

Figure 3.34
QR of *who*$_x$.

The verb *likes* requires a direct object. That explains the contrast between (43) and (44). In (45), the verb has a direct object, *Vladimir*, but it has been moved from object position to the front of the sentence. Merely placing *Vladimir* in front of a grammatical sentence doesn't work, as (46) shows. It has to have been moved there. Turning now to (47), we see that again the verb *likes* appears to have no direct object, yet it is grammatical. This is explained by the idea that *who* is generated as the object of *likes* and then is moved. (47) starts as *Jack met every actor Sue likes who* and then *who* is moved. We'll assume that the **relative pronoun** *who* is indexed, and that the movement is an instance of QR, as shown in figure 3.34.[7]

Exercise (3.24)

In each of the examples below there are two relative pronouns, *who*$_x$ and *who*$_y$. These pronouns have been moved from the position of subject or object of *cured* or of *rescued*.

(i) Natchaya knows the doctor [who$_x$ cured the woman [who$_y$ the boy rescued]].

(ii) Natchaya knows the doctor [who$_x$ cured the woman [who$_y$ rescued the boy]].

(iii) Natchaya knows the boy [who$_x$ the doctor cured the woman [who$_y$ rescued]].

[A] Below is a list showing what position the relative pronoun has moved from. The first entry is filled in. Read '*x*:subject of *cured*' as "*who*$_x$ was moved from the subject of *cured*". Complete the list.

(i) *x*:subject of *cured*   *y*:

(ii) *x*:   *y*:

(iii) *x*:   *y*:

[B] Given the constraint on movement discussed in section 3.3.3, one of the examples in (i)–(iii) is predicted to be ungrammatical. Which one is it? Which pronoun has moved incorrectly?

The relative clause itself plausibly forms a constituent with the noun it modifies giving us the result shown in figure 3.35. We now have to devise a translation for the structure in

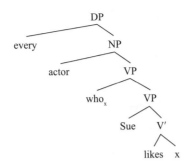

Figure 3.35
Structure of *every actor who Sue likes* after QR of *who$_x$*.

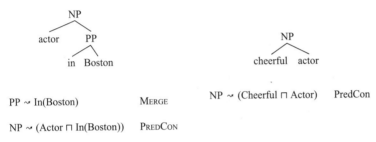

Figure 3.36
Translation of *actor in Boston* and *cheerful actor*.

figure 3.35 in which quantification is restricted to those actors who satisfy the condition imposed by the relative clause.

We've already seen instances of restrictive modification in *every actor in Boston* and *every cheerful actor*. So let's remind ourselves how those cases work (see figure 3.36). Restrictive NP-modifiers are one-place predicates that combine via predicate conjunction. This tells us what rule of translation will be used for the NP in figure 3.35. The challenge now is to have the relative clause translate as a one-place predicate. This will take some innovation because the translation of the VP *Sue likes x* in figure 3.35 is a formula. In SL, quantifiers combine with formulas to form new formulas. We'll use some of that machinery to define a new expression that combines with a formula to form a predicate. We'll make use of that new expression to translate relative clauses.

3.5.2 Defining the λ Operator
First, we add a new rule to the syntax of SL.

(48) If ϕ is a formula and u is a variable, then '$\lambda u.\phi$' is a one-place predicate.

Next we define the semantics of these newly formed predicates

(49) $[\![\lambda u.\ \phi]\!]^M = \{o' : \phi$ is true with respect to $M + \langle u,o' \rangle\ \}$.

We'll illustrate how this works with examples from exercise (2.7) in chapter 2. It might be helpful to review your results from that exercise before continuing.

Instantiating the rule in (51) with 'z' for u, 'Broken(z)' for ϕ, and 'L' for M, we get:

(50) $[\![\lambda z.\ \text{Broken}(z)]\!]^L = \{o' : \text{'Broken}(z)\text{'}$ is true with respect to $L + \langle z,o' \rangle\ \}$.

(51) 'Broken(z)' is true with respect to $L + \langle z,o' \rangle$ iff o' is broken.

Now using (51) to perform REPLACE in (50) we get:

(52) $[\![\lambda z.\ \text{Broken}(z)]\!]^L = \{o' : o'$ is broken$\}$.

Likewise, since

(53) 'Above(z)(Alan)' is true with respect to $L + \langle z,o' \rangle$ iff Alan is above o',

by REPLACE,

(54) $[\![\lambda z.\ \text{Above}(z)(\text{Alan})]\!]^L = \{o' : \text{Alan is above } o'\}$.

The equation in (54) says that '$\lambda z.$ Above(z)(Alan)' is a one-place predicate true of anything that Alan is above. Here is another result from exercise (2.7):

(55) '[$\exists z$: Broken(z)](Above(z)(y))' is true with respect to $L + \langle y,o' \rangle$ iff o' is above something that is broken.

Using (55) to perform REPLACE in (56), we get (57):

(56) $[\(y))]\!]^L = \{o' : \text{'}[\exists z: \text{Broken}(z)](\text{Above}(z)(y))\text{'}$ is true with respect to $L + \langle z,o' \rangle\ \}$.

(57) $[\(y))]\!]^L = \{o' : o'$ is above something that is broken.$\}$.

The equation in (57) says that '$\lambda y.\ [\exists z: \text{Broken}(z)](\text{Above}(z)(y))$' is a one-place predicate true of entities that are above something that is broken. Finally, by a similar calculation, we get

(58) $[\![\lambda x.\ \text{Likes}(x)(\text{Sue})]\!]^L = \{o' : \text{Sue likes } o'\}$.

'$\lambda x.$ Likes(x)(Sue)' is a one-place predicate true of any entity that Sue likes.

Exercise (3.25)

Fill in the blanks below in a way that doesn't use any technical vocabulary. Use only colloquial English:

Natchaya $\in [\![\lambda y.(\text{Hungry}(y)\ \&\ \text{Tired}(y))]\!]^L$ iff _____.

Amaya$\in [\(z))]\!]^L$ iff _____.

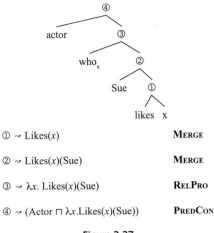

① ⁓ Likes(x)   **MERGE**

② ⁓ Likes(x)(Sue)   **MERGE**

③ ⁓ $\lambda x.$ Likes(x)(Sue)   **RELPRO**

④ ⁓ (Actor $\sqcap$ $\lambda x.$Likes(x)(Sue))   **PREDCON**

Figure 3.37
Translation of *actor who Sue likes*.

3.5.3 Translating Relative Clauses Using the λ Operator

Now that SL has a device for forming one-place predicates from formulas, we can use it in a new rule of translation:

(59) RELPRO $\{who_u, \alpha\} \rightsquigarrow \lambda u.\ \alpha'$

We now translate the NP in figure 3.35 as shown in figure 3.37.

The original sentence containing this relative clause receives the following translation:

(60) Jack met every actor who Sue likes $\rightsquigarrow$

$[\forall z: (\text{Actor} \sqcap \lambda x.\text{Likes}(x)(\text{Sue}))(z)](\text{Met}(z)(\text{Jack})).$

Exercise (3.26)

What extensions are assigned to the SL expressions below relative to the lexicon L?

(i) $\lambda z.(\text{Smiles}(z)\ \&\ \text{Sings}(z))$

(ii) $(\text{Farmer} \sqcap \lambda z.[\forall y: \text{Politician}(y)](\text{Likes}(y)(z)))$

(iii) $\lambda z.\text{Admires}(z)(z)$

(iv) $\lambda z.\neg(\text{Admires}(z)(z))$

Exercise (3.27)

Our grammar assigns the translation in (i) below to what English sentence?

(i) $[\exists x: (\text{Man} \sqcap \text{From}(\text{Belgium}) \sqcap \lambda z.\ [\forall y: \text{Answer}(y)](\text{Knew}(y)(z)))(x)]\ (\text{Resigned}(x))$

Exercise (3.28)

Provide the LF and translation for the missing reading of (29) below, discussed in section 3.3.3. Treat *was included in our survey* as a simple intransitive verb with the translation 'IncludedInSurvey'.

(29) A student [who solved every problem] was included in our survey.

Exercise (3.29)

[A] Provide an LF for the sentence *A child who Sue hired survived.* Figure 3.38 shows the base structure for that sentence.

[B] Provide the translation that gets assigned to the LF you provided in [A].

[C] The bracketed subject of the sentence in (i) below is called a *free relative.*

(i) [Whoever Musya hired] survived.

Propose a way to modify or expand the grammar so that it assigns a translation to (i) that captures your intuitions about its truth conditions. You may need to make a guess about the base structure for that sentence, but there is no need to justify the base structure you propose. The modified grammar should produce a translation for (i) as well as for the sentence in (ii) below.

(ii) Musya called whoever knew Vladimir.

[D] Provide the LF and translation assigned by your grammar to (i).

[E] Provide the translation your modified grammar assigns to (ii).

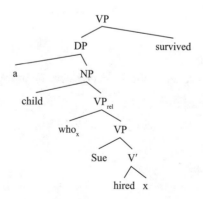

Figure 3.38
Base structure of *A child who Sue hired survived.*

3.6   Coordination and Narrative Progression

Up to this point, we have focused on the role of syntax and word meaning in the inter-pretation of expressions of natural language. In this section and the next, we'll start to acknowledge other factors that influence interpretation. Our narrow goal in this section is to arrive at the proper analysis of *and*, but along the way, we'll discover a new princi-ple of interpretation that will be of importance in our discussion in later chapters on verb meanings, tense and aspect.

The conjunction *and* connects many types of expressions. We will focus here on its use as a sentence conjoiner. We'll assume a simple syntax as illustrated in figure 3.39.

Here is a proposal for assigning translations to conjunctions:

(61)   CONJUNCTION $\{and, \alpha, \beta\} \rightsquigarrow (\alpha' \& \beta')$

Given (61) and the other rules of translation listed in table 3.7, we have

Maria sings and Fred dances $\rightsquigarrow$ (Sings(Maria) & Dances(Fred))

Exercise (3.30)

Provide an LF for *Aparajita didn't dance and Gadarine didn't sing* along with the trans-lation that our grammar assigns to that LF. Recall that our SPECIFICVOCAB rule says that *not* translates as '¬'. A base structure for a simple negated sentence is given in figure 3.21.

We consider first a well-known challenge to the accuracy of the analysis of *and* embodied in the rule in (61) and the SL interpretation for '&'. It is often said that conjunctions with English *and* usually mean the same as conjunctions with symbolic logic '&', but that in

Figure 3.39
Syntactic structure of *Maria sings and Fred dances.*

Table 3.7
Current rules of translation applicable at nodes with two daughters

MERGE	$\{\alpha, \beta\} \rightsquigarrow \alpha'(\beta')$
INDEXEDDAUGHTER	$\{\alpha_u, \beta\} \rightsquigarrow [\alpha'u: \beta'(u)]$
PREDCON	$\{\alpha, \beta\} \rightsquigarrow (\alpha' \sqcap \beta')$
CONJUNCTION	$\{and, \alpha, \beta\} \rightsquigarrow (\alpha' \& \beta')$

some contexts an English conjunction has a meaning best captured using the phrase *and then*. For example, consider the contrast between (62) and (63) from exercise (2.5):

(62) They got married, and they had a baby.

(63) They had a baby, and they got married.

Clearly, these sentences could be used to communicate the claim that two events happened in a certain order, with different order for each sentence—hence, the contrast between them. There is nothing about order in the semantics of conjunctions with '&', so one might suggest that this shows that *and* conjunctions shouldn't be translated with '&' and that in general *and* conjunctions convey temporal succession. One problem with this idea is that *and* isn't always synonymous with *and then*. For example, if I utter the sentence

(64) She walked in, and Arash was sitting there.

it does not seem like I am communicating the idea that she walked in and then *some time after that* Arash was sitting there. Instead, the tendency is to understand that he was sitting there when she walked in. So the data is a bit complicated.

A key difference between the baby examples (62)–(63) and the walking in example in (64) has to do with the kind of eventuality described in the second sentence. In (62) and in (63) the second sentence in the conjunction describes an event that occurs—a wedding or a birth. In (64), the second sentence describes a state that Arash was in. This contrast illustrates a general rule we follow in interpreting stories. The phenomenon is called **narrative progression**, and the rule is as follows:

NARRATIVE PROGRESSION In the course of a narrative, when an event is described, it is usually understood to follow in time a previously mentioned event. When a state is described, it is usually understood to hold at the time of a previously mentioned event.

In (62), first a marriage is described and then a birth is described. The rule of NARRATIVE PROGRESSION leads us to the understanding that the birth followed the marriage. In (63), first a birth is described and then a marriage is described. The rule of NARRATIVE PROGRESSION leads us to the understanding that the marriage followed the birth. In (64), an entering is described and then a state of sitting is described. In this case, the rule of NARRATIVE PROGRESSION leads us to the understanding that the sitting state is understood to hold throughout the time of the entering. For the event sentences, NARRATIVE PROGRESSION amounts to the idea that the order in which events are described follows the order in which they occurred.

The text in (i)–(ix) serves as further illustration of NARRATIVE PROGRESSION. As you read it, consider how you perceive the order of events:

(i) She walked in.

(ii) He was sitting there.

(iii) She looked around the room.

(iv) It was dark and gloomy.

(v) There was nothing to lighten the mood.

(vi) He got up saying, "I'm glad you're here."

(vii) She replied, "I'm glad I could come."

(viii) Her reply didn't sound sincere to him.

(ix) It didn't sound sincere to her either.

Each of these sentences tells us what is going on at a certain past time, which is sometimes called a **reference time**[8]. Most people interpret the reference times as advancing from earlier to later as the narrative progresses. But not every sentence in the narrative triggers such an advance. Normally, sentences (iii), (vi), and (vii) are interpreted as advancing the reference time, and sentences (ii), (iv), (v), (viii), and (ix) are interpreted as leaving it unchanged. In other words, if someone were to claim that this story were a completely true one, then one would expect there to be five successive past times such that

At time 1, she walks in.
At time 1, he is sitting there.

At time 2, she looks around the room.
At time 2, it is dark and gloomy.
At time 2, there is nothing to lighten the mood.

At time 3, he gets up and says, "I'm glad you're here."

At time 4, she replies, "I'm glad I could come."
At time 4, her reply doesn't sound sincere to him.
At time 4, it doesn't sound sincere to her.

The sentences that advance the reference time describe events and the ones that don't advance the reference time describe states. The NARRATIVE PROGRESSION rule contains the phrase "a previously mentioned event." In our implementation, we understood the events to follow, and the states to hold, at the time of the <u>immediately</u> previously mentioned events. The rule doesn't require this, and in more elaborate discourses it may not work this way. Also, above we said that the state of being dark held at the time of looking around the room (time 2). Most likely it held also at the time of entering (time 1). States can last a while and the rule requires only that they at least held at the time of one previously mentioned event.

Once we recognize the phenomenon of narrative progression, we have a new way to understand the contrast between (62) and (63):

(62) They got married, and they had a baby.

(63) They had a baby, and they got married.

In both sentences, two events are reported. In both cases, the events are understood to have occurred in the order in which they are reported. This can be attributed to the NARRATIVE PROGRESSION rule. In that case, our semantics of conjunction can remain as originally proposed in (61) above. This way of viewing things also explains why the "and-then effect" is absent in (64).

(64) She walked in, and Arash was sitting there.

The second conjunct of (64) is stative so by the rule of NARRATIVE PROGRESSION, it should not introduce a later reference time.

This analysis fits into a picture of language according to which there are rules of grammar that associate sentences of the language with truth conditions. These come under the narrow heading of **semantics**. On top of that, there are conventions governing the use of language which may allow a speaker to convey more information than is captured by truth conditions alone. The rule of NARRATIVE PROGRESSION is one such example. It governs how we interpret sequencing of sentences. These conventions come under the heading of **pragmatics**.

Separating the data in this way, as opposed to revising our translation for conjunction, also helps to explain the fact that a speaker can explicitly cancel the effect. It is felicitous to say:

(65) He rented an apartment, and he found a job, but not necessarily in that order.

Here the speaker is removing the effect of a pragmatic rule with the *but*-clause. There is a strong contrast between this cancellation and an attempt by a speaker to deny or question an <u>entailment</u>. The following sounds contradictory (note that '#' indicates that the sentence is contradictory or infelicitous. This differs from '*', which is used to indicate that a sentence is ungrammatical).:

(66) #He rented an apartment, and he found a job, but I'm not sure if he found a job.

Stepping back now, there is an important lesson to be learned from our discussion of *and*. The perceived meaning of a sentence may be the product of several forces. In addition to syntax and word meaning, conventions of language use, or pragmatics, can be at play. A convincing hypothesis about the pragmatics will often lead us to adopt a simpler semantics and hopefully a more correct account of our intuitions about meaning.

Exercise (3.31)

In section 3.4, we showed that our rules assigned the translation in (ii) to an LF for the sentence in (i) in which *in Boston* is a VP modifier.

(i) Jack discussed a wedding in Boston.

(ii) $[\exists x : \text{Wedding}(x)]((\text{Discussed}(x) \sqcap \text{In(Boston)}))(\text{Jack})$.

The translation in (ii) fails to capture the fact that on the relevant reading, (i) entails that the discussion of the wedding and Jack's being in Boston were simultaneous. Discuss the possibility of appealing to the rule of NARRATIVE PROGRESSION to solve this problem.

Exercise (3.32)

Below are four brief narratives. For each one, draw a timeline, mapping out how time moves in the narrative. Reflect on which cases depart from the rule of NARRATIVE PROGRESSION and which conform to it and why. For each narrative, submit

- a list of the verbs that appear in the phrases that <u>advance</u> the reference time;
- your observations about departures from NARRATIVE PROGRESSION.

Each narrative below is given twice. The second time it is numerically annotated. This is to indicate which units you should be focusing on when you map out the timeline.

(i) One day Willie was sitting at his desk in the boarding house. He heard a knock on the door. He got up and opened the door. A boy stood there, drinking a glass of orange juice. The boy stopped drinking, studied Willie for a moment, and then began to sing.

One day Willie was [sitting]$_1$ at his desk in the boarding house. He [heard]$_2$ a knock on the door. He [got up]$_3$ and [opened]$_4$ the door. A boy [stood]$_5$ there, [drinking]$_6$ a glass of orange juice. The boy [stopped drinking]$_7$, [studied]$_8$ Willie for a moment, and then [began to sing]$_9$.

(ii) A tall doctor entered the room. She was opening a can of Pepsi. She had heard the crying patient and had come to investigate. She paused, drank the Pepsi and left. It was all quite mysterious.

A tall doctor [entered]$_1$ the room. She [was opening]$_2$ a can of Pepsi. She [had heard]$_3$ the crying patient and [had come to investigate]$_4$. She [paused]$_5$, [drank]$_6$ the Pepsi and [left]$_7$. It [was]$_8$ all quite mysterious.

(iii) Yesterday morning I was standing around, waiting for my car. Suddenly, this odd-looking truck pulls into the garage. Its roof is covered with colored lights. A little girl jumps out of the back. She's eating an apple, and she throws it at me. I jumped out of the way, and the apple went flying through the shop window, just missing Sam.

Yesterday morning I [was standing]$_1$ around, [waiting]$_2$ for my car. Suddenly, this odd-looking truck [pulls]$_3$ into the garage. Its roof [is covered]$_4$ with colored lights. A little girl [jumps]$_4$ out of the back. She's [eating]$_5$ an apple, and she [throws]$_6$ it at me. I [jumped]$_7$ out of the way and the apple [went]$_8$ flying through the shop window, just [missing]$_9$ Sam.

(iv) Alan sat in the front seat. A violent jerk woke him. The train was moving slowly. He wiped the misty windowpanes, shaded his eyes, and tried to look out into this new country. The moon was full. He saw arching hills, stumps of burnt trees, and a lonely road. It was strange. He turned to look at Elham. She gave him a deprecatory smile.[9]

Alan [sat]$_1$ in the front seat. A violent jerk [woke]$_2$ him. The train [was moving]$_3$ slowly. He [wiped]$_4$ the misty windowpanes, [shaded]$_5$ his eyes, and [tried]$_6$ to look out into this new country. The moon [was]$_7$ full. He [saw]$_8$ arching hills, stumps of burnt trees, and a lonely road. It [was]$_9$ strange. He [turned]$_{10}$ to look at Elham. She [gave]$_{11}$ him a deprecatory smile.

Exercise (3.33)

[A] Consider the following bit of narrative:

(i) The team renovated the beach house yesterday.

(ii) Nadir painted the door.

(iii) Baboloki fixed the toilet.

(iv) Akna rebuilt the porch.

(v) At the end of the day, they went for a long swim.

It is natural to understand the painting, fixing, and rebuilding as simultaneous, which is not what is expected by our Narrative Progression rule. Formulate a hypothesis about what distinguishes this case from the ones discussed above.

[B] Consider the following two mini-narratives:

(i) Baboloki was dead. Akna shot him.

(ii) Akna shot Baboloki. He was dead.

(i) and (ii) contain the same event and state descriptions, but in different order. This affects the temporal interpretation. Describe how (i) and (ii) differ in their interpretation and whether this difference is expected by our Narrative Progression rule. If not, formulate a hypothesis about what distinguishes (i) and (ii) from the narratives discussed in this chapter. Finally, state whether your hypothesis also explains the temporal interpretation of (iii)–(iv) and (v)–(vi):

(iii) The barn was red. Nadir painted it.

(iv) Nadir painted the barn. It was red.

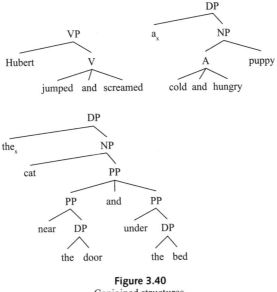

Figure 3.40
Conjoined structures.

(v) It was pitch dark. Nadir turned off the lights.

(vi) Nadir turned off the lights. It was pitch dark.

Exercise (3.34)

In the text, we looked at examples of sentential conjunction. In the structures in figure 3.40 *and* conjoins constituents that are not sentences. Write a rule of translation that, along with our other rules, will allow us to assign good translations to the structures shown in figure 3.40.

✪ Thinking about Movement Out of Conjunctions ✪

In section 3.3.3, we observed that movement out of relative clauses is prohibited, which explains why quantifiers cannot take scope out of relative clauses. Movement out of conjunctions is also prohibited. This prohibition is the topic of the next exercise.

Exercise (3.35)

The sentence in (i) is formed by applying Wh-movement to *which fireman* and pulling it out of a conjunction as illustrated in figure 3.41, in which '*x*' marks the original position of *which fireman*.

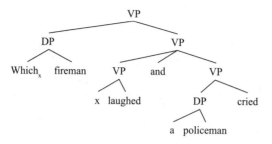

Figure 3.41
*Which fireman laughed and a policeman cried?

Table 3.7
Current rules of translation applicable at nodes with two daughters

MERGE	$\{\alpha, \beta\} \rightsquigarrow \alpha'(\beta')$
INDEXEDDAUGHTER	$\{\alpha_u, \beta\} \rightsquigarrow [\alpha'u: \beta'(u)]$
PREDCON	$\{\alpha, \beta\} \rightsquigarrow (\alpha' \sqcap \beta')$
CONJUNCTION	$\{and, \alpha, \beta\} \rightsquigarrow (\alpha' \,\&\, \beta')$

(i) *Which fireman laughed, and a policeman cried?

The aim of this exercise is to show that, as predicted, a quantifier cannot move out of a conjunction. Before proceeding, it might be useful to review the quantifier terminology introduced in section 3.3.1.

[A] Produce an LF for (ii) that captures a reading in which *no fireman* has scope over *a policeman*.

(ii) No fireman laughed, and a policeman cried.

[B] Provide the translation that our grammar assigns to the LF you provided in [A]. Our current rules of translation for branching nodes are shown in table 3.7.

[C] Describe a situation in which the translation you provided in [B] is true, but where intuitively the sentence in (ii) would not be true on any reading.

[D] Why is the following ungrammatical?

(iii) *The man who laughed and a policeman cried was arrested.

Exercise (3.36)

In section 3.3.3, we observed that the sentence below has only two readings.

(36) A dog chased every cat, and a squirrel did too.

If QR were completely unconstrained, we would have expected there to be four readings.

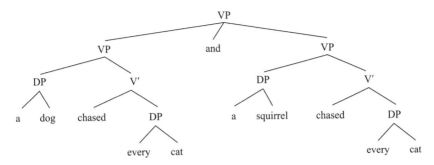

Figure 3.42
Base structure of *A dog chased every cat and a squirrel chased every cat.*

[A] Provide an LF for one of the missing readings. To do that, assume that the LF is formed from the base structure in figure 3.42, even though a rule of deletion is applied to that base structure on its way to surface structure.

[B] Assume that the sentence in (36) is the result of a deletion operation that applies to the base structure above, separately from the LF, as part of forming the surface structure. State the deletion rule.

[C] Try to state a constraint on syntactic structures that would effectively rule out the missing interpretations.

Exercise (3.37)

In this section, we've introduced a special rule for translating sentential conjunctions. Suppose instead we merely added '&' to our SPECIFICVOCAB with this rule:

SPECIFICVOCAB *and* ⤳ &

[A] Explain why this rule would not be enough to get a well-formed formula.

[B] Propose a revision to the syntax and semantics of SL so that MERGE and the SPECIFICVOCAB rule would produce good translations for sentential conjunctions assuming the binary branching structure in figure 3.43.

3.7 Pronouns

In the previous section we introduced a division of labor between semantics and pragmatics. On this view, an expression is assigned a meaning determined by its syntax and by the content of the lexical items in the expression. When the expression is uttered, rules of conversation may enrich the message. NARRATIVE PROGRESSION is one such rule. Pronouns give rise to a different kind of phenomenon in which the message conveyed is

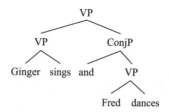

Figure 3.43
Syntactic structure of *Ginger sings and Fred dances.*

determined in part semantically, based on syntax and word meaning, and in part prag-
matically, the result of a contribution from the speech context.

   To appreciate this phenomenon we need to first establish some basic facts about pronouns, some of which were discussed in the previous chapter (section 2.3 and exercise
(2.15) in particular). Compare the sentences in (67) and (68):

(67) Every musician nominated himself.

(68) She smiled.

Intuitively, the pronoun *himself* in (67) does not refer to any particular individual. It has
the kind of meaning that a bound variable has in SL. Its value varies with the choice of
musician. It is called a **bound pronoun**. Now consider the pronoun *she* in (68). Whoever
might have used this sentence would have had a particular individual in mind and the
pronoun would be used to refer to that individual. Since it is used to refer, it's called a **ref-
erential pronoun**. It's also called a **free pronoun**, a label that contrasts with *bound pronoun*. Although we have the intuition that *she* was used to refer to a particular individual,
we also feel that, despite our competence as English speakers, we do not know who *she*
was meant to refer to; nor could we know unless we knew more about the discourse in
which it was used. Focusing on this pragmatic aspect, **discourse pronoun** is a third label
applicable to *she* in (68). Our first goal is to give some account of how the bound pronoun
gets its interpretation in (67). Our second goal will be to explain why *she* in (68) is unin-
terpretable out of the blue and how it is able to get an interpretation when the sentence is
embedded in a discourse.

   Before turning to these goals, let's round out the story by pointing out that (69) below is
ambiguous with respect to how the pronoun *she* is interpreted.

(69) No child discussed a story that she had read in class.

Here, *she* could be a bound pronoun, in which case its interpretation varies with the
children. Or *she* could be used as a free/referential/discourse pronoun in which case it
would refer to an individual salient in the discourse.

Exercise (3.38)

Sentence (69) uses the pronoun *she*. What effect would there be if *he* or *they* were used instead of *she*? Divide your answer into two parts. First describe the effect on a reading where the pronoun is free, then describe the effect on a reading where the pronoun is bound.

3.7.1 Pronoun Indexing
To incorporate pronoun interpretations into our grammar, first we'll add a syntactic indexing rule that applies specifically to pronouns:

(70) Pronoun Indexing   Pronouns are indexed with a variable.

We'll also need a translation rule for pronouns:

(71) Pronoun   A pronoun with index u is translated as u.

We illustrate how this works, beginning with an LF for (67), which was arrived at by indexing *every* and *herself* and applying QR, as shown in figure 3.44. The result is a good translation for *Every musician nominated herself*, leaving aside the issues raised in exercise (3.38).

Syntactic theories of the distribution and interpretation of pronouns are usually spelled out in terms of indexation and co-indexation within a syntactic structure. By first indexing the pronoun in the syntax, (70), and then referring to that index in the rules of translation, we make it possible to integrate our results with those theories.

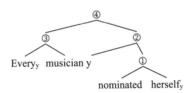

herself$_y$ ⤳ y **Pronoun**

① ⤳ Nominated(y)   **Merge**

② ⤳ Nominated(y)(y)   **Merge**

③ ⤳ [∀y: Musician(y)]   **IndexedDaughter**

④ ⤳ [∀y: Musician(y)] (Nominated(y)(y))   **Merge**

Figure 3.44
LF and translation of *Every musician nominated herself.*

Exercise (3.39)

The sentence *Herself nominated every musician* is ungrammatical. State syntactic constraints governing the distribution of indices that will rule it out. Specify whether or not your constraints need to hold prior to QR, after QR or both.

Exercise (3.40)

This exercise is about a perceived difference in the interpretations allowed for the pronoun *him* in this pair of examples:

(i) No fireman saw a reporter near him.

(ii) No fireman cried, and a reporter photographed him.

(i) has a reading in which *him* is a bound pronoun ranging over firemen. On that reading, (i) says that there is no fireman such that that fireman saw a reporter who was near that fireman. It would be falsified if there was a reporter next to a fireman, and the fireman saw the reporter. By contrast, (ii) does <u>not</u> have a reading in which *him* is a bound pronoun ranging over firemen. In other words, (ii) can <u>not</u> be used to say that there was no fireman such that that fireman cried, and a reporter photographed that fireman.

[A] Provide an LF and translation for (i) for the reading in which *him* is a bound pronoun ranging over firemen.

[B] Decide whether our grammar correctly captures the fact that (ii) fails to have a reading in which *him* is a bound pronoun ranging over firemen. In making your decision, consider various possible LFs for (ii) and the corresponding translations. In doing so, keep in mind the ban on movement out of a conjunction discussed in exercise (3.35).

• If you conclude that the grammar correctly captures the fact that (ii) fails to have a reading in which *him* is a bound pronoun ranging over firemen, then explain how the reading is excluded.

• If you conclude that the grammar incorrectly assigns the missing reading to (ii), then propose amendments to the grammar that will block that reading.

Next, we use PRONOUN INDEXING and our new translation rule PRONOUN on the sentence in (68), *She smiled*, and we get the result shown in figure 3.45. The formula 'Smiled(y)' is undefined with respect to L. That's because $L(y)$ is undefined. Recall that L assigns meanings only to individual constants and to simple one- and two-place predicates. The fact that 'Smiled(y)' is undefined with respect to L is bad news and good news. On the one hand, the English sentence is perfectly meaningful, so the translation should also be meaningful. On the other hand, as noted above, merely knowing English is not sufficient to interpret (68). We'd like to say that the sentence is not meaningful unless the discourse makes it meaningful. What we need to spell out now is the contribution of the discourse.

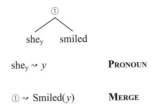

she$_y$ ⤳ y PRONOUN

① ⤳ Smiled(y)   MERGE

Figure 3.45
Application of PRONOUN INDEXING and translation rule PRONOUN.

Recall how variables work in SL. They are not defined by L, and yet they don't always lead to undefined formulas, and that's because quantifiers can step in and augment L with values for variables. We'd like a similar effect here, but instead of a quantifier triggering the augmentation, we want a way to let the discourse do it. Moreover, we'd like a mechanism that is general enough to apply to several free pronouns. The sentence *She told him that it was in the car* has three free pronouns (*she, him, it*). Since pronouns in our grammar get translated as variables, what we are looking for is a discourse-based mechanism that assigns values to variables. Since this mechanism assigns meanings to basic symbols, it is a kind of lexicon. We will call it a **context lexicon**, and we'll combine it with the fixed lexicon L using the '+' operation introduced in our chapter 1 discussion of bilingualism:

[M+N] notation

Let M and N be two sets of pairs.
If M and N have no first elements in common, then [M+N] is defined.
If [M+N] is defined, then it consists of all the pairs in M along with all the pairs in N.

In the next subsection, we'll nail down the details on context lexicons. Before doing that, though, let's sketch how a discourse including an utterance of *She smiled* might proceed.

Suppose that Jack is telling us a story and at some point he mentions Jill. Since Jill is now salient, she will be paired with a variable. We'll choose 'y' for that purpose so that now our current context lexicon contains the pair ⟨y, Jill⟩ . The discourse continues, and Jack mentions Ellen. Again a variable, let's say 'z', is paired with Ellen, so our current context lexicon consists of the set of pairs { ⟨y, Jill⟩ , ⟨z, Ellen⟩ }. At some point in the story, it transpires that Ellen told a bad joke, and Jack reports Jill's polite reaction to the joke with the sentence *She$_y$ smiled*. As explained above, that sentence is translated as '$Smiled(y)$'. And now since we are interpreting that formula relative to the combination of L and the context lexicon, it will come out true if and only if Jill smiled. That's because the variable 'y' is assigned to Jill. If the pronoun had been indexed 'z' instead of 'y', the sentence would have been translated as 'Smiled(z)', and it would be true iff Ellen smiled. If the pronoun had been indexed 'x' instead of 'y', the sentence would have been translated as 'Smiled(x)'. Since 'x' is not paired with anything in the context lexicon, the result would be undefined.

What about the intuition that an out-of-the-blue utterance of *She$_y$ smiled* is odd? If no discourse has preceded the utterance, then the context lexicon is empty; it contains no pairs. In particular, there is nothing paired with 'y' and so 'Smiled(y)' is undefined, and we correctly predict that the sentence is not felicitous.

Exercise (3.41)

At some point in a discourse the sentence *She$_x$ told him$_y$ that it$_z$ was open* is uttered and is understood by the participants in that conversation as meaning that Kim told Chris that their front door was open. What set of pairs would have to have been included in the context lexicon for that utterance to be understood in that way?

3.7.2   Context Lexicon

As a discourse progresses, entities become salient and are associated with variables. We represent the state of a discourse at any point as a set of variable-entity pairs. We call this a **context lexicon**, and we'll use the letter 'K' to stand for a context lexicon. Unlike the fixed lexicon L, there is in principle a different context lexicon for each point in any discourse, depending on what individuals have become salient at that point. So we'll need to add a subscript to 'K' to distinguish different context lexicons. In other words, we'll have different context lexicons, K_1, K_2, K_3, and so on, or one context lexicon for each point in each discourse. To make general statements about context lexicons, we'll use the letter 'p' to stand for a point in a discourse.

Summarizing then, 'K_p' will stand for the context lexicon for point p in a discourse. 'K_p' records all the individuals salient in the discourse at point p. It does this in the form of pairs of individuals and variables. Next, we'll want to set up rules that make the felicity of an utterance dependent on what is in 'K_p' and we'll want to make the interpretation of an utterance dependent on 'K_p'. The rules follow in (72) below. The term **infelicitous** appears in those rules. That's a technical term from pragmatics. If a sentence is unacceptable for syntactic reasons, we call it *ungrammatical*. If it is unacceptable for pragmatic reasons we call it *infelicitous*.

(72)   FELICITY AND TRUTH

As a discourse progresses, individuals become salient and are associated with variables. K_p is a set of variable-individual pairs that represent the state of the discourse at point p. K_p is the context lexicon for point-in-a-discourse p.

If an utterance is made at point p in a discourse, then:

(a) an LF for that utterance is <u>infelicitous</u> if its translation is not defined with respect to K_p+L.

(b) If an LF for that utterance is <u>felicitous</u>, then it is true if its translation is true with respect to K_p+L, and it is false if its translation is false with respect to K_p+L.

Let's now apply this definition to the conversation mentioned earlier in which Jack related that Ellen had told a joke (see table 3.8). The points in the discourse are numbered arbitrarily.

Following the rules of the grammar, we make some calculations:

She$_y$ smiled. $\rightsquigarrow$ 'Smiled(y)'

'Smiled(y)' is true with respect to K_{61}+L iff Jill smiled.

'Smiled(y)' is not defined with respect to K_{59}+L.

Given these calculation and the rules in (72), it follows that

She$_y$ smiled would be <u>infelicitous</u> if uttered at point [59].

She$_y$ smiled is felicitous when uttered at point [61], and it conveys that Jill smiled.

With wider coverage of English, we can now extend our list of correspondences between syntactic and semantic categories to include pronouns, as shown in table 3.9.

Table 3.8
Conversation

Utterance	Point in time when utterance ended	Context lexicon at that point
Here's what happened yesterday.	[59]	$K_{59} = \varnothing$
Jill was present.	[60]	$K_{60} = \{ \langle y, \text{Jill} \rangle \}$
Ellen told a bad joke.	[61]	$K_{61} = \{ \langle y, \text{Jill} \rangle, \langle z, \text{Ellen} \rangle \}$
She$_y$ smiled.	[62]	$K_{62} = \{ \langle y, \text{Jill} \rangle, \langle z, \text{Ellen} \rangle \}$

Table 3.9
Correspondence between syntactic and semantic categories

Syntactic category of English	Syntactic category of SL	Semantic category (extension)
Name	Individual constant	Entity
Intransitive verb, adjective, noun, NP	One-place predicate	Set of entities
Transitive verb, preposition	Two-place predicate	Sets of pairs whose first element is an entity and whose second element is a set of entities
Sentence (VP)	Formula	Truth value
Variable	Variable	Entity
Pronoun	Variable	Entity

Exercise (3.42)

[A] Fill in the blanks based on the discourse mapped out in table 3.8.

$[K_{61}+L](y) = $ _____.

She$_z$ *smiled* is true with respect to $K_{61}+L$ iff _____.

[B] In the previous chapter, exercise (2.15) explored the sentence below:

(i) *Phil tickled Stanley, and Liz poked him.*

Recall that this sentence has a reading in which the pronoun *him* is used to refer to Phil, and another reading in which *him* is used to refer to Stanley. The goal of this exercise is to make sense of the ambiguity in light of the ideas developed in this section. Begin by providing an LF for the sentence in (i) and the translation assigned by the grammar to that LF. Next, describe two different conversations using the format found in table 3.8. In one conversation, the pronoun *him* is naturally used to refer to Phil, and in the other conversation, *him* is naturally used to refer to Stanley.

[C] Consider the conversation in table 3.10. *She*$_y$ *frowned* will work the way that *She*$_y$ *smiled* did in the conversation in table 3.8. But *It*$_x$ *wasn't funny* will incorrectly be predicted to be infelicitous. How should the context lexicon be adjusted to rectify this problem? What would happen if the index on *it* was changed to '*z*', and everything else in table 3.10 was left as is?

3.8 Semantics and Pragmatics

3.8.1 Pragmatics

Although the term *semantics* is said to refer to the study of meaning, its use is often restricted to truth conditions and the contribution that word meaning and syntax make to truth conditions. That's the sense in which it is used in this chapter. The term *pragmatics* is then used to refer to other factors that influence interpretation. There are at least three

Table 3.10
Conversation

Utterance	Point in time when utterance ended	Context lexicon at that point
Here's what happened yesterday.	[59]	$K_{59} = \varnothing$
Jill came over.	[60]	$K_{60} = \{ \langle y, \text{Jill} \rangle \}$
Alan told a joke.	[61]	$K_{61} = \{ \langle y, \text{Jill} \rangle, \langle z, \text{Alan} \rangle \}$
She$_y$ frowned.	[62]	$K_{62} = \{ \langle y, \text{Jill} \rangle, \langle z, \text{Alan} \rangle \}$
It$_x$ wasn't funny.	[63]	$K_{63} = \{ \langle y, \text{Jill} \rangle, \langle z, \text{Alan} \rangle \}$

seemingly distinct kinds of phenomena that fall into this category, two of which we've just seen: conventions of language use such as the rule of NARRATIVE PROGRESSION and the dependence on context in the interpretation of free pronouns. *Pragmatics* is also used to refer to considerations of plausibility. Given several situations in which a sentence might be true, hearers may tend to fix on those that are most plausible. This idea was briefly alluded to at the end of our discussion of constraints on quantifier scope (see section 3.3.3). The following text illustrates all three of these phenomena:

(73) Baboloki and Rihanna entered the laboratory at noon. Baboloki immediately went inside the testing room and locked the door. He pressed a button on the outside of the testing room, and oxygen began to flow in.

There is something odd about this text. Here's a pragmatic explanation:

• The free pronoun *he* is context dependent. Since Baboloki is mentioned in the second sentence, Baboloki is salient when the pronoun occurs and the context supplies Baboloki as the referent of the pronoun.

• There is a <u>convention of use</u> according to which we describe events in the order in which they occurred. So we understand the pressing of the button to have followed Baboloki's having entered the testing room.

• Given the way rooms work, a person locked inside can't press a button on the outside. Hence the scenario described is not *plausible*, so the text is judged odd.

✪ Thinking about Movement Out of Conjunctions, Part 2 ✪

In exercise (3.35) we observed that movement out of conjunctions is prohibited. This prohibition helped us explain the data not only in exercise (3.35), but also in exercise (3.40). As it turns out, there are some exceptions to the prohibition. The goal of exercise (3.43) is to consider whether the prohibition is subject to pragmatic constraints.

Exercise (3.43)

In exercise (3.35), we observed that the question below is ungrammatical.

(74) *Which fireman laughed and a policeman cried?

Recall that this example is formed by applying Wh-movement to *which fireman*, thereby pulling it out of a conjunction in which '*x*' marks the original position of *which fireman*. This is illustrated in figure 3.41, which we have reproduced below.

Now consider the examples in (75)[10] which suggest that movement out of conjunctions is sometimes possible:

(75) a. What book did Akna buy and read?
      b. What did Natchaya go to the store and buy?

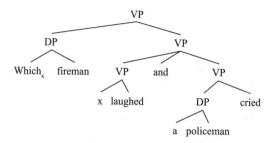

Figure 3.41
*Which fireman laughed and a policeman cried?

c. What dress did Amaya go and ruin now?
d. Who did Gardine pull out her phone and call?
e. How much can Baboloki drink and stay sober?
f. How small a meal can Musya eat and feel satisfied?
g. What did Sam go to the store, buy, load in his car, drive home and unload?

In this exercise we will consider whether there is a pragmatic component to the prohibition against movement out of conjunctions which may explain why the question in (74) is ungrammatical but the questions in (75) are grammatical. To do so, let us consider a proposal by David Hume about human psychology, and in particular, the ways in which two ideas can be associated to form a complex idea.[11] Hume proposed that there are only three ways to associate two ideas: via contiguity in time or place, cause and effect, or resemblance. This trichotomy has been useful to characterize pragmatic inferences in several domains. When applied to natural language, the trichotomy manifests as **coherence relations**, which relate **discourse units**, or descriptions of events and states. Below, you will find definitions of four coherence relations.[12]

Given two discourse units π_1, π_2,

• Occasion(π_1, π_2) iff π_1 describes an event e_1 that is a precondition for an event e_2 described by π_2.

• Result(π_1, π_2) iff π_1 describes an event e_1 that causes an e_2 described by π_2.

• Parallel(π_1, π_2) iff π_1 describes an event e_1 that is similar in some way to an event e_2 described by π_2.

• Contrast(π_1, π_2) iff π_1 describes an event e_1 that is different in some way from an event e_2 described by π_2.

Occasion is a Humean contiguity relation. We can make an argument that it is exemplified by the question in (75)a. Take π_1 to correspond to the discourse unit *Akna bought book x*, and take π_2 to correspond to the discourse unit *Akna read book x*. We can infer that the described book-buying event by Akna is a precondition for her reading that book. In other words, Akna's book-buying "occasioned her" to read it. The question in (75)a, then, amounts to asking which book Akna came to have in her possession, which in turn "occasioned her" to read it.

Result is a Humean cause relation. We can make an argument that it is exemplified by the question in (75)f. Take π_1 to correspond to the discourse unit *Musya eats a meal*, and take π_2 to correspond to the discourse unit *Musya feels satisfied*. We can infer that the event of Musya's eating a meal causes her to feel satisfied. The question in (75)f, then, amounts to asking about the smallest quantity of the meal that causes her to feel satisfied.

Parallel is a Humean resemblance relation. We can make an argument that it is exemplified by the question in (76) below. Take π_1 to correspond to the discourse unit *Fireman x smiled*, and take π_2 to correspond to the discourse unit *Policeman y grinned*. We can infer that both events are similar in being a humorous response. Moreover, the individuals described, namely x and y, are similar: they are both law enforcement officers. The question in (76) amounts to asking about the value of x—that is, which fireman participated in an event that is parallel to that of the policeman's?

(76) *Which fireman smiled and a policeman grinned?

Contrast is the negation of parallel, and is also seen as a Humean resemblance relation.[13] We can make an argument that parallel is exemplified by the question in (74), repeated below:

(74) *Which fireman laughed and a policeman cried?

Take π_1 to, once again, correspond to the discourse unit *Fireman x smiled* and take π_2 to correspond to the discourse unit *Policeman y cried*. We can infer that while smiling is a humorous response, crying is not. The question in (74) amounts to asking about the value of x—that is, which fireman participated in an event that contrasts with that of the policeman's?

[A] Notice that the ungrammatical questions in (74) and (76) exemplify Humean resemblance relations, while the grammatical questions in (75)a and (75)f exemplify Humean contiguity and cause relations, respectively. This leads to the following hypothesis:

(i) The prohibition against movement out of conjunctions applies only to questions that exemplify a Humean resemblance relation (parallel and contrast).

Test this hypothesis by considering the other questions in (75) not discussed thus far and arguing that they exemplify not a Humean resemblance relation (parallel and contrast), but rather a Humean contiguity (occasion) or a cause relation (result).

[B] Above, we considered the Humean cause relation (result). There is also an effect relation called **explanation**, which is the inverse of result:

• Explanation(π_1, π_2) iff π_2 describes an event e_2 that causes an e_1 described by π_1.

EXAMPLE *Nadir fell down. Gadarine pushed him.*

The hypothesis in (i) predicts that movement out of conjunction is possible when explanation is exemplified. Create an example that tests this prediction, justifying that your example does, in fact, exemplify explanation, as defined above. Then state whether your example supports the hypothesis in (i).

[C] Above, we considered two Humean resemblance relations (parallel and contrast). There is a third resemblance relation called **elaboration**:

- Elaboration(π_1, π_2) iff π_2 describes an eventuality e_2 that provides more information about an event e_1 described by π_1.

EXAMPLE *Gadarine wrote a letter. She wrote it using classical Armenian orthography.*

The hypothesis in (i) predicts that movement out of conjunction is impossible when elaboration is exemplified. Create an example that tests this prediction, justifying that your example does, in fact, exemplify elaboration, as defined above. Then state whether your example supports the hypothesis in (i).

[D] Create other examples to further test the hypothesis in (i). Then, based on your examples, as well as your answers to [A]–[C], provide an argument as to whether the prohibition against movement contains a pragmatic component. If you think that it does not, explain how our grammar could explain the data that you have considered in this exercise. If you think there is a pragmatic component to the phenomenon, provide a rule that would aide in explaining the data that you have considered in this exercise. Before stating your rule, you may want to consider how our NARRATIVE PROGRESSION rule was stated in connection with (62)–(64) above.

Note: This is an open problem. You're not expected to solve it. Success lies in coming up with an interesting hypothesis that can be tested further with more data.

✪ Thinking about Constraints on the Interpretation of Pronouns ✪

In exercise (3.42) we considered a discourse in which a pronoun can refer to either the subject or the object of the previous sentence. The task was to provide an analysis of the ambiguity by providing an LF for the discourse in question with two different context lexicons. While this allowed us to analyze the ambiguity, the question that was left unanswered is what will determine how the context lexicon looks. This question is pragmatic in nature. The goal of the exercise below is to take some steps in thinking about this question.

Exercise (3.44)

In exercise (3.42) we discussed the sentence below:

(i) Phil tickled Stanley and Liz poked him.

Recall that this sentence has a reading in which the pronoun *him* is used to refer to Phil, and another reading in which *him* is used to refer to Stanley. Further recall from exercise (3.43) that according to the philosopher David Hume, there are only three possible ways that two ideas can be associated to form a complex idea: via contiguity in time or place, cause and effect, and resemblance. When applied to natural language, this trichotomy manifests as coherence relations, which were defined in exercise (3.43). With these two ideas in place, attempt the following tasks.

[A] State which coherence relation from exercise (3.43) is exemplified by one of the readings of (i) above. Then do the same for the other reading of (i).

[B] Create three other discourses in which a pronoun can refer to more than one possible individual. For each reading of each discourse, state which coherence relation is exemplified. Note: if possible, attempt to create discourses that exemplify coherence relations not found in (i) above. If it's not possible, provide a hypothesis concerning why it's difficult to create ambiguous discourses that exemplify coherence relations not found in (i) above.

[C] Based on your answers in [A] and [B], provide an argument in favor of the generalization in (ii).[14] Then state how this generalization could be helpful for answering the following question: What determines how the context lexicon looks?

(ii) Determining the referent of a pronoun and establishing a coherence relation between two discourse units are two mutually correlated tasks.

[D] Consider the discourse below, in (iii). Observe that on one reading of the discourse, Liz's poking is understood to precede Stanley's scream. This reading is salient if, for example, Liz's poking caused Stanley to scream. In this case, explanation (defined in exercise (3.43)) is inferred: *Stanley screamed with pain in his eyes because Liz poked him*. On another reading of the discourse, Liz's poking is understood to follow Stanley's scream. This reading is salient if, for example, Stanley's screaming caused Liz to poke him. In this case, result (defined in exercise (3.43)) is inferred: *Stanley screamed with pain in his eyes and this resulted in Liz poking him*.

(iii) Stanley screamed with pain in his eyes. Liz poked him.

Revise our NARRATIVE PROGRESSION rule, repeated below, in order to account for the two readings found in (iii). When revising your rule, attempt to incorporate your answer to [C]. You may also need to revise the definitions of the coherence relations defined in exercise (3.43), which currently involve events, but not states (which coherence relations involve events, which involve states, and which involve both events and states?).

NARRATIVE PROGRESSION

In the course of a narrative, when an event is described, it is usually understood to follow in time a previously mentioned event. When a state is described, it is usually understood to hold at the time of a previously mentioned event.

Note: This is an open problem. You're not expected to solve it. Success lies in coming up with an interesting hypothesis that can be tested further with more data.

3.8.2 Truth Conditions

At this point we have a theory about the semantic component of grammar, and we can examine it in light of the goals set in the introduction, in chapter 1. Let's begin with words. Words have extensions, and these extensions are determined by the meanings of the words and the facts, the way the world is. If Alex practices medicine, then she is in the extension of the noun *physician*. If the facts were different and Alex instead spent her days painting murals, she would not be in the extension of *physician*. Or, if the word meaning were different, if *physician* applied to someone who studies physics, then despite the fact that Alex practices medicine, she would not be in the extension of *physician*. Competent speakers of English often know the meanings of English words but do not possess all the facts of the world. For that reason, they do not know what the full extension is for most English words. You do not know for every entity whether or not it's in the extension of *physician*. However, you do have an idea about what conditions an entity has to meet in order to be in the extension. Given the way we've tied word extensions to what L assigns to their translations, everything just said about *physician* carries over to the SL symbol 'Physician'. Its extension is jointly determined by the meaning of *physician* and the facts as they are. Together these ingredients determine that Alex, who practices medicine, is in L(Physician).

Declarative sentences have truth values. A number of ingredients go into determining the truth value of a sentence. One ingredient is syntactic structure, which, via rules of translation, determines which SL formula is assigned to the sentence. Word meanings and facts are also ingredients. Via the semantic rules of SL, they contribute to determining the truth value assigned to the sentence's translation. Competent speakers of English know the meanings of English words but do not possess all the facts. For that reason, they do not know the truth values of many English sentences. But even when they don't know the truth value, they do know what conditions would have to hold in order for the extensions to be such as to make the sentence true. You may not know if the sentence *A yellow submarine exploded* is true. But you do know what conditions would have to hold for an entity to be in the extension of *yellow*, and likewise for *submarine* and for *exploded*. Therefore, because you know what translation that sentence gets and how that translation is interpreted, you know what conditions have to hold in order for *A yellow submarine exploded* to be true. In general then, speakers know the truth conditions of sentences and

(77) truth conditions + facts about the world → truth value.

There is an aspect of meaning that came up in this chapter that was not anticipated in the introduction, namely context dependence. To determine the truth value of an utterance, one needs to know what discourse it was uttered in, in addition to knowing its syntax, the meaning of the words, and the relevant facts about the world. That added feature was captured in the rule in (72) assigning truth values to utterances. We should now revise our statements from chapter 1 about facts and meanings as follows:

(78) word meanings + facts about the world + context → extensions;
       extensions + syntax → truth value.

This picture of our semantic competence helps to resolve a puzzle about dictionary definitions mentioned in chapter 1 at the end of section 1.1. Dictionary definitions seem to be our first idea about what word meanings are, yet they can't easily be combined. According to the theory developed here, they don't need to be. Their role is to determine extensions, and it is these extensions that are combined. The semantic rules of SL tell us how.

Exercise (3.45)

There are two problems with the reference to word meanings in the discussion above. First, words themselves are often composed of meaningful parts—**morphemes**. Speakers know the meanings of morphemes, and from that they get to the meanings of complex words. Second, we often look up words in the dictionary, so it can't be that a competent speaker knows the meanings of *all* the words in the language. How should the discussion above, connecting the theory proposed here to knowledge of truth conditions, be modified to address these problems?

Exercise (3.46)

The discussion above focused on the determination of a truth value for a sentence. Detectives and scientists use language that way. They begin with a statement and try to discover facts that will make it true or false. But language has other uses also tied to truth conditions. In an everyday conversation, sentences are uttered to <u>communicate information</u>. In fictional storytelling, sentences are used to <u>evoke a scene</u>. Describe one of these uses highlighting the role played by the semantic component of grammar as analyzed here.

Exercise (3.47)

Musya knows that the sentence *Some ice-cube melted* is true. And yet, she does not know the full extension of the noun *ice-cube* nor does she know the full extension of the verb *melted*. Explain how that is possible, given the discussion above of truth conditions and the way our grammar works.

Exercise (3.48)

Up to now, we've been ignoring lexical ambiguity, and this simplification will continue in subsequent chapters. This simplification allows us to define L as the lexicon that assigns to the symbols of SL <u>the same extension</u> as the corresponding word of English. Explain what goes wrong when lexical ambiguity is acknowledged. Think, for example, about an SL translation with respect to L of *The soup is hot*. Suggest a method for dealing with this problem. This exact exercise appears at the end of chapter 2, but now the question has changed a little from one about defining a lexicon for SL to designing a grammar for a natural language that displays lexical ambiguity.

3.9   Chapter Summary

Indirect Interpretation (section 3.2)

In this chapter, we set out a general format for interpreting sentences of English. We adopted the method of indirect interpretation. This means that we have rules that map English into a symbolic language, SL, with lexicon L. Formulas of SL are assigned truth values. So we indirectly assign to syntactic structures of English the truth values of their SL translation, relative to L. A sentence of English has one or more base structures depending on whether or not it is structurally ambiguous. Base structures are mapped into LFs, and LFs are translated into formulas of SL.

Quantificational Determiner Phrases (section 3.3)

We developed the hypothesis that scopal ambiguity is a kind of structural ambiguity. The account makes use of syntactic rules that index and move quantificational DPs. These operations can lead to multiple LFs for a single base structure, thereby capturing the ambiguity. We gave evidence that scopal ambiguity is structural by showing that it is sensitive to constraints on movement.

Prepositional Phrases, Adjectives, and Adverbs (section 3.4)

Modification was interpreted in terms of predicate conjunction. This works well with modifiers inside of DPs (*an expensive wedding in Boston, a person who speaks French*). It was not successful with adverbial modifiers (*he discussed it in Boston, he drove quickly*).

Pragmatics (sections 3.6–3.8)

A distinction was introduced between semantics and pragmatics. In semantics, expressions are interpreted based on their syntax and the meanings of the words from which they are formed. For this we used the mechanism of translation into SL. We looked at two pragmatic phenomena. The first is narrative progression, in which events are under-

Table 3.9
Correspondence between syntactic and semantic categories

Syntactic category of English	Syntactic category of SL	Semantic category (extension)
Name	Individual constant	Entity
Intransitive verb, adjective, noun, NP	One-place predicate	Set of entities
Transitive verb, preposition	Two-place predicate	Sets of pairs whose first element is an entity and whose second element is a set of entities
Sentence (VP)	Formula	Truth value
Variable	Variable	Entity
Pronoun	Variable	Entity

stood to have occurred in the order in which they are described. Identifying this principle allowed us to maintain a simple rule of translation for conjunction. The second phenomenon was discourse pronouns. These are pronouns whose referent is determined by the speech context. We posited a mechanism that records individuals mentioned in the discourse and deploys these records to interpret pronouns.

Our list of correspondences between syntactic and semantic categories in table 3.9 is a handy way to summarize what the grammar achieves through indirect interpretation.

Ambiguity is a useful tool for organizing the phenomena covered so far. We have discussed four kinds of ambiguity:

1. Lexical ambiguity: If a word has more than one meaning, phrases containing that word will be ambiguous.

EXAMPLE *The soup is hot.*

2. Attachment ambiguity: If there are multiple sites in a structure for attaching a phrase, all of which result in the same string, the string is ambiguous.

EXAMPLE *Jack discussed a wedding in Boston.*

3. Scopal ambiguity: When two quantificational DPs appear in the same sentence or when a quantificational DP appears in the same sentence as a negation, their relative scope may affect truth conditions. In that case, if both relative scopes are available, the sentence is ambiguous.

EXAMPLES *Some person ordered every dish.*
    Every character did not survive.

4. Pronoun resolution: The interpretation of a pronoun depends on how its index is interpreted. When more than one option is available, ambiguity arises.

EXAMPLES *No child discussed a story that she had read in class.*
    I introduced Sarah to Elizabeth. She smiled.

Applications

Upon completing this chapter, you should be able to do the following:

• Assign a base structure, LF and translation to sentences of English formed using negation, transitive and intransitive verbs, PP and adjectival modifiers inside DPs, conjunction, and one or more DPs formed from a name, a pronoun, or a determiner plus NP. Here are examples of such sentences:

Nadir knows Gadarine.
The clever clerk doesn't know her.
Every organization in Portland supports itself.
At least one politician called Nadir, and Nadir called Gadarine.

• Show step by step that the rules of translation apply to the LF to produce the interpretation.

• Show how our grammar assigns two truth-conditionally distinct translations to sentences with multiple quantifying DPs or a quantifying DP and negation:

Every passenger didn't run.
At least one triangle touches every circle.

• Identify the effect of the rule of NARRATIVE PROGRESSION.

• Say what a context lexicon would look like at a point in a discourse where a free pronoun is felicitously uttered, say how it might come to have that look, and say how that enters into the interpretation of the free pronoun. An example with a free pronoun is: *She met Norman Baldy.*

3.10 The Grammar

Syntax

Quantifier Indexing	Quantificational determiners are indexed with a variable.
Pronoun Indexing	Pronouns are indexed with a variable.
Quantifier Raising (QR)	If a node has an indexed daughter, then the constituent corresponding to that node can be adjoined to a node that dominates it, with a copy of the index inserted in the position formerly occupied by the adjoined constituent.

Translation

Lexicon A symbol of SL is a translation for an English word if the extension of the SL symbol relative to L is the same as the extension of the English word.

SpecificVocab

every, all ⤳ ∀, *no* ⤳ No, *the* ⤳ The
a ⤳ ∃, *at least one* ⤳ ∃, *some* ⤳ ∃, *not* ⤳ ¬

Pronoun	A pronoun with index u is translated as u.
Variable	A variable in an LF is translated as the corresponding variable in SL.
Merge	$\{\alpha, \beta\}$ ⤳ $\alpha'(\beta')$
PredCon	$\{\alpha, \beta\}$ ⤳ $(\alpha' \sqcap \beta')$
IndexedDaughter	$\{\alpha_u, \beta\}$ ⤳ $[\alpha'u: \beta'(u)]$
Conjunction	$\{and, \alpha, \beta\}$ ⤳ $(\alpha' \& \beta')$
Wellformedness Filter	Any potential translation of an expression of English that is well formed is a translation of that expression. The rules of translation produce some expressions that are well formed and some that are not. Applying the WELLFORMEDNESS FILTER leaves only the well-formed ones as translations of the English expressions.

Note: Not listed here is the rule for relative clauses, introduced in section 3.5.3.

Pragmatics

NARRATIVE PROGRESSION

In the course of a narrative, when an event is described, it is usually understood to follow in time a previously mentioned event. When a state is described, it is usually understood to hold at the time of a previously mentioned event.

FELICITY AND TRUTH

As a discourse progresses, individuals become salient and are associated with variables. K_p is a set of variable-individual pairs that represent the state of the discourse at point p. K_p is the context lexicon for point-in-a-discourse p. If an utterance is made at point p in a discourse, then:

(a) an LF for that utterance is infelicitous if its translation is not defined with respect to $K_p + L$.

(b) if an LF for that utterance is felicitous then it is true if its translation is true with respect to K_p+L and false if its translation is false with respect to K_p+L.

Further Reading

Altshuler, Daniel. *Events, States and Times. An Essay on Narrative Discourse in English*. Berlin: De Gruyter, 2016.

Altshuler, Daniel, and Robert Truswell. *The Syntax-Discourse Interface. Extraction from Coordinate Structures*, Oxford Surveys in Syntax and Morphology. Oxford: Oxford University Press, forthcoming.

Asher, Nicholas, and Alex Lascarides. *Logics of Conversation*. Cambridge, UK: Cambridge University Press, 2003.

Dekker, Paul. "Predicate Logic with Anaphora." In *Proceedings from Semantics and Linguistic Theory 4*, edited by M. Harvey and L. Santelmann, pp. 79–95. Ithaca, NY: Cornell University, CLC Publication, 1994.

Dowty, David. "The Effects of Aspectual Class on the Temporal Structure of Discourse: Semantics or Pragmatics?" *Linguistics and Philosophy* 9 (1986): 37–62.

Elbourne, Paul. "The Interpretation of Pronouns." *Language and Linguistics Compass* 2 (2008): 119–50.

Karttunen, Lauri. "Discourse Referents." In *Syntax and Semantics*: *Notes from the Linguistic Underground*, Vol. 7, edited by J. McCawley, pp. 363–85. New York: Academic Press, 1976.

Lasnik, Howard. "The Forms of Sentences." In *An Invitation to Cognitive Science*: *Language*, Vol. 1, 2nd ed., edited by L. Gleitman and M. Liberman, pp. 283–310. Cambridge, MA: MIT Press, 1995.

Stanford Encyclopedia of Philosophy, The. https://plato.stanford.edu. See especially the following entries: Anaphora (by Jeffrey King and Karen Lewis); Dynamic Semantics (by Rick Nouwen, Adrian Brasoveanu, Jan van Eijck and Albert Visser); Pragmatics (by Kepa Korta and John Perry).

Szabolcsi, A. *Quantification*. Cambridge, UK: Cambridge University Press, 2010.

Szabolcsi, Anna. *Ways of Scope Taking*, Studies in Linguistics and Philosophy, Vol. 65. Dordrecht: Springer, 1994.

4 Events and States

4.1 Events and Thematic Roles

Our grammar assigns translations such as the ones in figure 4.1. Notice that verbs in these translations are treated as predicates of individuals. As predicates of individuals, verb extensions are sets of individuals or pairs formed from sets of individuals. These extensions get assigned to verbs indirectly via the extensions assigned to their translations:

(1) $L(\text{Fell}) = \{x : x \text{ fell}\}$
   $L(\text{Called}) = \{\langle x, Y \rangle : Y = \{z : z \text{ called } x\}\}$

The meanings in (1) fail to capture intuitions like the ones recorded in these remarks from *English Grammar* by George O. Curme:[1]

(2) A transitive verb denotes an action which passes over from the doer of the action to the object of it: The boy *struck* his dog.
   An intransitive verb denotes a state or simple action without any reference to an object: John *is sleeping*. I *dream* every night.

Our goal in this chapter is to revise the grammar to capture the intuition that verbs like *fall* and *call* describe **events**. One of the outcomes of this revision will be an analysis of adverbial modifiers, something that was beyond our reach in the last chapter.

We'll start with the assumption that verbs are predicates of events, so instead of the extensions in (1), we'll have those in (3):

(3) $L(\text{Fell}) = \{e : e \text{ is an event of falling}\}$
   $L(\text{Called}) = \{e : e \text{ is an event of calling}\}$

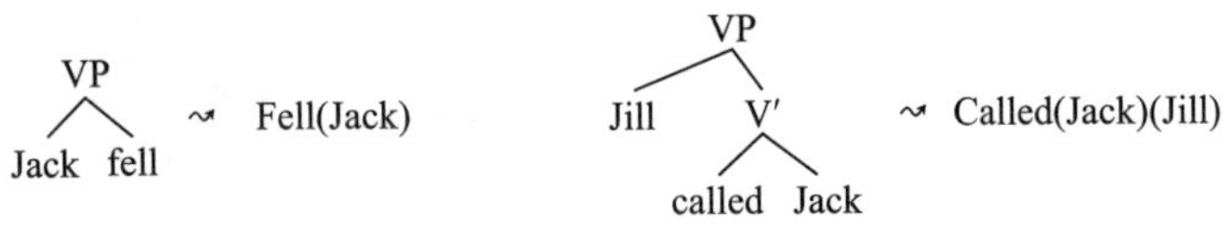

Figure 4.1
Translations of *Jack fell* and *Jill called Jack*.

If a verb describes an event, then the DP arguments of that verb describe participants in the event. For example, in the sentence *Jack fell* we understand Jack to be a participant in the event of falling described by the verb. The presence of the DP *Jack* in that sentence must lead to a translation that includes a statement about Jack's participation. But associating mere participation with a DP is insufficient, as consideration of transitive clauses shows. If Jack called Jill, then there was an event of calling, and Jack and Jill were the participants in that event. Similarly, if Jill called Jack, there was an event of calling, and Jack and Jill were the participants in that event. But these events are different, and the language distinguishes them. The sentence *Jill called Jack* tells us not only <u>that</u> Jill participated, but also <u>how</u> she participated. It tells us what role Jill played as compared with Jack. In this case, Jill is the one who is actively doing something; she controls the event while Jack is having something done to him. We say that Jill is the **agent** of the event and Jack is the **patient** of the event.[2] Summarizing, the sentence *Jill called Jack* tells us that

(4) there is an event *e*:

Jill is the agent of *e*, Jack is the patient of *e* and *e* was an event of calling.

To encode statements like *Jill is the agent of e* in our translations we'll add 'Agent' to our stock of two-place predicates in SL, we'll add *e* to our stock of variables, and we'll write

Agent(Jill)(*e*).

To encode statements like *Jack is the patient of e* in our translation we'll add 'Patient' to our stock of two-place predicates, and we'll write

Patient(Jack)(*e*).

Now, we can translate the statement in (4) above as

(5) [∃*e*: Event(*e*)] ((Agent(Jill)(*e*) & (Patient(Jack)(*e*) & Called(*e*)))).

Summarizing now, verbs are predicates of events and DPs characterize participants in the event described by the verb with which they are combined. Different kinds of participation are linguistically encoded. The two types of participant we've seen so far are agent and patient. An agent undertakes willful activity within the event, and without that activity, the event would not occur. A patient is affected in the event and could be said to undergo the action. These kinds of participation motivated us to add the two-place predicates 'Agent' and 'Patient' to SL.

Often a preposition is used to signal the type of event participation associated with a DP. In (6) below, *to* indicates that Jill participates in the event as a **goal**, while in (7), *from* indicates that Jill participates as a **source**.

(6) Jack sent the package <u>to</u> Jill.   (*to* goal)

(7) Jack received the package <u>from</u> Jill.   (*from* source)

Other types of participation that are signaled by prepositions include

(8) **Instrument**: entity used to perform an action
Jack clipped the hedge <u>with</u> a scissors.

(9) **Benefactive**: the entity that benefits from the action or event.
Jack threw a party <u>for</u> Jill.

(10) **Location**: where the event takes place
Jack danced <u>in</u> Union Square.

While *to* and *for* may be used to indicate goal and benefactive, respectively, these kinds of participation are sometimes conveyed without the aid of a preposition. Alongside (11)a below, we have (11)b, in which there is no *to* to tell us that Jill participated as the goal. Alongside (12)a, we have (12)b, in which there is no *for* to tell us that Jill participated as the benefactive.

(11) a. Jack sent the package to Jill.
     b. Jack sent Jill the package.

(12) a. Jack threw a party for Jill.
     b. Jack threw Jill a party.

The coming and going of these prepositions leads one to wonder how it is that we understand what kind of participation is at stake when there is no preposition present. This question applies to (11)b and (12)b as well as to our earlier examples with agents and patients (*Jack fell, Jill called Jack*). There are two broad approaches to this question to which we now turn.

One possibility is that the verb itself incorporates participant information. Compare (13) and (14).

(13) Jack fell.

(14) Jack ran.

In (13), *Jack* combines with the intransitive verb *fell*, and Jack is understood to be the patient of a falling event; he could intentionally fall, but falling per se doesn't require intention. In (14), *Jack* combines with the intransitive verb *ran*, and Jack is understood to be the agent of a running event. From these two examples, it would appear that the verb determines the role associated with its argument: patient with *fall* and agent with *ran*. Further evidence comes from pairs like *Jack heard the music* and *Jack listened to the music*. They describe very similar events, but with the verb *listen* we understand Jack to be the agent: that is, he undertakes willful activity, something that is not implied when the verb *heard* is used.

A different idea about the source of participant information arises in reaction to a phenomenon called **linking** in which participant information is correlated with grammatical roles (subject, object, indirect object). The most robust linking generalization correlates subject with agent. Here is a statement of the generalization from David Dowty:[3]

(15) A linking generalization: If a transitive verb has one argument that is a highly prototypical Agent and one argument that is a highly prototypical Patient, the Agent-argument is always the subject.

"highly prototypical Agent" : acts physically (not just cognitively) and volitionally.

"highly prototypical Patient" : is causally affected by the Agent and undergoes some specific change of state as a result, including coming into existence and going out of existence.

Examples that fit the generalization: *kill, eat, smash, build, move, break, cook*

It is hard, if not impossible, to find counterexamples to this generalization both within English and across a wide variety of languages. This generalization and others like it have led to the idea that the agent relation is determined not by choice of a particular verb, but by something in the syntax of subjects. It is interesting to note that something like this generalization seems to extend as well to intransitive verbs. Across a range of syntactic phenomena, intransitive verbs divide into two classes.[4] There are those whose single argument patterns with the object of a transitive. They're called **unaccusatives**. And there are those whose single argument patterns with the subject of a transitive verb. They're called **unergatives**. By and large, when the single argument of an intransitive verb patterns syntactically with transitive subjects, it is interpreted as agent denoting. *Run* is in that class, while *fall* is in the class of unaccusatives.

Summarizing now, we've seen that prepositions can be used to indicate the kind of event participation associated with a DP argument of a verb. Often, however, we understand that a particular kind of participation is involved even though no preposition is present. We considered two possible explanations for this. The verb itself may encode information about event participation associated with its arguments. Alternatively, the information about event participation could be determined by features of the syntactic structure. It is likely that the truth lies in the middle and that some types of participation are syntactically determined and others are lexically encoded. We will follow Christopher LaTerza and assume that information about event participation is always present in the form of a preposition, leaving open the question of what determines the choice of preposition: the verb itself or features of the syntactic structure.[5] For sentences that have no overt preposition, we'll assume a null preposition and indicate this with capitalization. The base structure we'll use for the VP *Jill called Jack* is shown in figure 4.2.

The types of event participation that we've been discussing (Agent, Patient, Goal, Source, Benefactive, Instrumental) are referred to as **thematic relations**. And the syntactic reflexes of these relations are called **θ-roles**. For that reason, we used 'ΘP' to label

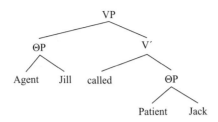

Figure 4.2
New structure for *Jill called Jack.*

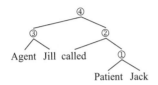

Agent ~ Agent, Patient ~ Patient, Jack ~ Jack, Jill ~ Jill   Lexicon

① ~ Patient(Jack)   MERGE

② ~ (Called ⊓ Patient(Jack))   PREDCON

③ ~ Agent (Jill)   MERGE

④ ~ (Agent (Jill) ⊓ (Called ⊓ Patient(Jack)))   PREDCON

Figure 4.3
Structure and translation for *Jill called Jack.*

the nodes above 'Agent Jill' and above 'Patient Jack', and we'll use the term **thematic role head** to refer to the null prepositions Agent and Patient.

Like overt prepositions, the null prepositions have extensions, and these extensions are the meanings of the corresponding symbols of SL. So thematic role heads are subject to the translation rule called LEXICON. Applying our rules of translation to *Jill called Jack* we get the result shown in figure 4.3.

Recall that we are now translating verbs as one-place predicates of events. That's why PREDCON was used to translate node ②, and not MERGE. The entire structure translates as a one-place predicate true of an event just in case Jill is the agent of that event, it's a calling event and Jack is the patient. Here are the meanings of the simple one- and two-place predicates making up the complex predicate translating ④:

(16) L(Called) = {$e : e$ is an event of calling}.

(17) L(Agent) = { $\langle x,Y \rangle : Y =$ {$e : e$ is an event whose agent is x}}.

(18) L(Patient) = { $\langle x,Y \rangle : Y =$ {$e : e$ is an event whose patient is x}}.

Exercise (4.1)

[A] Review the discussion of the thematic roles assigned to *Jack* in the sentences *Jack fell* and *Jack ran*. Provide the base-structures for those sentences.

[B] Provide the translations that are assigned by our grammar to the base structures you provided in [A].

[C] The structures with which we began the chapter are shown in figure 4.4. We've abandoned those structures for more elaborate ones with thematic role heads. Let's remind ourselves why. Assuming the meanings adopted in (3), repeated below, what translations, if any, are assigned to the old structures? If a translation is assigned, say what truth conditions it has. If a translation is not assigned, explain why not.

(3) L(Fell) = {$e : e$ is an event of falling}.
      L(Called) = {$e : e$ is an event of calling}.

Exercise (4.2)

In the following examples, prepositions are used to signal the type of event participation that is associated with a DP. Interestingly, in these examples, the event in question is described with a noun, not a verb.

(i) The delivery <u>to</u> Jill was in error.

(ii) The entry <u>into</u> Jerusalem surprised many.

(iii) The exit <u>from</u> Egypt was hurried.

Using the descriptions in (6)–(10) above, decide which types of event participation are indicated. Provide meanings for 'To', 'Into', and 'From' following the pattern in (17)–(18).

Figure 4.4
Abandoned structures for *Jill called Jack*.

Exercise (4.3)

The linking generalization in (15) holds in English as well as in many other languages. For this exercise, you will need to choose a language other than English for which you have access to semantic and syntactic judgments.

[A] The generalization comes with a list of transitive verbs (*kill, eat, smash, build, move, break, cook*). To the extent that they translate into the language you chose, determine if the position of the argument that describes the agent is consistent across those verbs.

[B] Find other examples of transitive verbs with one argument that is a highly proto-typical Agent and one argument that is a highly prototypical Patient. Determine if the position of the argument that describes the agent is consistent across those verbs. If there isn't consistency, note any subgeneralizations.

[C] If you have experience with syntactic theory and/or the language you chose, try to find a distinct pattern of syntactic behavior that can be used as basis for deciding whether or not a given DP is a subject. Use that and what you found in [A] and [B] to evaluate the linking generalization.

4.2   Event Phrase

According to the analysis developed so far, the VP *Jill called Jack* has the translation in (19):

(19) (Agent(Jill) $\sqcap$ (Called $\sqcap$ Patient(Jack))).

According to this translation, the entire VP is a one-place predicate. It is true of an event e if Jill is the agent of e, e is a calling event, and Jack is the patient of e. Compare (19) with the formula in (5) below, which we arrived at by consulting our intuitions about what the sentence *Jill called Jack* says.

(5) [$\exists e$: Event(e)] ((Agent(Jill)(e) & (Patient(Jack)(e) & Called(e))))).

The difference between (19) and (5) is not as great as it at first seems. Given *conjunction equivalence* discussed at the end of chapter 2, (20)a. is equivalent to (20)b. and so by REPLACE, (5) is equivalent to (21).

(20) a. (Agent(Jill)(e) & (Patient(Jack)(e) & Called(e))).
       b. (Agent(Jill) $\sqcap$ (Patient(Jack) $\sqcap$ Called))(e).

(21) [$\exists e$: Event(e)] ((Agent(Jill) $\sqcap$ (Patient(Jack) $\sqcap$ Called))(e)).

And since $\sqcap$ is commutative (you can reverse the order without affecting the truth-value), (21) is equivalent to

(22) [$\exists e$: Event(e)] ((Agent(Jill) $\sqcap$ (Called $\sqcap$ Patient(Jack)))(e)),

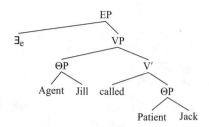

Figure 4.5
Illustrating the event phrase.

and now (22) differs from the translation for the VP given in (19) only by the presence of the existential quantifier and the final '*e*' argument. As mentioned above, without the existential quantifier, the translation is a one-place predicate.

If we want to assign a truth-value to *Jill called Jack*, we must modify our grammar so that *Jill called Jack* is translated into a formula. We'd like to achieve that result in a way that builds on the speaker intuition that led to (5)/(22), as well as the compositional work we've already done with VPs. This means that there must be an existential quantifier in the structure. Lisa deMena Travis argues on syntactic and morphosyntactic grounds that across languages VPs are generated immediately inside an **event phrase** (EP).[6] We'll assume that an EP consists of an indexed event–existential symbol whose sister is the VP that we developed up to now. This is illustrated in figure 4.5.

Having added that piece of structure, we now need to ask about its translation. Assuming that '∃' in English translates into SL '∃', INDEXEDDAUGHTER applies at the EP node and it yields the translation in (23) below:

(23) [∃*e*: (Agent(Jill) ⊓ (Called ⊓ Patient(Jack)))(*e*)].

Unfortunately, (23) is not a formula, which is what we need for the translation of a sentence. The problem in (23) is that we have a quantifier but no scope for that quantifier. To solve this problem, we assume a special rule that assigns EP a translation that is a formula:

(24) EvExist {∃$_u$, α} ↝ [∃*u*: Event(*u*)](α'(*u*))

To see the force of EvExist, recall that in the previous section, we showed that the VP under EP is translated as in (25) below:

(25) VP ↝ (Agent(Jill) ⊓ (Called ⊓ Patient(Jack))).

Hence, applying EvExist at the EP node in *Jill called Jack* gets us (26), as desired.

(26) EP ↝ [∃*e*: Event(*e*)] ((Agent(Jill) ⊓ (Called ⊓ Patient(Jack)))(*e*)).

Translations like the one in (26) will be common in subsequent discussion, so it pays to get comfortable reading them. There are two logical moves that can help. First, as noted above, '⊓' is commutative: the order in which two predicates are conjoined does not affect

Table 4.1
Current rules of translation applicable at nodes with two daughters

MERGE	$\{\alpha, \beta\} \rightsquigarrow \alpha'(\beta')$
INDEXEDDAUGHTER	$\{\alpha_u, \beta\} \rightsquigarrow [\alpha'u: \beta'(u)]$
PREDCON	$\{\alpha, \beta\} \rightsquigarrow (\alpha' \sqcap \beta')$
CONJUNCTION	$\{and, \alpha, \beta\} \rightsquigarrow (\alpha' \& \beta')$
EVEXIST	$\{\exists_u, \alpha\} \rightsquigarrow [\exists u: \text{Event}(u)](\alpha'(u))$

the meaning. This means that we can reorder them whenever doing so aids in understanding. Secondly, there are a lot of parentheses in (26) cluttering up the formula. To simplify we'll adopt an abbreviatory convention commonly adopted by logicians:

(27) SL abbreviatory convention: Optionally omit parentheses in repeated conjunctions.
   EXAMPLE: ((Clever $\sqcap$ Tall) $\sqcap$ Young) *abbreviates to* (Clever $\sqcap$ Tall $\sqcap$ Young)

Now, we can rewrite (26) as

(28) EP $\rightsquigarrow$ [$\exists e$: Event(e)] ((Agent(Jill) $\sqcap$ Patient(Jack) $\sqcap$ Called)(e)),

which by conjunction equivalence is the same as

(29) EP $\rightsquigarrow$ [$\exists e$: Event(e)] ((Agent(Jill)(e) & Patient(Jack)(e) & Called(e)).

And now we have a translation for *Jill called Jack* that can be read like the initial statement that guided the development of a semantics based on events:

(30) There is an event e:
   Jill is the agent of e, Jack is the patient of e, and e was an event of calling.

To arrive at the translation in (30), we stipulated a rule of translation, EVEXIST, that can apply to an EP. Stipulations often have a negative connotation in scientific theorizing. However, they need not. As we shall see in the next chapter, there is still more structure above the EP (higher tense and aspect nodes), which will allow us to explain in a more insightful way how we get to (26). Until then, our stipulation will allow us to develop our grammar, while keeping in mind that we will get rid of the stipulation in due time. A list of our current rules of translation that apply to nodes with two or more daughters is given in table 4.1.

Exercise (4.4)

[A] Provide the translation that our grammar assigns to *Jack ventured into Hollywood*, assuming the structure shown in figure 4.6. Assume that *into* is translated as 'Into'—a two-place predicate relating entities to sets of events.

[B] Provide the meaning that L assigns to 'Into' following the pattern in (17)–(18), repeated below:

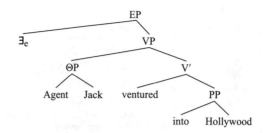

Figure 4.6
Structure for *Jack ventured into Hollywood*.

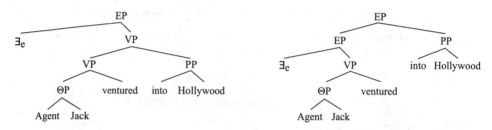

Figure 4.7
Structures alternative to the one in figure 4.6.

(17) $L(\text{Agent}) = \{ \langle x, Y \rangle : Y = \{e : e$ is an event whose agent is $x\}\}$.

(18) $L(\text{Patient}) = \{ \langle x, Y \rangle : Y = \{e : e$ is an event whose patient is $x\}\}$.

[C] In the tree in figure 4.6, *into Hollywood* is attached to the verb. The word order in the sentence is compatible with either of the alternative structures shown in figure 4.7. What <u>semantic</u> considerations come into play in deciding among the three alternatives?

[D] Provide a syntactic structure and translation for *Jack fell*.

✪ Important Practice and Looking Ahead ✪

Exercise (4.5) below explores relative scope between a quantificational DP and the existential quantifier in EP. This exploration provides an understanding of how our grammar constrains movement, which is crucial for what is to follow in later sections and in chapter 5.

Exercise (4.5)

The base structure for the sentence *Every tourist smiled* is shown in figure 4.8. Draw two structures for the sentence *Every tourist smiled*. Both structures should be arrived at by indexing *every* and applying QR to [DP *every tourist*]. Adjoin the DP to the VP

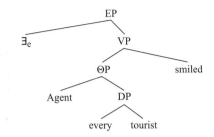

Figure 4.8
Base structure for *Every tourist smiled.*

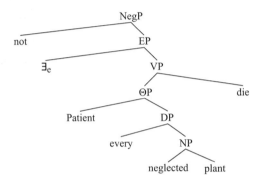

Figure 4.9
Base structure for *Every neglected plant didn't die.*

in one structure and adjoin it to the EP in the other structure. One of the structures is assigned a translation, and one is not. Provide the translation for the one that has a translation and explain what goes wrong in the other structure.

Exercise (4.6)

[A] Provide two LFs for *Every neglected plant did not die*. The LFs should receive distinct translations. The base structure is shown in figure 4.9.

[B] Provide the translations that our grammar assigns to the LFs you provided in [A].

✪ Thinking about Ditransitives ✪

The verb in the sentence *Jack sent Jill a letter* is **ditransitive**: it takes an indirect object in addition to the direct object. Up to now, we've avoided ditransitive verbs because they take three arguments, while SL has only one- and two-place predicates. With our revised grammar, new possibilities open up, which we'll explore below, in exercise (4.7).

Exercise (4.7)

In an influential paper on double objects, Richard Larson proposed an analysis for ditransitives that makes use of the idea that a verb can have a VP complement.[7] On a slightly updated version of Larson's analysis, our sentence begins with the structure shown in figure 4.10, where *Jill* is the subject of the lower VP, which is a complement of the higher V. The verb *sent* is then copied into the higher V as in the structure in figure 4.11. Only the higher copy of *sent* is pronounced, which gives us *Jack sent Jill a letter.*

In more recent work, Larson added a mechanism by which the verb licenses thematic role features on DP arguments.[8] We will represent these as thematic role heads, and we'll embed the whole thing in an EP giving us the structure in figure 4.12.

[A] Provide the translation that our rules assign to the structure in figure 4.12. To get to the translation, you'll have to apply QR to *a letter* and then apply the rules of translation to the result.

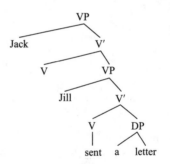

Figure 4.10
Initial structure for *Jack sent Jill a letter.*

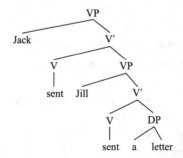

Figure 4.11
Structure involving a copy of *sent.*

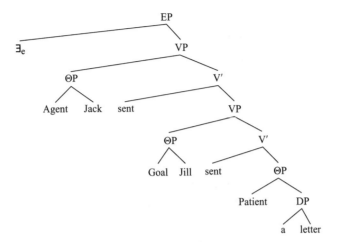

Figure 4.12
Structure for *Jack sent Jill a letter* with thematic role heads.

[B] Does the translation you provided in [A] capture the intuitive truth conditions of the sentence?

[C] As noted above, we avoided ditransitives in chapter 3 because SL has only one- and two-place predicates. Given your answer to [A], is it a virtue of SL that it allows only one- and two-place predicates? Justify your answer, then consider how our semantic rules could be extended to cover 3-place predicates. ATOMIC-1 and ATOMIC-2 are repeated below. If possible, provide a new rule called ATOMIC-3 that allows SL to have three-place predicates. If it's not possible, state why not.

ATOMIC-1
If π is a one-place predicate, then '$\pi(\alpha)$' is true with respect to M iff $[\![\alpha]\!]^M \in [\![\pi]\!]^M$.

ATOMIC-2
If π is a two-place predicate, then $[\![\pi(\alpha)]\!]^M = [\![\pi]\!]^M ([\![\alpha]\!]^M)$.

Exercise (4.8)

[A] The abbreviatory convention in (27) allows us to use the expression in (i) below to abbreviate (ii) or (iii):

(i)   (Clever ⊓ Tall ⊓ Young)

(ii) ((Clever ⊓ Tall) ⊓ Young)

(iii) (Clever ⊓ (Tall ⊓ Young))

But this means then when we write the abbreviated (i), there is no way for a reader to know whether it's meant to stand for (ii) or for (iii). (ii) and (iii) are syntactically distinct expressions of SL. A design goal of SL and logics like it is to eliminate ambiguity. Why doesn't this convention threaten that goal?

[B] Our quantifier notation follows Stephen Neale in enclosing the scope in parentheses.[9]

(iv) $[\exists u: \phi](\psi)$

(v) $[\exists x: \text{Dog}(x)](\text{Clever}(x))$

Other authors omit these parentheses.[10]

(vi) $[\exists u: \phi] \, \psi$

(vii) $[\exists x: \text{Dog}(x)] \, \text{Clever}(x)$

Propose an abbreviatory convention that will allowing us to write (vii) instead of (v). In composing your proposal, decide whether those parentheses could be omitted everywhere or only in limited cases. The decision is based on concerns like those raised in [A].

[C] How would MERGE have to have been stated if we had adopted the parenthesisless notation in (vi)?

4.3 Thematic Uniqueness

Our development of a semantics based on events commenced with the statement in (31) below.

(31) There is an event e:
      Jill is the agent of e, Jack is the patient of e, and e was an event of calling.

(31) says that Jill was the agent of e, not merely an agent of e. Likewise, Jack is the patient of e, not just a patient. To see the importance of this distinction, consider a situation in which a group of soldiers killed a dragon. If Jill was one of the soldiers, then it is true that

(32) there is an event e:
      Jill is an agent of e, the dragon is the patient of e, and e was an event of killing.

But it isn't true that

(33) Jill killed the dragon.

It follows that (32) doesn't accurately capture the content of (33). (33) requires that Jill be the only agent of the killing event, and since she wasn't, (33) is false. To accurately capture the content of (33), (32) should be amended to say that Jill is the agent of e.

Here's another example. Suppose that Rihanna decides to get rid of her car, and she gives it to her kids, Jack and Jill. In that case, it isn't true that

(34) Rihanna gave the car to Jill.

But it is true that

(35) there was an event e:

Rihanna was the agent of e, the car was the patient of e, Jill was a goal in e, and e was a giving event.

It follows that (35) doesn't accurately capture the content of (34). (34) requires that Jill be the only goal in the giving event, and since she wasn't, (34) is false.

In general, then, thematic role heads pick out unique agents, patients, goals, and so on. This feature of thematic role heads is known as **thematic uniqueness**. It is encoded in our meanings for the corresponding predicates of SL. Here are some calculations showing how thematic uniqueness propagates:

(36) $L(\text{Agent}) = \{ \langle x, Y \rangle : Y = \{e : x \text{ is } \underline{\text{the}} \text{ agent of } e\}\}$.

(37) $[\![\text{Agent}(\text{Jill})]\!]^L = \{e : \text{Jill is } \underline{\text{the}} \text{ agent of } e\}$.

(38) $[\![(\text{Called} \sqcap \text{Agent}(\text{Jill}))]\!]^L = \{e : \text{Jill is } \underline{\text{the}} \text{ agent of } e \text{ and } e \text{ was a calling event}\}$.

4.4   Summary of Event Semantic Foundation

Syntactic Innovations

(39) Arguments are introduced with thematic role heads.

We've replaced the base structures on the left with those on the right, as shown in figure 4.13.

(40) VP is embedded inside EP, which is headed by an indexed '∃', as shown in figure 4.14.

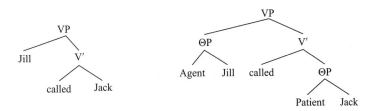

Figure 4.13
Structures from chapter 3 versus those from chapter 4.

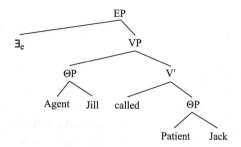

Figure 4.14
Illustrating an event phrase.

Semantic Innovations

(41) Verbs are one-place event predicates.
  EXAMPLE: $L(\text{Defibrillate}) = \{e : e \text{ is an event of defibrillation}\}$.

(42) SL contains two-place predicates for thematic relations.
  EXAMPLE $L(\text{Patient}) = \{\ \langle x, Y \rangle : Y = \{e : x \text{ is \underline{the} patient of } e\}\}$.

(43) Temporary rule for translating EPs.
  EVEXIST $\{\exists_u, \alpha\} \rightsquigarrow [\exists u: \text{Event}(u)](\alpha'(u))$.

What These Changes Achieve

- Verbs describe events.
- Sentences (eventive ones) are used to assert the existence of events.
- DPs describe event participants.

4.5   States

In the previous sections, we restricted our attention to verbs like *call* and *fall*, which describe events. An event is something that happens. People, animals, and objects (abstract and concrete) participate in these happenings. There are also verbs that describe states that an individual or an object can be in. Such verbs are called **stative verbs**. Each of the following examples contains one.

(44) Sentences with verbs describing states.
  Akna has a cold.   *The milk smells bad.*
  Akna owns a bike.   *Akna feels sick.*
  Akna lives in Chiapas.   *This music sucks.*

Akna owes me $40.   *A solution exists.*
Akna likes me.   *A small gift will suffice.*
Akna trusts me.

Adjectives and prepositional phrases also describe states.

(45) Sentences with adjectives and prepositional phrases describing states:
   Gadarine is cold.   *Gadarine is in his room.*
   Gadarine is afraid.   *The article is about hair dryers.*
   Gadarine is Armenian.   *This gift is for Gadarine.*

The state/event distinction has a wide range of syntactic and semantic consequences. One of these we saw in section 3.6 on coordination and narrative progression. There we observed that eventive sentences tend to advance the time in a narrative, while stative sentences do not. Another difference between statives and eventives has to do with the use of the progressive. In the example

Akna is calling Gadarine,

the verb ends with *-ing* and is preceded by a form of *be*. This configuration is called the **progressive**. In our dialects of English, many statives do not sound good when they are in the progressive:

#Akna is owning a bike.
#Akna is owing me $40.

There is a corresponding fact in English that has to do with verbs that are <u>not</u> in the progressive form. Nonprogressive statives can be used in the present tense to describe a state that holds at the time the sentence is uttered, as in

Akna owns a bike.

But if a nonprogressive eventive is used in the present tense, it cannot describe an event occurring at the time when the sentence is uttered. If you are watching Akna fry an egg, you cannot use the first sentence below to describe what you are seeing. Likewise, if you are watching Gadarine swim across the pond, you cannot use the second sentence below to describe what you are seeing.

Akna fries an egg.
Gadarine swims.

The present tense nonprogressive form of the verb is called the **simple present**, and so the generalization we've just discussed can be summarized as follows:

(46) The simple present can be used to describe a state that holds at the time of utterance, but the simple present cannot be used to describe an event occurring at the time of utterance.

The sentence *Gadarine swims* is most readily interpreted as **habitual**. It describes events that Gadarine engages in habitually, without saying anything about what she might be doing at the present.

Another difference between eventives and statives concerns sentences of the form *what X did was* ____ which are called **clefts**. The blank in the cleft can be filled with an eventive VP but not a stative VP. Compare the following examples, the first with eventive *call* and the second with stative *owe*:

What she did was call Gadarine.
#What she did was owe me $40.

A final difference between eventives and statives concerns the way in which events and states play out in time. Suppose that Dylan owned a horse as of the first day of October 2006 and he sold it on the last day of that month. In that case, Dylan owned a horse for that month and for any period within that month. Thus, it is true, for example, that Dylan owned a horse during the second week of October 2006. Now, suppose that on the first of October 2006, Dylan began work on a barn, and he finished it on the last day of that month (and he did no other building during that period). In that case, Dylan built a barn in October 2006, but the same is not true for every period of that month. Thus, it is false, for example, that Dylan built a barn during the second week of October 2006. In general, if a state holds for some period of time, then a state of that kind holds for any part of that period. That is not true in general for events.

Summarizing now, the state/event distinction plays a role in a range of natural language phenomena. Five of them were reviewed here and are shown in table 4.2.

Exercise (4.9)

The phenomena listed in table 4.2 can be thought of as diagnostics for determining whether a verb is an eventive or a stative. They tend to converge on the answer to that question, but there are several interesting cases in which they disagree. Ultimately, we'd like to understand the phenomena themselves. Once we do, we might find out

Table 4.2
Events versus states

	Eventives	Statives
Narrative progression: moves the narrative forward.	✓	✗
Progressive verb form (*is singing*)	✓	✗
Use of simple present to describe what is happening at the time of utterance	✗	✓
do-clefts (*what Gadarine did was* ____)	✓	✗
Truth at a period of time implies truth at any part of the period.	✗	✓

that some of them target distinctions that often but not always map onto the event-state distinction. Two verbs that lead to diverging results are *wear* and *sit*. For each of these verbs, indicate which of the diagnostics leads to a categorization as stative and which as eventive. List other verbs for which there are diverging results. See if there is some generalization across your examples, and on that basis suggest a possible way to fine-tune the categorization of verbs to eliminate disagreements.

Earlier, when we began discussing events, we talked about the roles that an individual can play in an event and these included 'Agent' and 'Patient'. The agent controls the event. The agent engages in willful activity without which the event would not occur. The patient doesn't control the event. Something is done to the patient in the event. These roles do not make sense for states such as owning, owing, being sick or being at home. That means we need a new thematic relation for the entity that is in the state described by the verb. We'll use 'Hold' to denote that relation, which gives us translations like the one in (47):

(47) Natchaya is nervous.

$[\exists s: \text{State}(s)]\ ((\text{Hold}(\text{Natchaya}) \sqcap \text{Nervous})(s))$.

Nervous describes a psychological state, and the SL predicate 'Hold' is used to describe Natchaya's relationship to the state. Analogously, *Aparan is deserted* describes a state that holds of the Armenian town, Aparan. So we can write:

(48) Aparan is deserted.

$[\exists s: \text{State}(s)]\ ((\text{Hold}(\text{Aparan}) \sqcap \text{Deserted})(s))$.

Oftentimes a stative verb or adjective comes with an additional argument that denotes what we'll call the **theme** of the state. We'll translate these with a two-place predicate 'Theme':

(49) Gadarine owns Fido.

$[\exists s: \text{State}(s)]\ ((\text{Hold}(\text{Gadarine}) \sqcap \text{Own} \sqcap \text{Theme}(\text{Fido}))(s))$.

Following our practice with eventives, we now assume that sentences with stative verbs include null 'Hold' and 'Theme' prepositions.[11]

Exercise (4.10)

[A] Provide a base structure for *Avi knows Natalie*.

[B] Provide the translation that our grammar assigns to the structure you provided in [A].

Key Ideas

• Stative verbs describe states, which differ from events.

• The distinction between a state and an event appears to be relevant to natural language syntax and semantics (see the list in table 4.2 for evidence).

- A stative describes a state that *holds* of the individual denoted by the DP subject. The holding relation is described with the two-place predicate 'Hold'.

- The DP object of a stative describes the theme of the state and is introduced with the two-place null preposition 'Theme'.

New Terminology

- states
- stative verb
- eventuality
- Hold
- Theme

4.6   Adverbial Modifiers

In the previous chapter (section 3.4), we discussed the ambiguity present in the example *Jack discussed a wedding in Boston*. We entertained the idea that the ambiguity was structural. The PP *in Boston* adjoins either to *wedding* or to *discussed a wedding*. The two options are illustrated in figure 4.15.

It turned out that the structure on the left in figure 4.15 worked as expected, but there were problems arising from the interpretation of the structure on the right. The NP in the structure on the left was translated as follows:

PP $\rightsquigarrow$ In(Boston)   MERGE

NP $\rightsquigarrow$ (Wedding $\sqcap$ In(Boston))   PREDCON

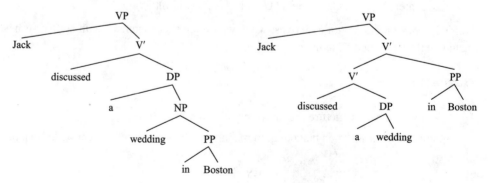

[PP *in Boston*] as NP modifier   [PP *in Boston*] as VP modifier

Figure 4.15
Chapter 3 structures for *Jack discussed a wedding in Boston*.

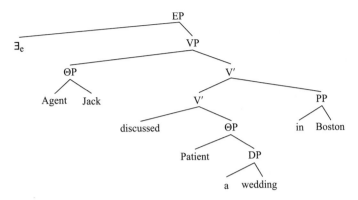

Figure 4.16
Base structure for *Jack discussed a wedding in Boston*.

Given this translation, the NP is a predicate that is true of something if it is a wedding and it is in Boston. This is as desired. This along with other rules of translation correctly deliver the interpretation according to which there was a wedding in Boston and Jack discussed it.

Several problems were raised by the translation we arrived at for the structure on the right in which *in Boston* is a VP modifier. Among other things, we weren't capturing the intuition that *in Boston* describes the location of the discussion. Now that we are working with an event semantics, we can remedy that.

The base structure for the sentence on the reading where *in Boston* is an adverbial adjoined to V′is given in figure 4.16. This structure differs from the one in figure 4.15 in keeping with the syntactic innovations introduced in sections 4.1–2 and summarized in section 4.4. The VP is now part of an EP headed by an indexed '∃', and DPs combine with thematic role heads. To arrive at a translation, we first index the object DP and apply QR, as shown in figure 4.17.

Let us now apply our rules of translation to the binary nodes in the tree:

⑧ $\rightsquigarrow$ Patient(x)   MERGE

⑦ $\rightsquigarrow$ (Discussed $\sqcap$ Patient(x))   PREDCON

⑨ $\rightsquigarrow$ In(Boston)   MERGE

⑥ $\rightsquigarrow$ ((Discussed $\sqcap$ Patient(x)) $\sqcap$ In(Boston))   PREDCON

⑤ $\rightsquigarrow$ Agent(Jack)   MERGE

④ $\rightsquigarrow$ (Agent(Jack) $\sqcap$ (Discussed $\sqcap$ Patient(x)) $\sqcap$ In(Boston)))   PREDCON

③ $\rightsquigarrow$ [∃e: Event(e)]((Agent(Jack) $\sqcap$ (Discussed $\sqcap$ Patient(x)) $\sqcap$ In(Boston))) (e))   EVEXIST

② $\rightsquigarrow$ [∃x : Wedding(x)]   INDEXEDDAUGHTER

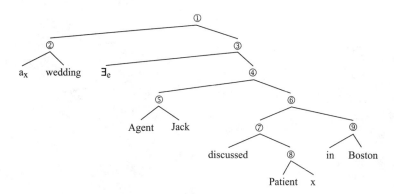

Figure 4.17
LF structure for *Jack discussed a wedding in Boston*.

① ↝ [∃x : Wedding(x)]([∃e: Event(e)]((Agent(Jack) ⊓ (Discussed ⊓ Patient(x)) ⊓
In(Boston))) (e)))   MERGE

According to this translation, there is a wedding and there is an event that is a discussion, whose agent is Jack, whose patient is the wedding, and which is in Boston. This is the desired interpretation. Unlike the failed analysis in the previous chapter, this one extends easily to nonlocative modifiers. *Jack walked toward the door* says that the event is toward the door, not that Jack is.

✪ Thinking about Adverbs ✪

In the previous chapter, in section 3.4, an analysis was proposed for adverbs that incorrectly predicted that *Jack sang quietly and Jack walked noisily* entails *Jack sang noisily*. This motivated the event-semantic analysis developed in this chapter. The exercises below provide further exploration of adverbs within our analysis.

Exercise (4.11)

[A] Provide an LF for *Jack sang quietly* along with the translation assigned to your LF by the rules of translation. Translate *quietly* as a one-place event predicate 'Quiet'.

[B] Assuming the analysis in [A] of *Jack sang quietly* and the corresponding analysis for *Jack walked noisily*, explain why *Jack sang quietly and Jack walked noisily* does <u>not</u> entail *Jack sang noisily*.

[C] In the previous chapter, in section 3.4, an analysis was proposed for adverbs that incorrectly predicted that *Jack sang quietly and Jack walked noisily* entails *Jack sang noisily*. Given your results in [B], we now have an argument in favor of the events analysis and against the nonevent analysis. Let's call this a "jump argument"—since in the rejected analysis the adverb *noisily* jumps from modifying *walked* to modifying *sang*. This argument relies on the use of the manner adverbs *quietly* and *noisily*. Find another pair of *-ly* adverbs and provide your own jump argument. Your argument will make use of two examples sentences, one of which will contain a conjunction. Describe a situation in which one of your sentences, the one with the conjunction is true and the other is false.

[D] The phrase *on February 4, 2000*, functions as a **temporal adverbial** in the sentence *Jack cried on February 4, 2000*. *February 4, 2000*, is a name for a day, so it has the syntax of a DP like *Jack* and its translation is an individual constant. Use 'Feb42000'. Propose an analysis for the sentence *Jack cried on February 4, 2000*. Your analysis should consist of an LF, a translation, and a meaning for 'On', the SL translation for *on* (do this by filling in the equation: $L(On) = \underline{\hspace{1cm}}$).

[E] The sentence *Jack cried quietly on February 4, 2000*, contains a manner adverbial and a temporal adverbial. Provide the translation our grammar assigns to this sentence, assuming the analyses in [A] and [D].

[F] Below are examples of potential jump arguments. In the first, *noisily* jumps from one clause to the next, and the entailment is not valid ($\nvDash$ means 'doesn't entail'). In the second, *in Central Park* jumps, and the entailment is valid:

Jack cried softly at 4 p.m. on February 4, 2000, and Jack walked noisily at 4 p.m. on February 4, 2000, $\nvDash$ Jack cried noisily at 4 p.m. on February 4, 2000.

Jack cried softly at 4 p.m. on February 4, 2000, and Jack walked in Central Park at 4 p.m. on February 4, 2000, $\vDash$ Jack cried in Central Park at 4 p.m. on February 4, 2000.

Assume for the purposes of this exercise that *4 p.m. on February 4, 2000*, is the name of a time and is translated as an individual constant. Why is the first entailment invalid and the second valid? What does our grammar have to say about these entailments?

Exercise (4.12)

Alongside *Jack left on February 4, 2000*, one can also say *Jack left February 4, 2000*, omitting the preposition *on*. This is known as a **bare-NP adverb**. Sometimes prepositions can be omitted from adverbial PPs and sometimes not.

[A] Discover and report generalizations about when the omission is possible and when it's prohibited.

[B] How should we develop our grammar so that it interprets sentences with bare-NP adverbs?

Exercise (4.13)

In chapter 1, the concept of entailment was introduced with the following pair of examples:

(i) On July 11, Nadir clumsily assembled a metal bookcase.

(ii) Nadir assembled a bookcase on July 11.

[A] Provide an LF for the example in (i). In forming your LF, you'll need to make a choice about where to attach the temporal adverbial. Explain how you chose. You will also need to QR the object *a metal bookcase*.

[B] Provide the translation assigned by our rules to the LF in [A]. Check carefully that the translation you provide indeed follows from the LF and our rules of translation.

[C] Briefly explain how our grammar accounts for the entailment from (i) to (ii).

Exercise (4.14)

Within every day, there is a point in time known as 4 p.m. When I say *Nadir cried at 4 p.m. on February 4, 2000*, I report a crying event that occurred at the particular 4 p.m. point of the day specified. But it is also possible in discourse to simply say *Nadir cried at 4 p.m.* In that case, hearers follow pragmatic rules to determine the intended day on which that particular 4 p.m. occurred. Which day is chosen will depend on prior discourse and possibly other factors involving the discourse participants. It follows then that the context lexicon will play a role in interpreting *at 4 p.m.* in this example. Provide an analysis of the syntax and semantics of this example. Your analysis should include an LF and a translation for the sentence as well as some discussion of how discourse influences the content of a context lexicon so your translation gets the intuitively correct truth conditions.

Exercise (4.15)

The sentence *Jack slowly ruined every phone* may describe a situation in which Jack stands before a line of cellphones with a hammer, and, one after another, he gives each phone a quick, sharp pounding, pausing between poundings to smile at his audience. In that reading, it appears that *slowly* has a scope over *every phone*. It isn't true for each phone, that he ruined it slowly. Explain why this reading cannot be captured with our grammar.

Exercise (4.16)

Graham Katz argues from examples like those in (i)–(iv) that stative verbs cannot be modified by adverbs like *slowly*, *enthusiastically*, and *revoltingly*[12]:

(i) *Natchaya resembled Akna slowly.

(ii) *Akna desired a raise enthusiastically.

(iii) *They hate us revoltingly.

(iv) *Akna was slowly tall.

[A] Why do you think the adverbs in (i)–(iv) can modify eventive verbs, but not-stative verbs?

[B] In (v) and (vi) below, stative verbs are modified by PPs (*in the subway* and *in the back seat of the car*).[13] In (vii) and (viii) below, stative verbs are modified by the adverbs *passionately* and *eerily*.[14] Provide a hypothesis that explains the contrast between (i)–(iv) and (v)–(viii).

(v) In New York, I am scared in the subway. (In Paris, I am not).

(vi) In Germany, John was nauseous in the back seat of the car because of the speed at which we drove.

(vii) John loves Mary passionately.

(viii) The house is eerily quiet.

Note: The contrast between (i)–(iv) and (v)–(viii) is still not well understood. In doing this exercise, try your best to state a hypothesis that can be tested with more data.

✪ Important Practice and Looking Ahead ✪

In this chapter, verbs are understood to be one-place event predicates. Nouns can also be used to describe events. Nominal event predicates are used in exercise (4.17) below to introduce talk about *events in progress*. This idea will form the basis for the analysis of the progressive in the next chapter.

Exercise (4.17)

In this exercise, we'll be interested in DPs which are formed with nouns that describe events, such as *the closing of a small private school*, *the closing of the case by the court* and *the rejection of every proposal*. To keep things simple, we'll use an example in which names are used for the objects of the prepositions *of* and *by*:

(i) Jack observed the closing of UCLA by Nixon.
The sentence in (i) entails that

(ii) Nixon closed UCLA.

Our goal here is an analysis of (i) that captures the entailment to (ii). Begin by constructing LFs for yourself for (i) and (ii), using the base structure for the DP object of (i) shown in figure 4.18.

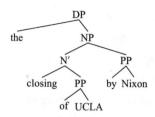

Figure 4.18
Base structure for *the closing of UCLA by Nixon*.

[A] Provide the translations assigned by our rules to your LFs.

[B] Provide extensions for the translations of *closing*, *of*, and *by*. These will come in the form of equations where to the left of '=' you have *L*(*Closing*), *L*(*Of*), and *L*(*By*).

[C] Given your translations and extensions, state whether the entailment from (i) to (ii) is captured or not. If it is captured, state in a few sentences how it is that if the translation of (i) is true, the translation for (ii) must be true as well. If the entailment is not captured, describe a situation in which the translation for (i) is true while that for (ii) is false.

[D] The following sentences describe events that are in progress:

The game was already in progress when we took our seats.

A dance was in progress when the quake occurred.

A dig was in progress when we were at Sungai Batu.

An unusual high-water rescue was underway when television crews went to survey the flooding.

A criminal investigation was ongoing.

What revolution was underway when Descartes was a child?

The interview was underway when I pulled into your driveway.

The event was underway when fire broke out. We ran to save our lives.

The third world steel LCI data collection is currently underway. It will be completed by the end of 2008.

Provide a translation for the sentence in (iii) below. Your translation should be one that is assigned to an LF for (iii). Treat *was in progress* as a single-word, stative verb translated as 'InProgress'.

(iii) The closing of UCLA by Nixon was in progress.

[E] Unlike (i), (iii) does not entail (ii). Is this fact compatible with your answer in [C]? Discuss the difference between (i) and (iii) and why only (i) entails (ii).

[F] Consider the following piece of discourse:

(iv) At 4 p.m., an unusual high-water rescue was underway. It was completed by 9 p.m.

Provide a translation for the second sentence in (iv), treating *was completed* as a single-word, stative verb and translating *9 p.m.* as an individual constant that stands for a point in time. Your translation should be one that is assigned to an LF of that sentence. Describe the content lexicon at the point at which the sentence is interpreted. Provide the extension for the two place predicate 'By' used in your translation.

4.7 Chapter Summary

In this chapter we revised our grammar so that it captures the intuition that verbs describe events and states. Our grammar has the following features:

• Verbs are treated as one-place eventuality predicates.

• Thematic role heads connect the meanings of DPs to the events and states described by the verbs with which they combine.

• Adverbs are treated as one-place eventuality predicates. They add further descriptive information about the events described by the verbs they modify.

• VPs are embedded inside EPs, which are headed by '∃'.

• We have a new temporary rule of translation:

EvExist $\{\exists_u, \alpha\} \rightsquigarrow [\exists u: \text{Event}(u)](\alpha'(u))$.

These features are illustrated in the structure and translation in figure 4.19.

Applications

When you have completed this chapter, you should be able to

• Assign a base structure, an LF, and a translation to English sentences formed using: negation, transitive and intransitive verbs, adjectives, adverbs, prepositions, conjunction, and one or more DPs formed from a name, a pronoun, or a determiner and a noun phrase. Here are examples of such sentences:

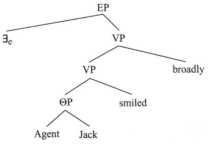

$[\exists_e: \text{Event}(e)]((\text{Agent}(\text{Jack}) \sqcap \text{Smiled} \sqcap \text{Broadly})(e))$

Figure 4.19
Structure for *Jack smiled broadly.*

Table 4.2
Events versus states

	Eventives	Statives
Narrative Progression: moves the narrative forward.	✓	✗
Progressive verb form (*is singing*)	✓	✗
Use of simple present to describe what is happening at the time of utterance	✗	✓
do-clefts (*what Gadarine did was ____*)	✓	✗
Truth at a period of time implies truth at any part of the period.	✓	✓

- *Aparajita didn't praise Baboloki loudly.*
- *Some ignominious farmer beat a donkey with a stick.*
- *At least one politician carefully avoided Arash and no doctor spoke to him.*

• You should be able to show how our grammar assigns two distinct translations to sentences such as those listed below and then derive their truth conditions using the semantic rules of SL. The third sentence displays a scopal ambiguity and an attachment ambiguity, so it should receive four distinct translations.

- *Every passenger didn't run quickly.*
- *Baboloki bought a gift for every student.*
- *No manager called every athlete from Miami.*

• Understand the difference between eventives and statives. Be acquainted with natural language phenomena in which they behave differently, as summarized in table 4.2.

• Understand why thematic roles are needed in an event semantics. Understand thematic uniqueness and how it is encoded.

• Understand the motivation for positing an indexed '∃' heading an EP.

4.8   The Grammar

Our grammar consists of

- rules of syntax
- rules of translation
- rules defining SL
- pragmatic rules.

Below is a list of the rules of syntax and translation introduced in this chapter and the previous one.[15] The definition of SL can be found at the end of chapter 2.

Syntax

Any DP-argument of a verb is sister to a preposition or a thematic role head such as 'Agent' or 'Patient'.

An EP node has two daughters, an indexed '∃' and a VP. 'EP' stands for event phrase.

Quantifier Indexing	Quantificational determiners are indexed with a variable.
Pronoun Indexing	Pronouns are indexed with a variable.
Quantifier Raising (QR)	If a node has an indexed daughter, then the constituent corresponding to that node can be adjoined to a node that dominates it, with a copy of the index inserted in the position formerly occupied by the adjoined constituent.

Translation

A verb translates as a one-place predicate of events or a one-place predicate of states.

Manner adverbs translate as one-place predicates of events.

Lexicon	If the meaning of a symbol of SL relative to L is the extension of the corresponding word of English, then that symbol is a translation for that word.
SpecificVocab	*every, all* ⤳ $\forall$, *no* ⤳ No, *the* ⤳ The, a ⤳ $\exists$, *at least one* ⤳ $\exists$, *some* ⤳ $\exists$, *not* ⤳ $\neg$
Pronoun	A pronoun with index u is translated as u.
Variable	A variable in an LF is translated as the corresponding variable in SL.
Merge	$\{\alpha, \beta\} \rightsquigarrow \alpha'(\beta')$
PredCon	$\{\alpha, \beta\} \rightsquigarrow (\alpha' \sqcap \beta')$
IndexedDaughter	$\{\alpha_u, \beta\} \rightsquigarrow [\alpha'u\colon \beta'(u)]$
Conjunction	$\{and, \alpha, \beta\} \rightsquigarrow (\alpha' \,\&\, \beta')$
EvExist	$\{\exists_u, \alpha\} \rightsquigarrow [\exists u\colon \text{Event}(u)](\alpha'(u))$
Wellformedness Filter	Any potential translation of an expression of English that is well formed is a translation of that expression.

Pragmatics

NARRATIVE PROGRESSION

In the course of a narrative, when an event is described, it is usually understood to follow in time a previously mentioned event. When a state is described, it is usually understood to hold at the time of a previously mentioned event.

FELICITY AND TRUTH

As a discourse progresses, individuals become salient and are associated with variables. K_p is a set of variable-individual pairs that represent the state of the discourse at point p. K_p is the context-lexicon for point-in-a-discourse p.

If an utterance is made at point p in a discourse, then

(a) an LF for that utterance is infelicitous if its translation is not defined with respect to K_p+L and

(b) if an LF for that utterance is felicitous, then it is true if its translation is true with respect to K_p+L, and it is false if its translation is false with respect to K_p+L.

Further Reading

Dowty, David. "Thematic Proto-Roles and Argument Selection." *Language* 67 (1991): 547–619.

Krifka, Manfred "Thematic Relations as Links between Nominal Reference and Temporal Constitution." In *Lexical Matters*, edited by I. Sag and A. Szabolsci, pp. 29–53. Palo Alto, CA: Center for the Study of Language and Information, 1992.

Maienborn, Claudia. "Events and States." In *Handbook of Event Structure*, edited by R. Truswell, Oxford: Oxford University Press, forthcoming.

Parsons, Terence. *Events in the Semantics of English: A Study in Subatomic Semantics*. Cambridge, MA: MIT Press, 1990.

Williams, Alexander. *Arguments in Syntax and Semantics*. Cambridge, UK: Cambridge University Press, 2015.

5 Tense and Aspect

5.1 Tense

In keeping with the syntactic innovations from the previous chapter, the sentence *Jack fell* has the structure shown in figure 5.1. The verb form *fell* is past tensed. This morphological fact is indicative of the presence of a tense node above the EP, one that heads a **tense phrase** (TP), as shown in figure 5.2. Our goal in this section will be to figure out what contribution tense makes to the meaning of the sentence. Our strategy will be the same as in the previous chapter. We will first focus on formulas of SL. Once we have an idea of the kind of translations we want, we'll try to figure out how to connect the translations to the syntactic structure.

5.1.1 Meanings for Tenses

The translation we currently assign to figure 5.1 is in (1) below. It says that there is an event e, Jack is the patient of e, and e was a falling.

(1) $[\exists e: \text{Event}(e)]\,((\text{Patient}(\text{Jack}) \sqcap \text{Fell})(e))$.

In keeping with the way we often talk about the meaning of the past tense, we might replace "e was a falling" with "e is a falling, and e is in the past." This leads naturally to the following formula:

(2) $[\exists e: \text{Event}(e)]\,((\text{Patient}(\text{Jack}) \sqcap \text{Fall} \sqcap \text{Past})(e))$.

In (2), 'Past' is a one-place predicate of events. It has to be a one-place predicate since it is predicate-conjoined with 'Fall'. The intended meaning of 'Past' is

(3) $L(\text{Past}) = \{e : e \text{ is in the past}\}$.

While (2)–(3) accurately implement the idea expressed with "e is a falling, and e is in the past," it inherits a serious problem from that phrasing. The analysis in (2)–(3) fails to capture the fact that the truth of a tensed sentence depends on when it was uttered. *Neil Armstrong walked on the moon* could be truthfully uttered today, but it could not have

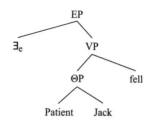

Figure 5.1
Structure of *Jack fell* from chapter 4.

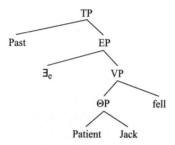

Figure 5.2
Incorporating the structure of *Jack fell* in a TP.

been truthfully uttered in 1812. *Twenty women landed on Mars* could not be truthfully uttered today, but there may be a future time at which it will be uttered truthfully. The reason the analysis misses this important fact has to do with (3), which makes reference to the set of all past events. There is no such set. Past is a relative notion. Events that were in the future at one time are in the past at another time. If there were a fixed set of events in the past, then we could inquire whether the event of Armstrong's walking on the moon was in that set. If it was, then *Neil Armstrong walked on the moon* would be true on this analysis, regardless of when it was uttered.

The practical ramifications of this discussion are that the predicate 'Past' should not get a meaning from our fixed lexicon, L; rather, it should get a meaning from the context lexicon, which is designed to allow sensitivity to facts about the discourse in which a sentence is uttered. Substituting 'K_p' for 'L' in (3), we arrive at the following proposal:

(4) For any point p in a discourse, K_p (Past) = {$e : e$ occurs before p}.

Now when the formula in (2) is interpreted with respect to K_p+L, it will be true iff there is an event e, Jack is the patient of e, e is a falling, and e occurs prior to p. If (2) is the translation of *Jack fell*, then by the FELICITY AND TRUTH rule from the previous chapter, p will be the point at which *Jack fell* is uttered, and so that sentence will be assigned TRUE just in case an event of Jack falling precedes the utterance, which conforms to our intuition.

This way of dealing with the past tense extends straightforwardly to the future and the present. Assuming that (5) is translated as (6), the SL predicate 'Fut', gets interpreted as in (7):

(5) Jack will fall.

(6) [∃e: Event(e)] ((Patient(Jack) ⊓ Fall ⊓ Fut)(e)).

(7) For any point p in a discourse, K_p (Fut) = {$e : e$ occurs after p}.

Turning to the present tense, since an eventive verb like *fall* cannot be used in the simple present to describe current events, as noted in chapter 4, section 4.5, we switch to stative *know*. Assuming that (8) is translated as (9), the SL predicate 'Pres' gets interpreted as in (10):

(8) Jack knows Jill.

(9) [∃s: State(s)] ((Hold(Jack) ⊓ Know ⊓ Theme(Jill) ⊓ Pres)(s)).

(10) For any point p in a discourse, K_p (Pres) = {$s : s$ co-occurs with p}.

The basic meaning ingredients are now in place. A compositional challenge awaits us in the next section.

Before going there, it's worth pointing out a technical feature of the account. Recall that our context lexicons consist of pairs of variables and individuals. When Akna is mentioned, a pair consisting of a variable and Akna becomes part of the context lexicon. The formalization in (4), (7), and (10) entails that a context lexicon will also contain pairs consisting of a predicate ('Past', 'Pres', or 'Fut') and a set. In other words, the SL expressions 'Past', 'Pres', and 'Fut' are being treated as variables over sets. They are one-place **predicate variables**.

Exercise (5.1)

[A] In (2), (6), and (9), we've offered SL translations for English sentences. These formulas are the result of taking the EP translations assigned by our grammar and inserting a tense predicate in them and changing the translation of the verb to one that is untensed. Following this recipe, provide formulas for *Jack will like Akna* and *Every pony jumped*.

[B] Following the same recipe as in [A] but for NegP instead of EP, provide a formula for *Jack didn't fall*. The NegP translation will come from applying the rules of translation to figure 5.3.

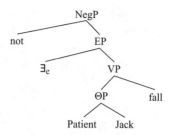

Figure 5.3
Base structure for *Jack didn't fall*.

✪ Thinking about Discourse Sensitivity of Nouns ✪

Above we observed the discourse sensitivity of tense. The exercise below introduces a related kind of sensitivity in the interpretation of nouns. This is an area of active current research. Students are invited to pursue the topic further. No attempt is made to incorporate this feature of noun semantics in the main text.

Exercise (5.2)

In the text, the meaning assignment in (i) below was criticized.

(i) $L(\text{Past}) = \{e : e \text{ is in the past}\}$.

Since it doesn't make sense to ask of an event whether it is a past event or not, there can't be a set consisting of all events that are past events, as (i) requires. It turns out that the same criticism could be directed at our analysis of other predicates. In this exercise we'll focus on nouns and their translations.

Tadpole, *child*, and *father* are all nouns whose extension changes over time. Freddie the frog was once a tadpole. Each of us was a child at one time but not at other times. Some individuals are fathers at a given time, and those same individuals are not fathers at other times. It seems then that the equations in (ii) below are no better than (i).

(ii) $L(\text{Tadpole}) = \{x : x \text{ is a tadpole}\}$.
   $L(\text{Child}) = \{x : x \text{ is a child}\}$.
   $L(\text{Father}) = \{x : x \text{ is a father}\}$.

A natural response to this observation, given our handling of tense, would be to replace 'L' with 'K_p'. For example,

(iii) for any point p in a discourse, $K_p(\text{Father}) = \{x : x \text{ is a father at the time of } p\}$.

If we make this change for all noun translations throughout the grammar, we arrive at the following generalization:

(iv) When a noun is used, its extension is calculated relative to the time at which it is uttered.

The following sentence is compatible with the generalization in (iv):

Exactly one tadpole lives in this lake.

There may be many frogs in the lake. They don't count, even though at one point they were tadpoles. All that matters is the number of individuals in the lake that are tadpoles at the time of utterance. In keeping with (iv), what matters for the truth of that sentence is the set of current tadpoles. That sentence is in the present tense.

The next one is a bit more interesting since the tense is past.

Natchaya's father was born in 1959.

When Natchaya's father was born, he was obviously not a father. But that doesn't matter. He is a father now, and so if we use the interpretation given in (iii), we get a set that includes Natchaya's father, and then the sentence goes on to discuss an event of being born that is in the past in which Natchaya's father participated. In this sentence, we calculate the extension of *father* relative to the time of utterance, as (iv) says.

It is interesting to note, though, that the generalization in (iv) has been shown to be wrong a lot of the time.

[A] Find examples that violate the generalization in (iv) as well as other examples that conform to the generalization. Examples that violate the generalization will be ones in which the truth of the sentence depends on facts about individuals who fit the description given by a noun in the sentence at some time other than the time of utterance and who do not fit it at the time of utterance.

[B] The generalization in (iv) is not completely wrong—it was correct at least for the sentences discussed above. Based on examples collected in [A], try to more accurately describe how the language works. What constraints are there on the time at which a noun's extension is calculated? Look at various potential factors such as the tense of the sentence, noun modifiers, the nature of the event being described, and the kind of DP that contains the noun or features of discourse.

Note: This is an open problem. You're not expected to solve it. Success lies in coming up with interesting generalizations correlating form and interpretation.

5.1.2   Tenses Treated as Pronouns

As noted at the end of the previous section, the SL expressions 'Past', 'Pres', and 'Fut' are predicate variables. They are variables in the sense that they don't get a fixed interpretation from L, but rather get their interpretation from the context lexicon, just like x, y, and z. But unlike x, y, and z, the interpretation they get is a set, not an individual. These predicate variables are going to be the SL translations for the English morphemes *Past*,

Present, and *will*. That means we are treating tense morphemes the way that we treated pronouns. They too are translated as variables. But whereas the pronouns we've looked at so far were singular (*he, she, himself, it*) and therefore got individual meanings, the tenses get set meanings. In that sense, they are more like plural pronouns such as *they* and *them*. Having made that connection, we can now identify a minor flaw in the meanings we assigned to the SL expressions 'Past', 'Pres', and 'Fut'. For free/discourse pronouns, all that our rules require is that they get assigned some individual. The choice of which individual is assigned is left open; it is to be decided in some way based on what is going on in the discourse. We haven't afforded the tenses that degree of freedom, but we should have. To see this point, let's focus on our meaning for 'Past':

(11) For any point p in a discourse, K_p (Past) = {$e : e$ occurs before p}.

(11) fixes the interpretation of 'Past' to the set of <u>all</u> events that precede p. There is only one such set! Nothing is left up to the discourse to decide except when p is. But the choice of past events should be left open as the following example shows. Imagine that Dhanvi and Chaha are on the highway together, and Dhanvi is complaining about Chaha's behavior:

(12) Dhanvi: You forgot to turn off the stove!
      Chaha: No, I didn't. You saw me turn it off.
      Dhanvi: No, I meant last week, when you rushed off to class.
      Chaha: Oh, that…

Dhanvi and Chaha are disagreeing about the truth of the sentence *You forgot to turn off the stove*, where *you* refers to Chaha. Dhanvi thinks it's true, while Chaha at first claims it is false and then realizes that they had different meanings in mind. Dhanvi meant that

(13) there is an event of Chaha forgetting to turn off the stove that was in the past, *at the time Chaha was rushing to class.*

Chaha at first understood Dhanvi to be saying that

(14) there is an event of Chaha forgetting to turn off the stove that was in the past, *at the time Dhanvi and Chaha left the house on the day of utterance.*

The disagreement had to do with what set of past events the sentence was about. Notice that Dhanvi and Chaha never disagreed about the more general statement that

(15) there is some event of Chaha forgetting to turn off the stove that was in the past.

But (15) is what our current analysis predicts are <u>the</u> truth conditions for Dhanvi's utterance. What we need to do is modify the analysis to say that 'Past' picks out <u>some</u> set of past events and then leave it to the discourse interpreters to decide which particular set is intended. The change is easy to make. We merely replace '=' with '⊆' (the subset symbol '⊆' was introduced in chapter 1, section 1.5) so that

(16) for any point p in a discourse, K_p (Past) ⊆ {$e : e$ occurs before p}.

For any point p, there are many subsets of the set of events past relative to p, and so we leave it up to the pragmatics to choose. Given the rule in (16), the truth conditions of (17) below relative to K_p+L are as in (18):

(17) [∃e: Event(e)] ((Patient(Jack) ⊓ Fall ⊓ Past)(e)).

(18) There is some salient set of events that precede p, and one of them is an event of Jack falling.

Corresponding changes are made for the other tenses:

(19) For any point p in a discourse, K_p (Fut) ⊆ {e : e occurs after p}.

(20) For any point p in a discourse, K_p (Pres) ⊆ {s : s co-occurs with p}.

Exercise (5.3)

Provide an example of a future tense sentence that would be judged false on the revised analysis in (19), but true on the original analysis in (7). Your sentence will need to come with relevant facts and a surrounding discourse. The discourse will be such as to narrow the space of relevant future events, something possible on the revised analysis but not on the original.

Exercise (5.4)

In (20) we modified the meaning for 'Pres' the way with did with 'Past' and 'Fut'. This was done for uniformity, but now we can wonder if this was good, bad, or just harmless. Take a position and argue for it.

Exercise (5.5)

The Dhanvi-Chaha dialogue in (12) is inspired by the following from Barbara Hall Partee.[1]

The deictic use of the Past tense morpheme appears in a sentence like (3):

(3) I didn't turn off the stove.

When uttered, for instance, halfway down the turnpike, such a sentence clearly does not mean either that there exists some time in the past at which I did not turn off the stove or that there exists no time in the past at which I turned off the stove. The sentence clearly refers to a particular time—not a particular instant, most likely, but a definite interval whose identity is generally clear from the extra-linguistic context, just as the identity of the *he* in *He shouldn't be in here* is clear from the context.

In exercise (5.1), part [B], you worked out a translation for a NegP. Assuming that type of translation for Partee's example, how can we account for her observation within our

grammar? In answering this question, treat *turn off the stove* as a unit, and replace the
first-person pronoun *I* with a name: *Barbara didn't turn-off-the-stove.*

○ **Thinking about Tense and Discourse Negation** ○

Exercise (5.5) is about how to interpret the tense in a negated sentence. The exercise
below is about how to interpret tense in a sentence uttered in the context of another negative sentence.

Exercise (5.6)

Consider first the following observation from Lauri Carlson:[2]

Negated sentences do not as a rule serve to introduce new individuals in a discourse.
Thus though

   (i) I did not catch all of the words.
is logically equivalent to

   (ii) I missed some of the words.
only (ii) is naturally continued with

   (iii) They were spoken too indistinctly.
meaning specifically the words missed, not the whole bunch.

Carlson illustrates his generalization by inquiring about the possible interpretations
for the plural pronoun *they*. If tenses are like plural pronouns, it seems as though his
generalization ought to hold in some way for tenses that follow negated sentences.
What are the facts? How are tenses interpreted in the context of negated sentences?
Does something like Carlson's generalization hold?

5.1.3 Translating Tense Phrases
At this point we have a proposed translation for *Jack fell* as well as a syntactic structure
that we're hoping will lead to that translation:

(21) Proposed translation for *Jack fell*:
$\quad$ [∃e: Event(e)] ((Patient(Jack) ⊓ Fall ⊓ Past)(e)).

Unfortunately, when our rules of translation are applied to the structure in figure 5.4, the
result is <u>not</u> the formula in (21). To see what goes wrong, we begin with the translation of
EP, calculated as in the previous chapter:

(22) $\quad$ EP ⤳ [∃e: Event(e)] ((Patient(Jack) ⊓ Fall)(e)).

Moving up to the TP now, 'Past' translates as a one-place predicate. We'd like to predicate-
conjoin 'Past' with 'Fall', but the closest we get is

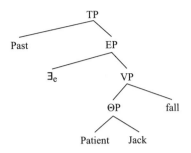

Figure 5.4
Base structure of *Jack fell.*

(23) TP ↝ (Past ⊓ [∃e: Event(e)]((Patient(Jack) ⊓ Fall)(e)))   PREDCON

The formula in (23) is not well formed. '⊓' can connect two predicates, but it cannot connect a predicate and a formula. Since a formula has to be well formed in order to be a translation, it follows that we don't have a translation for the structure in figure 5.4.

If we stop now, we not only don't get the hoped-for translation, but we appear not to have any translation! That's a bad result, since the sentence *Jack fell* and hence the structure in figure 5.4 must have a translation. The sentence intuitively can be true or false.

Luckily, there is a way to arrive at a well-formed formula, and it begins by noticing that the EP in the structure above fits the description for expressions to which QR applies, since EP is a node that has an indexed daughter:

(24) QUANTIFIER RAISING (QR)   If a node has an indexed daughter, then the constituent corresponding to that node can be adjoined to a node that dominates it, with a copy of the index inserted in the position formerly occupied by the adjoined constituent.

Applying QR to the EP in figure 5.4 gets us the structure shown in figure 5.5.

The next thing we observe is that the moved EP fits the description for the translation rule INDEXEDDAUGHTER repeated below (this fact was pointed out in the previous chapter—but there was nothing to be done with it at that point).

(25) INDEXEDDAUGHTER   {α$_u$, β} ↝ [α'u: β' (u)]

Applying that rule we get

(26) EP ↝ [∃e: (Patient(Jack) ⊓ Fall)(e)]   INDEXEDDAUGHTER

Continuing with the rules of translation, we have

(27) TP$_1$ ↝ Past(e)   MERGE

(28) TP$_2$ ↝ [∃e: (Patient(Jack) ⊓ Fall)(e)](Past(e))   MERGE

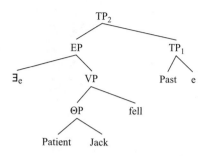

Figure 5.5
LF of *Jack fell*.

When interpreted relative to K_p+L, the formula in (28) requires that there be an event that is a falling of Jack and is in the past relative to p (and whatever other requirements come in with the choice of the value for 'Past'). We've ended up with a formula that has the desired truth conditions. It just came about in an unexpected way. Since we got to this translation via already existing rules of syntax and translation, our new proposal for the analysis of tense consists entirely of the translation of the tense morphemes. Let's now spell out the details of the proposal step by step.

First, we need to amend SL, as defined at the end of chapter 2:

(29) Amendments to SL

There are 3 kinds of one-place predicate:

• **Predicate constants** (formerly called "simple one-place predicates")

• **Predicate variables** (which include 'Past', 'Pres', and 'Fut').

• **Complex predicates** (formed with '∏' or by combining a two-place predicate with a variable or constant.)

There are two kinds of variables:

• **Individual variables** (formerly just called "variables")

• **Predicate variables**

If a variable is the first member of a pair in M, then the second member of that pair is the interpretation of the variable with respect to M.

• Individual variables are always paired with individuals.

• Predicate variables are always paired with sets.

The remainder of SL is unchanged—except that everywhere replace "variable" with "individual variable" and replace "simple one-place predicate" with "one-place predicate constant."

Next, we add a pragmatic rule governing the context lexicon, summarizing results from sections 5.1.1 and 5.1.2:

(30) For any point in discourse, p, the context lexicon K_p contains the predicates 'Past', 'Pres', and 'Fut' paired with sets of events, such that

K_p (Past) $\subseteq \{e : e$ occurs before $p\}$.
K_p (Fut) $\subseteq \{e : e$ occurs after $p\}$.
K_p (Pres) $\subseteq \{e : e$ co-occurs with $p\}$.

Next, we update the rule of FELICITY AND TRUTH so that it allows for predicate variables. We'll talk about the value of a variable: that's the set or individual that is assigned to the variable.

(31) FELICITY AND TRUTH
As a discourse progresses, individuals become salient and are associated with variables. K_p is a set of variable-*value* pairs that represent the state of the discourse at point p. K_p is the context lexicon for point-in-a-discourse p. If an utterance is made at point p in a discourse, then an LF for that utterance is infelicitous if its translation is not defined with respect to K_p+L. If an LF for that utterance is felicitous, then it is true if its translation is true with respect to K_p+L and it is false if its translation is false with respect to K_p+L.

Finally, the translation rule LEXICON needs to be modified. Currently it says:

(32) LEXICON A symbol of SL is a translation for an English word if the extension of the SL symbol relative to L is the same as the extension of the English word

But given what we have said about the tenses, one cannot ask what the extension of the *Past* is. One can only ask about the extension of *Past* when uttered at p. So we need to revise as in (33):

(33) LEXICON A symbol of SL is a translation for an English morpheme if the extension of the SL symbol relative to L or K_p is the same as the extension of the morpheme of English *when uttered at p*.

If the *Past* morpheme is uttered at point p, its extension is the set of salient events prior to p. That's exactly what K_p(Past) is, so (33) justifies the following translations:

Past $\rightsquigarrow$ Past

Pres $\rightsquigarrow$ Pres

will $\rightsquigarrow$ Fut

In sum, a tense morpheme is like a plural pronoun. It gets translated as a predicate variable in SL, with one of the meanings given in (30).

In the previous chapter, we adopted a stipulation in the form of the rule EvEXIST:

EvEXIST $\{\exists_u, \alpha\} \rightsquigarrow [\exists u: \text{Event}(u)](\alpha'(u))$

As noted in the previous chapter, EvEXIST was needed only because we hadn't gotten to the full TP. Now that we have the TP as part of our syntax, we can discard EvEXIST. Now we are back to having just the four rules from chapter 3 for translating branching nodes:

MERGE $\{\alpha, \beta\} \rightsquigarrow \alpha'(\beta')$

PREDCON $\{\alpha, \beta\} \rightsquigarrow (\alpha' \sqcap \beta')$

INDEXEDDAUGHTER $\{\alpha_u, \beta\} \rightsquigarrow [\alpha'u: \beta'(u)]$

CONJUNCTION $\{and, \alpha, \beta\} \rightsquigarrow (\alpha' \& \beta')$

The rule of EvEXIST made use of the predicate 'Event'. Compare these two translations for *Jack fell*:

(34) $[\exists e: \text{Event}(e)]((\text{Patient}(\text{Jack}) \sqcap \text{Fall})(e))$ chapter 4

(35) $[\exists e: (\text{Patient}(\text{Jack}) \sqcap \text{Fall})(e)](\text{Past}(e))$ chapter 5

The presence of 'Event' in (34) means that it will be true only if there is an <u>event</u> in which Jack fell. In fact, this follows from (35) as well. (35) requires there to be some object in the extension of 'Fall'. But since anything in the extension of 'Fall' is an event, it follows that (35) requires there to be an event in which Jack fell.

Exercise (5.7)

Provide the translation that our grammar assigns to *Jack will like Jill*.

Exercise (5.8)

Consider the base structure in figure 5.6.

[A] Provide an LF derived from this base structure. This will require applying QR to the EP and then applying QR to the DP.

[B] Provide the translation that is assigned by our grammar to your LF.

[C] Name the last rule of translation that you used to get the translation in [B].

[D] In the beginning of chapter 3, we mentioned that base structures are input to syntactic and morphological rules that produce surface structures. These include a rule that moves the subject from inside the VP to adjoin above TP. It also includes rules that produce the past tensed form of a verb in the scope of *Past*. Assuming those rules, provide the surface string that corresponds to this base structure.

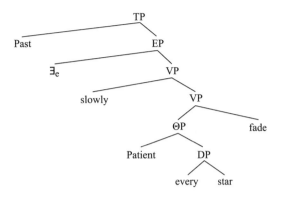

Figure 5.6
Base structure of a sentence.

[E] Provide a short discourse in which the sentence you gave in [D] is uttered. Say what set is assigned to 'Past' at the point at which it is uttered. Provide a paraphrase in English for the sentence that takes into consideration that set, as well as the translation you provided in [B]. (The paraphrase should begin with "there was an event..." along the lines of (14) above.).

❂ Thinking about Negation, Tense and Scope ❂

There is debate in the current literature about the relative order of tense and negation.[3] In our structures the tenses, Past, Pres and Fut, are higher in the structure than negation. This exercise explores the semantic consequences of that configuration.

Exercise (5.9)

Consider the base structure for *Jack didn't fall*, shown in figure 5.7.

[A] There is no LF for this structure. To discover what goes wrong, apply QR to the EP and then apply the rules of translation. Explain what the problem is.

[B] A possible solution might be to view *not* as a negative quantifier and to let it replace EP in negative sentences, giving us the base structure in figure 5.8. Provide an LF and translation for *Jack didn't fall* assuming this base structure, along with the SpecificVocab rule below, which replaces our current rule *not* ⤳ ¬.

SPECIFICVOCAB *not* ⤳ No

[C] Reconsider exercise (5.5), this time assuming a translation like the one you gave in [B]. If you did exercise (5.5) already, does this new kind of translation make a difference

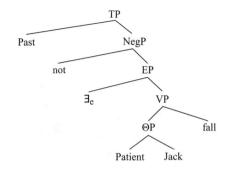

Figure 5.7
Base structure of *Jack didn't fall*.

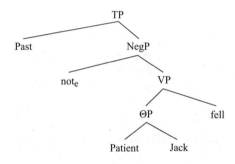

Figure 5.8
Base structure of *Jack didn't fall* treating *not* as quantifier.

for what you said? If you haven't done exercise (5.5) already, do it now, assuming the new translation.

[D] The following examples and observations are from a book by Hans Kamp and Uwe Reyle.[4]

(i) Mary looked at Bill. He smiled.

(ii) Mary looked at Bill. He was happy.

(iii) Mary looked at Bill. He didn't smile.

(iv) Mary looked at Bill. He wasn't happy.

The examples in (i)–(ii) display familiar narrative progression effects. The event of smiling is understood to follow the looking in (i), while the happiness state is understood to overlap with the looking in (ii). The negative sentences show corresponding effects. The lack of a smile is understood to follow the looking in (iii), while the lack of happiness is understood to overlap the looking in (iv). This is somewhat surprising given our formulation of the rule of NARRATIVE PROGRESSION:

Narrative Progression

In the course of a narrative, when an event is described, it is usually understood to follow in time a previously mentioned event. When a state is described, it is usually understood to hold at the time of a previously mentioned event.

Whereas in (i), a smiling event is described that follows the looking, all that (iii) says is that there was no smiling event. So what event or state could be following the looking? Likewise, for (iv), Bill is understood to not be happy while Mary is looking at him, but it is not immediately obvious how that could follow from the rule of Narrative Progression. There are at least two kinds of approaches to this problem; one pragmatic and the other semantic. On the pragmatic approach, the rule of Narrative Progression is replaced by a pragmatic rule governing the choice of value assigned by K_p to 'Past', the translation for the tense. This rule should do everything the Narrative Progression rule does, but it should also apply to (iii) and (iv). On the semantic approach, one defines a type of eventuality that is introduced in negative sentences and then Narrative Progression applies. Choose one of these approaches and spell out the details.

Exercise (5.10)

Two possible structures for *Jack fell yesterday* are shown in figure 5.9. The structure on the right makes use of a silent preposition 'On'. It allows us to treat *yesterday* uniformly as a name of time, as it would be in *after yesterday*, *yesterday was the best day of my life* or *yesterday's game*.

[A] Choose from among the two structures in figure 5.9. Provide the translation that our grammar assigns to that structure, assuming that the English word *yesterday* translates as a symbol of SL, 'Yest'.

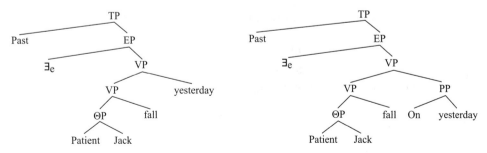

Figure 5.9
Two possible structures for *Jack fell yesterday*.

[B] Provide a meaning for the SL expression 'Yest' as it is used in your translation. Keep in mind that the extension of *yesterday* depends on when it is uttered.

[C] Given you answers in [A] and [B], what does our grammar say about the truth value of the sentences *Jack will fall yesterday* and *Jack has a cold yesterday*? Does that conform to your intuition?

Exercise (5.11)

[A] Provide the translation our grammar assigns to the sentence *You will sit here*, assuming that *you* and *here* translate into SL expressions 'You' and 'Here'. (You can assume a null preposition introducing *here* as with *yesterday* in exercise (5.10).)

[B] Provide meanings for 'You' and 'Here'. Keep in mind that the extensions of these words depend on when and by whom they are uttered.

Exercise (5.12)

Describe the contribution *now* makes to the truth conditions of sentences containing it. Begin by considering the examples below, some of which are marked with '#' to indicate that they are infelicitous.

(i) a. Rihanna is seeing my friend now.
    b. # Rihanna saw my friend now.
    c. Rihanna saw my friend just now.
    d. Rihanna will see my friend now.

(ii) I often think back to the summer of '82. #I was so happy now.

(iii) Rihanna came over to see me. It had been such a long time! I couldn't believe it. I was so happy now.

✪ Thinking about an Alternative Analysis of Tense ✪

The following is an exploration that leads to an alternative analysis of tense. Learning to seek an alternative theory and finding ways to discriminate among alternatives are core skills in doing natural language semantics.

Exercise (5.13)

In our analysis of tense, the context lexicon plays a crucial role. We proposed to interpret 'Past' as follows: For any point in a discourse, p, K_p (Past) $\subseteq \{e : e$ occurs before $p\}$. A consequence of this analysis is that the context lexicon K assigns values to predicate variables in addition to individual variables. The goal of this exercise is to consider an alternative analysis of tense in which we revert to our original idea that K assigns values only to individual variables. On this alternative analysis, *Past* is translated as a two-place predicate 'Past', where 'Past(a)(b)' when interpreted with respect to L says that $L(b)$ occurs before $L(a)$. Crucial to this proposal is the idea that the English morpheme *Past* occurs in the base structure along with a hidden pronoun, whose value is determined relative to K_p in the same way as any other free pronoun.

[A] Provide a base structure for *Baboloki ran*. Make sure to include a null indexed pronoun sister to the tense. Write the pronoun as pro_u (*pro* indicates it's null; u is the index on the pronoun)

[B] Provide an LF for the base structure in [A] along with the translation assigned to that LF. Give the meaning of the two-place predicate 'Past' relative to L.

[C] Under what conditions will the semantic rules of SL assign TRUE to the translation provided in [B] relative to K_p+L?

[D] This analysis depends on getting the correct interpretation for the index on the null pronoun. Provide any amendments to the grammar that will be needed to guarantee the correct interpretation. Say how your amendments apply to the translation in [B].

[E] Assuming this type of analysis of *Past* is extended to *Pres* and *will*, provide the translation of *Ava loves Anna* and provide an LF for *Baboloki will sing*.

[F] Under this analysis, the translation of *Past* follows from the old LEXICON rule in (32). The amended lexicon rule in (33) is not necessary. Explain why.

[G] Suggest a way to use the ingredients in this analysis of tense to address the issues raised in exercise (5.2) concerning the meanings of nouns.

[H] Up to now, we've assumed that the null pronoun attached to the tense is a free pronoun. Can you think of an example that would require the null pronoun to be bound? If so, say what its translation should be and how that translation could be produced.

[I] Can this analysis cope with the discourse freedom discussed in section 5.1.2, which motivated the use of subset ($\subseteq$) in the meanings of 'Past', 'Pres', and 'Fut'?

✪ Thinking about Variables and Domain Restriction ✪

The exercise below explores the idea that is that there is a domain over which a quantifier quantifies and the discourse restricts that domain. This is known as **domain restriction**. Exercise 5.14 seeks to account for domain restriction by positing a silent predicate variable, C, in the base structure.

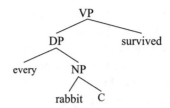

Figure 5.10
Chapter 3 base structure for *Every rabbit survived.*

Exercise (5.14)

This morning, Baboloki went outside and was delighted to discover that his rabbit friends had managed to make it through a recent cold snap. He said to Amaya:

(i) Every rabbit survived.

When Baboloki uttered (i), both he and Amaya knew he meant that every rabbit near their house had survived. He wasn't making a claim about every rabbit that exists. This is an example of *domain restriction*. The idea is that there is a domain over which a quantifier, in this case *every*, quantifies and the discourse restricts that domain. The goal of this exercise is to account for domain restriction by positing a silent predicate variable, *C*, in the base structure. For the purposes of this exercise, we revert to chapter 3 syntax. This gives us the base structure for (i) shown in figure 5.10.

[A] Construct an LF for yourself starting with the base structure in figure 5.10. Provide the translation assigned to your LF. State what rule of translation you used to translate *C* and what rule of translation was used to combine *C*'s translation with the translation of *rabbit*. Assume that *C* has been added to the stock of SL predicate variables.

[B] Does the rule of FELICITY AND TRUTH need to be revised with the addition of domain restriction variables? If so, how? If not, why not?

5.2   Aspect: The Progressive

5.2.1   The Meaning of the Progressive

Compare the following two sentences:

Henry opened the bottle.

Henry was opening the bottle.

They are both in the past tense; hence they both describe an eventuality that is located in the past relative to the time of utterance. And they both make reference to an opening event whose patient is a bottle and whose agent is Henry. Nevertheless, the sentences have slightly different meanings, and they are constructed using different forms of the verb.

The second sentence has the sequence *be* VERB+*ing*, known as the **progressive**. Since *be* is in the past tense (*was*), the second sentence is called a **past progressive**. Our goal here is to develop a semantics for the progressive. We'll begin by pinning down a difference in meaning between the two sentences above.

Compare the following two narratives:

Amaya walked in. She took off her coat. Henry opened a bottle of wine. They discussed the events of the day.

Amaya walked in. She took off her coat. Henry was opening a bottle of wine. They started to discuss the election.

In the first narrative, it is natural to understand Henry's opening the bottle as following Amaya's coat removal. As expected, the eventive sentence *Henry opened the bottle* moves the reference time of the narrative forward. By contrast, in the second narrative, it is natural to understand the bottle opening to be occurring while Amaya took off her coat. So the progressive sentence *Henry was opening the bottle* behaves like a stative. It does not move the narrative forward. We tentatively conclude that progressive *be* combines with a phrase headed by an eventive verb and forms a stative.

Further evidence for this conclusion comes from the use of the present tense. Recall that present tense eventive sentences may describe habits, but they are not good for describing an event that is happening at the moment of utterance. The odd sequence below illustrates this.

(36) Hey, look! Akna fries an egg.

By contrast, a stative sentence is generally fine in the present tense as a description of current facts. It follows then that if the progressive is stative, we should be able to fix (36) by putting the verb *fry* in the progressive. The result should be a present tense sentence that describes what is happening at the moment of utterance. This prediction is fulfilled in the sequence below:

(37) Hey, look! Akna is frying an egg.

A further piece of evidence for the stativity of progressive sentences comes from how states develop in time. A state can hold at a moment, and if it holds for a period of time, it holds for every moment in that period. Events, by contrast, usually do not occur in a moment. Given this difference in events and states, the entailment patterns in (38)–(39) below support the view that progressives are stative. (The symbol '$\nvDash$' means "doesn't entail", while '$\vDash$' means "entails").

(38) Akna made an omelette in 25 minutes, between 10:00 and 10:25.   (EVENTIVE)
$\nvDash$ Akna made an omelette at 10:15.

(39) Akna was making an omelette for 25 minutes, between 10:00 and 10:25.   (STATIVE)
$\vDash$ Akna was making an omelette at 10:15.

A final piece of evidence comes from sentences of the form *what X did was* ___, which are called clefts. As noted in chapter 4, the blank in the cleft can be filled with an eventive VP but not a stative VP. The contrast in (40)–(41) supports the view that progressives are stative.

(40) What Gadarine did was open the bottle.   (EVENTIVE)

(41) #What Gadarine did was opening the bottle.   (STATIVE)

   At the start of this section, we compared (42) and (43) below:

(42) Henry opened the bottle.

(43) Henry was opening the bottle.

Both sentences make reference to an opening event whose patient is a bottle and whose agent is Henry. Nevertheless, the sentences have different meanings. The data just reviewed suggest that the difference stems from a state introduced in (43) but not mentioned in (42). The data in (38) and (39) allow us to see more specifically what state is introduced in the progressive. If Akna makes an omelette, then some time passes from the beginning of the cooking process to the end, and we cannot say that Akna made an omelette at every moment in that period. However, at any point during the process, we can report that the event of omelette making is in progress. In (37), repeated below, we likewise report on an event in progress, and this is spelled out in the paraphrase in (44).

(37) Akna is frying an egg.

(44) There is an event of egg frying by Akna and that event is currently in progress.

   For an event to be in progress is for it to be in a certain state. An event is in such a state as soon as it begins, and when it stops, it goes out of that state. Let's refer to such a state as an *in-progress state* and modify our paraphrase of (37) so as to make our stativity discovery explicit:

(45) There is an event *e* of egg frying by Akna, and *e* is currently in an in-progress state.

Using the same type of paraphrase for (43) repeated below gets us (46):

(43) Henry was opening the bottle.

(46) There is an event *e* of opening the bottle by Henry, and *e* was in an in-progress state.

The paraphrases in (45) and (46) represent an analysis of the progressive that follows closely what you find in writing manuals and language learning textbooks. It goes beyond many of those discussions in being more precise about the role of events and states. Our grammar gives us the ability to be even more precise and to address the important question of compositionality. What are the bits of meaning that come together to produce the meanings in (45) and (46)? And how are these bits of meaning apportioned within the morphemes making up the paraphrased sentences, (37) and (43)? Since our grammar is based on indirect interpretation, we address these kinds of compositional questions by first producing paraphrases in the language of SL, so our next task is to go from paraphrases like (45) and (46) to SL formulas.

Since we are engaged now in a more technical exercise, and we're not concerned with tapping our speaker intuitions, it will be easier to proceed with the simpler example (47) paraphrased in (48):

(47) Jack is falling.

(48) There is an event e of falling by Jack, and e is currently in an in-progress state.

The first part of the paraphrase in (48) should be familiar to us from previous discussion. It is the meaning of the EP in *Jack fell*, which was calculated in (26) and is repeated here:

(26) $[\exists e: (\text{Patient}(\text{Jack}) \sqcap \text{Fall})(e)]$.

The second part of the paraphrase in (48) refers to <u>an</u> in-progress state. The indefinite article implies another existential quantifier in the scope of the first:

(49) $[\exists e: (\text{Patient}(\text{Jack}) \sqcap \text{Fall})(e)]([\exists s:$

The formula in (49) is in need of a predicate that describes a state. That predicate applied to s will form the restrictor of the quantifier and that predicate should say of s that it is an in-progress state that e is in. For this purpose, we'll introduce a new two-place SL predicate, 'InProgress':

(50) $L(\text{InProgress}) = \{ \langle e, Y \rangle : Y = \{s: s$ is a state e is in when it is in progress.$\}\}$

According to (50), 'InProgress' combines with an event-denoting expression to give a predicate true of states of that event being in progress. We can now use 'InProgress' to extend the formula in (49):

(51) $[\exists e: (\text{Patient}(\text{Jack}) \sqcap \text{Fall})(e)]([\exists s: \text{InProgress}(e)(s)])$.

The formula in (51) is not yet well formed. It is missing a scope for the second quantifier. The part of the paraphrase in (48) not yet accounted for is *is currently*. That is saying that the in-progress state holds at the time of utterance. We can capture that with our 'Pres' predicate:

(52) $[\exists e: (\text{Patient}(\text{Jack}) \sqcap \text{Fall})(e)]([\exists s: \text{InProgress}(e)(s)] (\text{Pres}(s)))$.

At last we have an SL formula that encapsulates the idea that the progressive describes a state of an event being in progress. It says there is an event of Jack falling, and there is a state of that event being in progress, and the state occurs at the time of utterance. This is a wordier version of what (48) says. By the same technique, we can now go from the paraphrase of (43) in (46) below to the formula in (53):

(43) Henry was opening the bottle.

(46) There is an event e of opening the bottle by Henry, and e was in an in-progress state.

(53) [The x: Bottle(x)]([$\exists e$: (Agent(Henry) $\sqcap$ Open $\sqcap$ Patient(x))(e)]([$\exists s$: InProgress(e)(s)] (Past(s)))).

Exercise (5.15)

[A] Provide an SL translation for (i) below that makes use of our new 'InProgress' predicate:

(i) There is an event e of making an omelette by Akna and e is currently in an in-progress state.

[B] Provide an SL translation for (ii) below that makes use of our new 'InProgress' predicate:

(ii) Akna will be feeding Baboloki.

Summarizing now, we observed that progressive sentences are stative even when their corresponding nonprogressive counterparts are eventive. We concluded that the progressive is used to describe a state that an event enters into when it starts and that it stays in until it stops. We called this kind of state an *in-progress state* and we've added a new two-place predicate, 'InProgress', to SL. 'InProgress(e)(s)' says that s is an in-progress state that e is in. Adding 'InProgress' to SL allowed us to write formulas that capture our intuitions about the meanings of progressives. In the next section, we turn to the compositional question of how that meaning is distributed within the morphemes making up progressives.

5.2.2 Translating Progressive *Be*

Figure 5.11 shows a base structure for the sentence *Jack was falling*. We analyze *was falling* as the result of combining the past tense with *be falling*. *Be falling* in turn results from having the progressive *be* take an EP complement.[5] As explained in section 5.1.3, the TP will not receive a translation unless QR is applied to the EP sister of tense. Applying QR gives us the result shown in figure 5.12.

It's a bit hard to see what to do next because we haven't yet said how to translate '$be_{[prog]}$'. We can get some guidance by studying a translation for *Jack was falling* along the lines sketched in the previous section:

(54) [$\exists e$: (Patient(Jack) $\sqcap$ Fall)(e)]([$\exists s$: InProgress(e)(s)] (Past(s))).

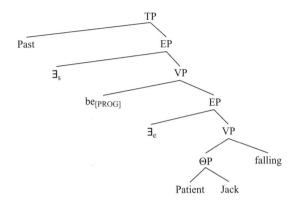

Figure 5.11
Base structure for *Jack was falling.*

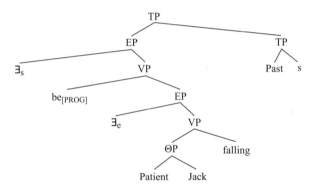

Figure 5.12
Applying QR to the EP sister of tense in figure 5.11.

Notice that the outermost quantifier in (54) is an event quantifier. That would come about by applying QR to the lower EP in the structure above, as we do in figure 5.13.

Comparing the VP '*be*$_{[\text{prog}]}$ *e*' with the restrictor in '[∃s: InProgress(*e*)(*s*)]' in (54), leads to the following proposal:

(55) *be*$_{[\text{prog}]}$ ↝ InProgress.

It now turns out that the structure in figure 5.13, arrived at through QR, leads to the desired translation. The calculation appears in figure 5.14. We translated *falling* as 'Fall'. The contribution of—*ing* is already part of 'InProgress'.

This completes our analysis of the progressive. The proposal in its entirety is in (56) below. The path from the sentence to the interpretation follows from (56), along with rules of syntax, translation, and interpretation that were in place before we started on the progressive.

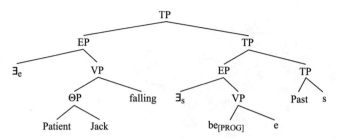

Figure 5.13
Applying QR to the EP sister of *be* in figure 5.12

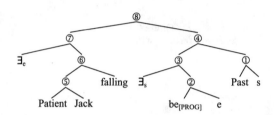

① ⤳ Past(*s*)   MERGE

② ⤳ InProgress(*e*)   MERGE

③ ⤳ [∃*s*: InProgress(*e*)(*s*)]   INDEXEDDAUGHTER

④ ⤳ [∃*s*: InProgress(*e*)(*s*)](Past(*s*))   MERGE

⑤ ⤳ Patient(Jack)   MERGE

⑥ ⤳ (Patient(Jack) ⊓ Fall)   PREDCON

⑦ ⤳ [∃*e*: (Patient(Jack) ⊓ Fall)(*e*)]   INDEXEDDAUGHTER

⑧ ⤳ [∃*e*: (Patient(Jack) ⊓ Fall)(*e*)]([∃*s*: InProgress(*e*)(*s*)](Past(*s*)))   MERGE

Figure 5.14
Translating the structure in figure 5.13.

(56) Proposal for the analysis of progressive *be*:

• Add 'InProgress' to SL.

• L(InProgress) = { $\langle e, Y \rangle$: Y = {s: s is the state e is in when it is in progress.}}

• $be_{[\text{prog}]} \rightsquigarrow$ InProgress   LEXICON

The proposal can be summarized in one line: progressive *be* is a two-place predicate relating events to their in-progress states.

Exercise (5.16)

[A] Provide the LF whose translation is given by (103), repeated below:

(53) [The x: Bottle(x)]([$\exists e$: (Agent(Henry) ⊓ Open ⊓ Patient(x))(e)]([$\exists s$: InProgress(e) (s)] (Past(s))))

[B] Provide the translation assigned by the grammar to *Every child was smiling*. Name the last rule of translation that you applied in arriving at your translation.

[C] There is at least one analysis (LF and translation) according to which if *Every child was smiling* is true when uttered, then for each child, there is some state which is in the past relative to the point in time when the sentence is uttered, and it's a state in which that child is smiling. That leaves open the possibility that each child was smiling at a different time. What are your intuitions about the sentence?

  ∘ Devise narratives in which *Every child was smiling* would occur naturally to try to discover what factors determine whether or not a quantified statement describes eventualities that are simultaneous.

  ∘ Is there a way to enforce simultaneity in our grammar? If so, describe your idea and say if it involves syntax, semantics (translation), and/or pragmatics. If not, state what problems you ran into in trying to enforce simultaneity.

Exercise (5.17)

In the previous chapter, it was noted that in our dialect of English, progressives formed from stative verbs do not sound good. *#Akna is owning Fido* is one such example. Provide the translation that is assigned to that sentence. Is there some way to explain the infelicity in terms of what the translation says?

✪ Thinking about Nested Quantifiers ✪

Figure 5.11 contains an EP quantifier, which contains within it another EP quantifier. In other words, we have a base structure with **nested quantifiers**. Exercise (5.18) below explores such quantifiers in more detail.

Exercise (5.18)

In chapter 3, exercise (3.21) you were asked for an LF for the sentence *Some bridge in every city collapsed*. A base structure is provided in the exercise, and it shows a DP quantifier *Some bridge in every city*, which contains within it a DP quantifier *every city*. Compare that to the base structure for *Jack was falling* in figure 5.11. In that structure, there's an EP quantifier, which contains within it another EP quantifier. In both cases, we have a base structure with nested quantifiers. Now notice that in the LF in figure 5.13, the nesting is undone, and the formerly innermost quantifier is now above the one that used to contain it. Compare that to the LF that you came up with in exercise (3.21). Did the quantifiers unravel there in the same way? If yes, how can we explain that commonality? If no, can you produce a different LF for *Jack was falling* along the lines of your solution to exercise (3.21)?

✪ Important Practice and Looking Ahead ✪

Duration adverbials figure prominently in the literature on verb meanings. These adverbials will come up in section 5.2.3. To better appreciate that discussion, it's helpful to form your own opinion about the semantic factors that govern the distribution of duration adverbials and about how they might be analyzed. The exercise below provides an opportunity to do that.

Exercise (5.19)

[A] In English, duration adverbials can be formed using the prepositions *for* and *in*. The choice is not random. Assess the examples below. Are both prepositions possible? If they are, does the choice affect the interpretation?

(i) Emily owned Fido for 3 years / in 3 years.

(ii) Emily swam for 20 minutes / in 20 minutes.

(iii) Emily opened the bottle for 10 minutes / in 10 minutes

(iv) Emily was opening the bottle for 10 minutes / in 10 minutes.

[B] Provide a base structure and a translation for *Emily swam for 20 minutes*. Translate *for 20 minutes* with a one-place predicate symbol 'For20'.

[C] Provide a meaning for 'For20' (i.e. L(For20) = _____).

[D] Suppose we translate *in 20 minutes* with a one-place predicate symbol 'In20'. Is there a way to interpret 'In20' and 'For20' that will allow us to account for the data in (i)–(iv)?

5.2.3   Different Kinds of Events: Aspectual Classes

The following describes what happened one day while Jack and Jill were spending their summer vacation with their Aunt Betty:

Before lunch, Jack was writing a letter to his friend Musya.
Before lunch, Jill was playing volleyball with the neighbors.
After lunch, they all went swimming.

That evening, Aunt Betty was on the phone with Jack and Jill's father, and she told him:

Jill played volleyball with the neighbors before lunch and Jack wrote a letter to his friend Musya. After lunch, we all went swimming.

Jack overheard this conversation and he politely corrected his Aunt Betty. He told her he was writing a letter to Musya but he hadn't finished it. Jack's correction is possible because *Jack was writing a letter* does not entail *Jack wrote a letter*. We can record this fact as

Jack was writing a letter before lunch $\nvDash$ *Jack wrote a letter before lunch.*

While Jack corrected Aunt Betty, there is no way that Jill could have made a similar correction. That's because if Jill <u>was playing</u> volleyball before lunch, then she <u>played</u> volleyball before lunch. We can record this fact as

Jill was playing volleyball before lunch $\vDash$ *Jill played volleyball before lunch.*

In the first case, the nonentailment makes some sense. There was an event of Jack's writing a letter that was <u>in progress</u> before lunch. Nothing guarantees that it was finished before lunch, and if it wasn't finished, then *Jack wrote a letter before lunch* is false, assuming all Jack's letter writing activities are as described above. This bit of reasoning reveals a fact about the simple past that hasn't been accounted for up to now. An event can be in progress or it can be suspended. In either case, it is not finished. Eventive sentences in the simple past are taken to be about events that are finished. Since the progressive *Jack was writing a letter* leaves open whether or not he finished, *Jack wrote a letter* doesn't follow. But now what do we say about the volleyball entailment? In that case, too, there was an event of Jill's playing volleyball that was <u>in progress</u> before lunch. Nothing guarantees that it was finished before lunch, and if it wasn't finished, then shouldn't *Jill played volleyball before lunch* be false?

In order to understand what's going on here, we need to provide some detail about the nature of volleyball playing events and about what it means for them to be in progress. One can conceive of an event of playing volleyball as consisting of a chain of smaller events of playing volleyball. Whatever it takes to be playing volleyball—serving the ball, preventing the ball from landing in your court, directing the ball back over the net, scoring points—those things go on again and again throughout the period of play. So any big, say hour-long, event of playing volleyball consists of a chain of smaller volleyball-playing events. That means that if one of those big events is in progress, it will follow that some of the smaller events have already occurred. So if Jill was playing volleyball before lunch, there was a big event of playing volleyball, it was in progress before lunch, and it may or may not have finished. Perhaps Jill and her friends were in the process of playing two games, and the second one was interrupted by lunch. But even if the big event wasn't finished, some of the smaller events were, and any one of them will make it true that Jill played volleyball before lunch.

In the previous chapter, we categorized VPs into eventives and statives based on speaker intuitions about grammaticality, felicity, and interpretation. The labels "eventive" and "stative" reflect the thought that the linguistic patterns are symptomatic of a distinction in the kinds of eventualities the VPs describe: events versus states. In the previous paragraph, we contrasted *Jack was writing a letter* and *Jill was playing volleyball* based on speaker intuitions about entailment. We went on to correlate the differential behavior with differences in the kinds of events described. This is then another classification of expressions based on the type of eventuality they describe. Such classifications are variously called **aspectual classes**, **aktionsarten**, or **Vendler classes**.[6] Two kinds of VPs that are frequently distinguished, which are relevant to our discussion of the progressive, are **accomplishments** and **activities**. *Jack wrote a letter* is an example of an accomplishment VP; its past progressive form (*Jack was writing a letter*) does not entail its simple past form (*Jack wrote a letter*). *Jill played volleyball* is an example of an activity VP; its past progressive form (*Jill was playing volleyball*) does entail its simple past form (*Jill played volleyball*). Related to this difference between accomplishment and activity VPs is that the former describes a particular culmination of an event in addition to a process leading up to the culmination, while the latter does not describe a culmination. For example, in the case of writing a letter, the culmination is reached when the letter is written. Before the culmination is reached, the event is not finished; after it's reached, the event is over.

One of the most cited phenomena connected with aspectual classes is the distribution of PPs describing the duration of an eventuality. *For*-PPs go with statives and activities, while *in*-PPs go with accomplishments:

(57) Durational PPs: *for* versus *in*
      Baboloki owned a Mercedes for a year   STATIVE
      Jill played volleyball for an hour   ACTIVITY
      Jack wrote the letter in an hour   ACCOMPLISHMENT

✪ Something to Think About ✪

There are two potential sources of confusion in the use of the terms naming aspectual classes. These terms are sometimes applied to eventualities and sometimes to expressions. You might read that the event of building the castle is an accomplishment, and you might read that *Jack built the castle* is an accomplishment. There is also variation in the type of

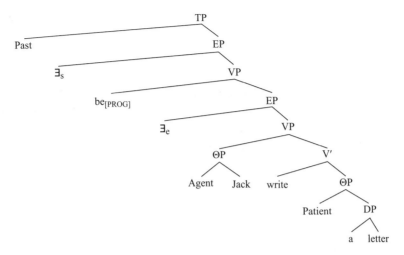

Figure 5.15
Base structure for *Jack was writing a letter.*

expression to which the terms are applied. Sometimes it's a verb, sometimes a verb phrase, and sometimes a whole sentence, and the classification can often yield different results depending on what phrase is classified. The base structure for *Jack was writing a letter* is shown in figure 5.15. The lowest VP could be classified as an accomplishment VP. But given our analysis of the progressive, the higher VP would be classified as a stative.

This section began with an explanation of a difference in entailment patterns for the sentences *Jill was playing volleyball* and *Jack was writing a letter*. The explanation turned on the nature of the entities on which our theory is based. It related the observed entailment difference to a difference between volleyball-playing events and letter-writing events. This type of explanation is **ontological**, or **metaphysical**; both terms that refer to the nature of things. Contrast that with our explanation for scopal ambiguities, where the key players are the syntactic structures and the rules of translation that apply to those structures.

Exercise (5.20)

In this section, we have been consulting our intuitions about entailment relations between a past progressive sentence and the corresponding simple past sentence. Here are two more examples of the kind of data discussed:

Musya was crossing the street.   ⊯   *Musya crossed the street.*
Baboloki was wearing a tuxedo.   ⊨   *Baboloki wore a tuxedo.*

[A] Provide three more examples of past progressive sentences that <u>don't</u> entail the corresponding simple past.

[B] Provide three more examples of past progressive sentences that <u>do</u> entail the corresponding simple past.

[C] In the text, an explanation was given for why the entailment goes through with *Jill was playing volleyball*. The explanation was based on the nature of volleyball-playing events. Does that type of explanation work for the three examples you gave in [B]? Pick one of your examples and say how the ontological explanation does or does not apply.

Exercise (5.21)

In our recent discussion of Jack's letter-writing above, we observed that eventive sentences in the simple past are taken to be about events that are finished. In the case of accomplishments, this means that the culmination point is reached.

[A] Provide the base structure for *Musya crossed Montana Avenue* and the translation assigned to an LF for that sentence.

[B] Recall that an event can be in progress or it can be suspended. In either case, it is not finished. Eventive sentences in the simple past are taken to be about events that are finished. Does it follow from the translation that you provided in [A] that the crossing event is <u>finished</u>? If yes, justify your answer by saying what in the translation leads to the entailment that the crossing event is <u>finished</u>. If no, suggest a way to modify our grammar so that that entailment is captured.

5.3   Aspect: The Perfect

5.3.1   The Meaning of the Perfect

The title of this chapter is *Tense and Aspect*. The term **aspect** is applied to constructions whose meaning has to do with the stage of development an event is in. The progressive is one such construction. It is used to describe an event in progress. We turn our attention now to another aspectual construction in English.

Compare the following two sentences:

(58) Jack spoke to Jill about her book.

(59) Jack has spoken to Jill about her book.

Both sentences report on a past speaking event, and yet, while (58) is in the past tense, as expected, (59) uses the present tense *has* (not past *had*), so it appears to be in the present tense! Evidence from adverbial modification suggests that this is not just a matter of form. Whereas it is fine to modify the past tensed (58) with *yesterday*—as in:

Yesterday, Jack spoke to Jill

present tensed (59) sounds odd when *yesterday* is added—as in:

#Yesterday, Jack has spoken to Jill

Yesterday is as incompatible with (59) as it is with any present tense sentence. Compare *#Jack has a cold yesterday*, from exercise (5.10). This is puzzling. (59) is morphologically and semantically present tensed, and yet it seems to describe an event in the past. To solve this puzzle, we'll need to pay attention to the fact that (58) and (59) are constructed with different verb forms. Whereas (58) has a simple past tense *spoke*, (59) has the sequence *has spoken*, known as the **perfect**.[7] Since the verb *has* is present tensed, (59) is a present perfect sentence. Our goal here is to get a syntax and semantics for the perfect that will explain how a present perfect sentence can come to describe an eventuality that occurred in the past.

Our first analytical clue is the very fact that (59) is present tensed, and yet, although it describes an event of speaking, it doesn't require any of the special interpretations attached to a present tense eventive—in particular, it doesn't have to have a habitual reading. This leads us to hypothesize that when we form a perfect, we create a stative. Further evidence for this hypothesis comes from clefts and progressives, both of which are not good with statives in general and are not good with perfects in particular.

(60) a. What Gila did was speak to Nadir.   (EVENTIVE)
     b. *What Gila did was know Armenian.   (STATIVE)
     c. *What Gila did was have spoken to Nadir.   (PERFECT)

(61) a. Gila was speaking to Nadir.   (EVENTIVE)
     b. *Gila was knowing Armenian.   (STATIVE)
     c. *Gila was having spoken to Nadir.   (PERFECT)

If it's true that in forming a perfect, we form a stative, we ought to see its effects on narrative progression. Just like other statives, we should expect that perfects do not move the reference time forward. In the following narratives, we test this prediction:

The Butler family arrived home from their vacation at 7 p.m. They quickly got out of the car and went in the house. Mr. Butler spoke to Billy about his poor performance in school. Everyone was tired, so they ate some cold pizza and went to bed.

The Butler family arrived home from their vacation at 7 p.m. They quickly got out of the car and went in the house. Mr. Butler had spoken to Billy about his poor performance in school. Everyone was in a bad mood, so they ate some cold pizza and went to bed.

In the first narrative, it is natural to understand Mr. Butler's speaking to Billy as following the entry into the house. As expected, the eventive sentence *Mr. Butler spoke to Billy...* introduces an event understood to follow in time a previously mentioned event. By contrast, in the second narrative, it is natural to understand Mr. Butler's speaking to Billy as preceding the entry into the house. This is unlike the eventive sentence, which supports the view that the perfect is stative. Still, it seems to work differently from other statives we've seen. With other statives, we understand the state to overlap a previously described event. But with the perfect *had spoken* the speaking <u>precedes</u> the previously mentioned entering event. So while the facts are compatible with a perfect not being eventive, it appears to work differently from other statives. We'll want our theory of the perfect to explain this as well.

We currently have two data points to explain about the perfect:

(62) a. How does a present perfect describe a past event?
     b. Why doesn't the perfect work like other statives with respect to narrative progression?

We also have an idea about the semantics of the perfect: It is used to create a stative. We had the same idea about the progressive. And the progressive and the perfect have similar syntax. So, we will now make use of our compositional analysis of the progressive to help guide us toward an analysis of the perfect.

To start, we have a base structure that has the perfect *have* heading a VP,[8] as in figure 5.16. Next, we apply QR, first to the higher EP then to the lower one, giving us the result showin in figure 5.17. As with the progressive, we'll assume that $have_{[perf]}$ is translated as a two-place predicate relating events and states. We'll use the metavariable π as a temporary placeholder for that predicate until we figure out more about what state the perfect introduces. Applying the rules of translation to the structure above exactly as we did for the progressive structure at the end of section 5.2.2, we get

(63) $TP_3 \rightsquigarrow [\exists e: (\text{Agent}(\text{Jack}) \sqcap \text{Speak})(e)]([\exists s: \pi(e)(s)](\text{Pres}(s)))$.

As we did with the progressive *speaking*, we translate *spoken* as 'Speak'. The contribution of—*en* will be part of whatever we fill π with. What remains is to determine the nature of the state that the perfect introduces and then to use that to fill in for π in (63). Let's look at a specific case.

Suppose that Musya decides to cross Montana Avenue. The event of crossing begins when she steps off the sidewalk and ends when she reaches the other side. As discussed in the previous section, at any moment between the stepping off and the reaching the other side, we can truthfully use the progressive to describe what is happening:

Musya is crossing the street.

And now we observe that as soon as Musya reaches the other side, we can truthfully use the present perfect to describe what happened:

Musya has crossed the street.

Whereas *cross* describes an event of crossing, *has crossed* describes a state that holds as soon as the crossing is completed.[9] This insight leads to the following proposal:

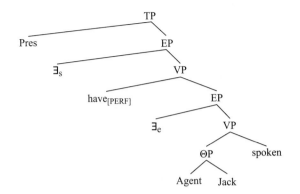

Figure 5.16
Base structure for *Jack has spoken.*

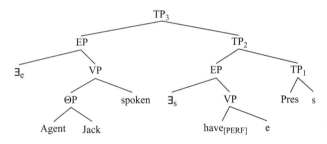

Figure 5.17
Applying QR, first to the higher EP then to the lower one in figure 5.16.

(64) Proposal for the analysis of the perfect:

- Add 'Completed' to SL.
- L(Completed) = { $\langle e,Y \rangle$: Y = {s: s is the state e is in once it is complete.}}
- $have_{[perf]} \rightsquigarrow$ Completed LEXICON

According to the second bullet in (64), 'Completed' combines with an event-denoting expression to give a predicate true of states of that event being completed. Using the translation in the last bullet in (64) to fill in for π in (63), our grammar now assigns the following translation to *Jack has spoken*:

(65) $TP_3 \rightsquigarrow [\exists e: (\text{Agent}(\text{Jack}) \sqcap \text{Speak})(e)]([\exists s: \text{Completed}(e)(s)](\text{Pres}(s)))$.

Given the translation in (65), it now follows that

(66) *Jack has spoken* uttered at point p in a discourse is true iff there is a state that holds at the time of p, which is a state of completion for an event of Jack speaking.

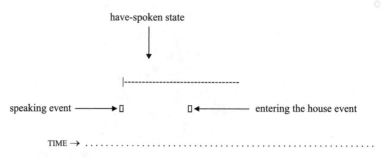

Figure 5.18
Diagraming eventualities in the bad mood narrative.

It follows from (66), that there has to be an event of Jack speaking and, moreover, that that event must be over by the time *Jack has spoken* is uttered. In other words, *Jack has spoken* describes a past event of speaking, but it is present tensed because it also describes a state, and that state holds when the sentence is uttered. This covers the first data point in (62).

Turning to the second data point in (62), we consider the perfect *had spoken* in the narrative discussed above, repeated here:

The Butler family arrived home from their vacation at 7 p.m. They quickly got out of the car and went in the house. Mr. Butler had spoken to Billy about his poor performance in school. Everyone was in a bad mood, so they ate some cold pizza and went to bed.

(67) *Mr. Butler had spoken to Billy* $\rightsquigarrow$
$[\exists e: (\text{Agent}(\text{Mr.B}) \sqcap \text{Speak} \sqcap \text{To}(\text{Billy})(e)]([\exists s: \text{Completed}(e)(s)](\text{Past}(s)))$.

The state that the perfect sentence describes is the state of the speaking event being complete. That state of completion begins after the speaking and continues on. That state <u>does</u> overlap with the going into the house, as the rule of NARRATIVE PROGRESSION predicts. This is illustrated in figure 5.18. The dashed line represents the state that commences with the completion of the speaking event. That event remains in a state of completion throughout the entering the house event. It is because the have-spoken state overlaps the entering that the speaking itself must precede the entering.

Exercise (5.22)

Provide the translation assigned by the grammar to *Every child had been smiling*. Name the last rule of translation that you applied in arriving at your translation.

❂ **Thinking about the Present Perfect Puzzle** ❂

Exercise (5.23) below is an opportunity to become acquainted with the *present perfect puzzle*, a topic of current research.

Exercise (5.23)

[A] Review the base structure for *Jack has spoken* in figure 5.16. It has two nodes labeled VP. An adverb describing an event could attach to either VP node. If an adverb is attached to the higher VP, the one headed by $have_{[perf]}$, we'll say it's attached high. If it's attached to the lower VP, we'll say it's attached low. Assuming that *on Monday* is translated as 'On(Monday)' and that 'On(Monday)' is a one-place predicate of events, provide the translation for *Jack has spoken on Monday* when *on Monday* is attached high and the translation for when it's attached low. Label your translations "High PP" and "Low PP."

[B] Describe a situation in which Jill utters the sentence *Jack had assembled a bookshelf on Monday* and in which what Jill says is predicted by our grammar to be false if *on Monday* is attached low and is predicted by our grammar to be true if *on Monday* is attached high. In your answer, you'll need to specify when Jill uttered the sentence, and you'll need to provide relevant facts about any bookshelves Jack may have assembled. Assume that *Monday* refers to a specific day (i.e., it is short for something like *Monday, April 19, 1997*).

[C] Explain why *#Jack has assembled a bookshelf yesterday* is odd, assuming *yesterday* is attached high.

[D] Describe a situation in which Jill utters the sentence *#Jack has assembled a bookshelf yesterday* and in which what Jill says is predicted by our grammar to be true. Assume the adverb is attached low. (Ignore the fact that the sentence is odd—we'll get to that in [E] below. For now, we just want to know what our grammar says)

[E] In English, the present perfect cannot be modified by an adverbial that locates eventualities in the past relative to the point of utterance. This prohibition is illustrated in the sentences *#Jack has assembled a bookshelf on Monday* or *#Jack has spoken yesterday*. This prohibition does not extend to all languages that have a perfect. Suggest a syntactic or semantic constraint that will capture and possibly explain the prohibition. In deciding on a constraint, keep in mind your answers in [B] as well as [C] and [D].

[F] Find a fluent speaker, possibly yourself, of a language other than English. Determine whether or not the language has a perfect. Explain what factors led you to determine that a given form was the perfect. Test whether the English prohibition applies in the language you described. (Some possible reasons to label a form the perfect are that the form is like an English perfect, consisting of a *have* verb with a participle; the language has a complex form that is present tensed but yet refers to past events; or the form behaves like an English perfect with respect to narrative progression.)

Exercise (5.24)

A sentence in the perfect has two VPs, and an adverbial can modify either one of them. Sentences in the progressive also have two VPs.

[A] Provide a base structure for each of the sentences below, assuming attachment of the adverbial to the higher VP for the first sentence and attachment of the adverbial to the lower VP for the second one.

On Thursday, Joshua was dancing.
Joshua was dancing on Thursday.

[B] Provide the translations that are assigned LFs formed from your base structures. Label your translations "High-adverb" and "Low-adverb."

[C] Describe any truth-conditional differences associated with the two translations.

[D] Do you perceive any truth-conditional differences between the English sentences? Can you think of an example of your own where the attachment site of the adverbial in the progressive affects the meaning?

5.3.2 Varieties of the Perfect

How long does a completion state last? It turns out that the perfect can be used in several different ways, leading to different answers to this question. Sometimes the perfect describes a state of completion that lasts as long as the effects of the completed event are around. Under that use *I have spilled my coffee on the table* would be a true thing to say while the coffee is on the table. It would be a funny thing to say after the coffee is cleaned up, and even odder to say the next day (assuming you didn't spill the coffee again in the meantime).[10] This is called the **perfect of result**, or a **resultative perfect**. There is another use of the perfect in which an experience is described. This is the use you find in examples such as *I've heard worse things than that* and in questions such as *Have you ever tasted eggplant?* In the **experiential perfect**, the completion state seems to last forever. A person can truthfully answer *yes* to the eggplant question, no matter how long ago the event of tasting eggplant occurred. There are languages that formally distinguish these two uses of the perfect.

The complement of perfect *have* can be stative. Perfects of statives have two kinds of readings. *Akna has owned a car* has an experiential reading according to which at some point Akna owned a car. Since this reading requires a past car-owning state, it is like the experiential reading described above, and indeed that term is used for perfects of statives as well. There is another reading that perfects of statives have that is called **universal**. This reading occurs in the presence of modifiers including *for-* and *since*-adverbials. *Akna has owned a car for four years* has a reading according to which Akna is currently in a four-year long car-owning state. *Akna has owned a car since her father died* has a reading according to which Akna is currently in a car-owning state that began when her father died. The label "universal" is meant to evoke the idea that car ownership covers every moment from the death until now.

Exercise (5.25)

Sentence (i) below is a present perfect progressive. Sentence (ii) is a present progressive perfect. ($\exists_e$ nodes and thematic role heads are omitted in the bracketted constituent structures.)

(i) Jack has been sleeping.   [Pres have$_{[perf]}$ been$_{[prog]}$ [Jack sleeping]]]

(ii) *Jack is having slept.   [Pres be$_{[prog]}$ having$_{[perf]}$ [Jack slept]]]

[A] As noted above, the perfect can be read in three different ways, dubbed resultative, experiential and universal. Which of these readings does (i) have? Provide discourses that bring out the varieties that apply.

[B] (i) is acceptable but (ii) is not. Is that expected given the way perfect and progressive behave when there is just one of them in the sentence?

5.4   The Grammar

Our grammar consists of

- rules of syntax
- rules of translation
- rules defining SL
- pragmatic rules

The grammar at the end of chapter 4 is extended as described below.

Syntax

Tense

Morphemes:	Combinations of *Past* and *Pres* are spelled out in
Past, Pres, will	tandem with verbs (e.g., Past+FALL → *fell.*)
Syntax:	A TP node has two daughters: a tense morpheme and an EP.

Aspect

The verbs *be*$_{[prog]}$ and *have*$_{[perfect]}$ both combine with an EP. They determine the form of the verb inside the EP (e.g., *speaking* goes with *be*$_{[prog]}$, and *spoken* goes with *have*$_{[perf]}$).

Rules of Translation

- LEXICON is redefined:

  ○ LEXICON A symbol of SL is a translation for an English morpheme if the extension of the SL symbol relative to L or K_p is the same as the extension of the morpheme of English *when uttered at p.*

- The temporary rule EVEXIST is eliminated.

Symbolic Logic

- Kinds of one-place predicate:

  ○ Predicate constants

  ○ Predicate variables; these include 'Past', 'Pres' and 'Fut'.

  ○ Complex predicates (formed with 'Π' or by combining a two-place predicate with a variable or constant)

- Kinds of variables:

  ○ Individual variables

  ○ Predicate variables

    Individual variables are always paired with individuals.

    Predicate variables are always paired with sets.

- If a variable is the first member of a pair in M, then the second member of that pair is the interpretation of the variable with respect to M.

- The remainder of SL is unchanged—except that everywhere replace "variable" with "individual variable," and replace "simple one-place predicate" with "one-place predicate constant"

- New one-place predicate constants:

  ○ $L(\text{InProgress}) = \{\, \langle e, Y \rangle : Y = \{s : s \text{ is a state of } e \text{ being in progress}\}\}$.

  ○ $L(\text{Completed}) = \{\, \langle e, Y \rangle : Y = \{s : s \text{ is a state that } e \text{ is in once it is completed}\}\}$.

Pragmatics

FELICITY AND TRUTH

As a discourse progresses, individuals become salient and are associated with variables. K_p is a set of variable-*value* pairs that represent the state of the discourse at point p. K_p is the context lexicon for point-in-a-discourse p. If an utterance is made at point p in a discourse, then

an LF for that utterance is infelicitous if its translation is not defined with respect to $K_p + L$. If an LF for that utterance is felicitous then it is true if its translation is true with respect to $K_p + L$ and it is false if its translation is false with respect to $K_p + L$.

For any point p in a discourse, the context lexicon K_p assigns values to tense predicate variables according to the following rules:

$K_p(\text{Past}) \subseteq \{e: e \text{ occurs before } p\}$.

$K_p(\text{Fut}) \subseteq \{e: e \text{ occurs after } p\}$.

$K_p(\text{Pres}) \subseteq \{e: e \text{ co-occurs with } p\}$.

✪ Thinking about Cessation Inferences ✪

Uttering a past tensed stative VP often triggers an inference to the effect that a state of the kind described doesn't hold at the moment of utterance. This is known as a **cessation inference**. The exercise below explores this inference in detail.

Exercise (5.26)

Consider the following discourse:

Aparajita: *How is your grandfather doing?*

Arash: *Oh, he's good. He still lives in Montréal. I speak to him at least once a week. He swims every Saturday. He was a member of an all-star bridge club. He has a brunch at his house with his friends every Sunday. What else can I tell you?*

Upon hearing Arash's response, Aparajita is likely to infer that Arash's grandfather is not currently a member of an all-star bridge club. This inference comes from Arash's use of the past tense stative sentence *He was a member of an all-star bridge club.* It's a cessation inference.

Here's another example. It's a question posed on an online forum:

What is the deal with hazel eyes? I can't find any satisfying scientific explanation for them everywhere I've looked, just speculation. Are they a brown/green crossover in eye color? My father, brother, and I all have hazel eyes, my mother had green eyes, and my sister has blue eyes. What populations are they most prevalent in?

Upon reading this, one naturally infers that the questioner's mother no longer has green eyes, and since for most people eye color doesn't change, one is likely to further conclude that the questioner's mother is dead. The cessation inference is triggered by the past stative *my mother had green eyes.*

In many cases, when a past stative is used, a cessation inference is triggered, but not in all cases. Consider the following discourse:[11]

Last week, I went to a party at Wolfram's house where I was introduced to Gregory and Eva-Lotta. I liked them. Gregory was from America, and Eva-Lotta was from Switzerland. Gregory had deep blue eyes, and I noticed a remarkable thing: he resembled Jörg Bieberstein.

There are several past statives in that text, none of which trigger cessation.

[A] Past tense statives can have cessation and noncessation construals. Given the interpretations our grammar assigns to a past tense stative, is cessation entailed? Is lack of cessation entailed? Are the truth conditions compatible with both possibilities?

[B] What are some of the circumstances that encourage or discourage a cessation inference? Provide examples of your own or from those above to justify your conclusion.

[C] The coming and going of cessation is a property of past statives. Past eventives don't allow for such a possibility. As noted in section 5.2.3, eventive sentences in the simple past are understood to be about events that have culminated. It makes no sense to ponder whether there is a completed event ongoing at the time of utterance. This means we should add cessation to our list of diagnostics for statives. The progressive and the perfect were said to create statives. Do they give rise to cessation inferences? Always, sometimes, never?

[D] Cessation inferences work somewhat differently in languages whose tense systems are unlike that of English and related languages. Seth Cable discusses cessation inferences in the Tlingit language (Na-Dene; Alaska, British Columbia, Yukon).[12] Determine how cessation works in languages for which you have access to speakers.

✪ Thinking About the Progressive and Narrative Progression ✪

Exercise (5.27)

Our analysis of the progressive began with the observation that it is stative as evidenced by how it interacts with narrative progression:

(i) Aparajita looked at Arash. He smiled.   (smile follows look)

(ii) Aparajita looked at Arash. He was smiling.   (smile simultaneous with look)

This led to an analysis captured in the following translation:

(iii) $[\exists e: (\text{Agent}(\text{Arash}) \sqcap \text{Smile})(e)]([\exists s: \text{InProgress}(e)(s)](\text{Past}(s)))$.

But notice that the translation introduces both a state and an event. One might ask why in (ii), it has to be the state that is ordered by the rule of NARRATIVE PROGRESSION around the event of looking. We do not get an interpretation in which the rule of NARRATIVE PROGRESSION orders the event of smiling after the looking. Given the rest of the formula, that would require an event of smiling that was in progress in the past and that followed the looking. That interpretation would make the formula true, but it's unavailable.

A possible explanation for this asymmetry may lie in the translation itself. Notice that the state is ordered in time by the tense and the event isn't. This suggests a possible line of analysis whereby the rule of NARRATIVE PROGRESSION is rethought as a pragmatic constraint on the choice of value assigned by K_p to 'Past'. If that were the case, it would necessarily affect the state and not the event.

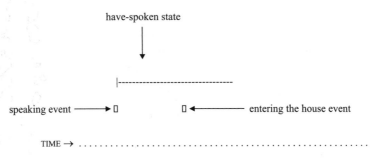

Figure 5.19
Diagraming a sequence of eventualities in the discourse.

[A] Propose a modification of the grammar along these lines.

[B] Does your modification in [A] make the right predictions for discourses including past perfects, such as the Butler example from section 5.3.1, repeated below, whose timeline is in figure 5.19?

The Butler family arrived home from their vacation at 7 p.m. They quickly got out of the car and went in the house. Mr. Butler had spoken to Billy about his poor performance in school. Everyone was in a bad mood, so they ate some cold pizza and went to bed.

[C] What happens in texts where there is a series of past progressives or a series of past perfects?

[D] In exercise (5.9) part [D], there is a puzzle about negation and narrative progression, illustrated with these examples:

(iii) Mary looked at Bill. He didn't smile.

(iv) Mary looked at Bill. He wasn't happy.

Will the grammar as modified in [A] solve the problem raised there?

✪ Thinking About Uses of the Present Tense Form ✪

The following exercise explores the many uses of the present tense in English and what these uses reveal about its meaning.

Exercise (5.28)

In the previous chapter, we introduced the following descriptive generalization:

(68) The simple present can be used to describe a state that holds at the time of utterance, but the simple present cannot be used to describe an event occurring at the time of utterance.

The sentences *Akna fries an egg* and *Baboloki swims* were used in that discussion as examples in which an eventive verb is in the simple present. The generalization says how simple present-tensed eventives can<u>not</u> be used, but nothing about how they can be used. In fact, there are a variety of possible uses, many of which are illustrated in the following:

(i) When Akna gets anxious, she fries an egg. When Baboloki gets anxious, he swims.

(ii) Akna fries eggs in olive oil. Baboloki swims in the ocean.

(iii) November 1492, Martín Alonso Pinzón, captain of the Pinta, deserts the expedition off Cuba. December 1492, Columbus arrives at Hispaniola.

(iv) Young gets the ball on his foot....Willard recovers the ball.... Johnson kicks the ball up field.... Roberts shoots ... and Johan scores!

(v) The other day I was walking down Montgomery Street on my way to the subway. I passed the CVS on the corner and made my way to the subway. I got there in time for the 9 a.m. train. Just then, a guy comes up to me and asks if I know where he can get a newspaper.

(vi) The plane arrives in Guam at 9:00. From there, we take a bus to the base. Amaya will meet us there.

[A] Come up with a name for any use identified while reading (i)–(vi) as well as in other examples you might imagine.

[B] For each use named in [A], describe the conditions under which it arises. What else must be in the sentence? What else is going on in the discourse? What kind of text is it?

[C] For each use, decide whether or not it is already covered by our analysis of present-tensed eventive verbs. If not, suggest an idea for an analysis that would predict that use.

[D] For each use not already covered by our analysis, comment on whether the idea you proposed comes under the heading of tense (locating eventualities in time) or aspect (describing the stage of development of an eventuality) or neither or both.

[E] For each use not already covered by our analysis, comment on whether in the interpretation characterized in [D] is also found with past and future tenses.

[F] In section 5.2.3, it was observed that eventive sentences in the simple past are understood to be about events that have culminated. Which, if any, of the uses of the present discussed in [D] also involve culmination?

[G] The generalization in (68) applies in English. Find a language other than English and determine whether the generalization applies there. Start by determining if the language has stative verbs. Next, determine whether it has a form for reporting states that hold at the time of utterance (e.g., *Rihanna is happy*; *Nadir feels sick*). Finally, discover what happens when an eventive verb is used in that form. Does (68) apply? How does the language convey the kind of meanings you found for the English simple present in [A]?

✪ Thinking about Bare Infinitive Complements ✪

This exercise explores **bare infinitive complements**, which syntactically bear a similarity to perfect and progressives, but differ in various interesting respects.

Exercise (5.29)

The bracketed portions of (i) and (ii) below are called *bare infinitive complements*: bare, because there is no *to*, infinitive, because the verb has no tense marking and complement, because their presence is governed by the verb that precedes them, *heard* or *make*. *Hear* is a perception verb. Other perception verbs that permit bare infinitive complements are *see*, *watch*, and *feel*. *Make* is causative verb. *Help* and *let* also permit bare infinitive complements and are often included among the causative verbs.

(i) Rihanna heard [Aparajita leave].
(ii) Rihanna made [Aparajita laugh].

Syntactically, these sentences bear a similarity to perfects and progressives, where you also find a higher verb *be* or *have*, and a lower complement with a verb and arguments.[13]
      The sentence in (i) entails that Aparajita left. That entailment is due in part to the fact that the complement of *heard* is a bare infinitive. The sentence *Rihanna heard that Aparajita left* does not entail that Aparajita left.

[A] Propose a base structure for (i) and provide a translation assigned by the grammar to an LF formed from your base structure.

[B] Provide a meaning for 'Hear', the translation of the verb *hear*.

[C] Explain why (i) entails that Aparajita left. Your explanation should make use of the translation you provided in [A] and the meaning in [B].

[D] Comment on the strangeness of the sentences *Rihanna heard Aparajita owe me $100* and *Rihanna heard Aparajita have spilled her coffee*. Is that expected given your analysis in [A]–[B]?

[E] Beginning with the base structure you provided in [A], provide two base structures for *Rihanna heard Aparajita laugh on Monday* that differ by the point of attachment of *on Monday*. Label your translations "High PP" and "Low PP." What is the relationship between the truth conditions associated with those two translations? How does that square with your intuitions about the sentence?

[F] If you did exercise (4.17) in chapter 4, you would have commented on the fact that *Jack observed the closing of UCLA by Nixon* entails *Nixon closed UCLA*. How does that compare with what you said in [C]?

[G] Repeat the steps in [A]–[E] for the sentence in (ii), replacing *heard* with *make* throughout.

5.5   Chapter Summary

In this chapter, we investigated the interpretation of tense and aspect. The fruits of our investigation are summarized in the additions to the grammar listed in section 5.4. Key features of the analysis are repeated below.

Tense

- Tense locates eventualities in time.
- Tenses are context dependent. They must be interpreted relative to the point in time at which they are uttered. They behave like plural event pronouns picking out discourse-salient sets of events. Technically, they translate as predicate variables assigned values by the context lexicon.

Aspect

- Aspects describe the stage of development an eventuality is in.
- A VP headed by $be_{[prog]}$ or $have_{[perf]}$ is stative.
- A progressive describes a state that an event is in when it is in progress.
- A perfect describes a state that an eventuality is in once it is completed.
- $be_{[prog]}$ and $have_{[perf]}$ are both two-place predicates relating events and states.

Composition of Meaning

We abandoned the temporary translation rule EvExist introduced in chapter 4. The Lexicon translation rule was modified to allow for context-dependent tenses. Otherwise, no new rules of translation were introduced. The compositional semantics relied on the application of QR to EPs along with the observation that EPs translate as quantifiers.

We can summarize much of what is listed above by focusing on the sentence *Jack was smoking*. Its base structure, LF structure and translation are shown in figure 5.20. Now, consider its use in the following dialogue:

(69)   Amy: It smelled funny in the break room yesterday.

Betty: Jack was smoking.

Carl: No, he wasn't. He stopped four years ago.

Carl claims that Jack stopped smoking four years ago, implying that there was a point in the past at which Jack smoked. That makes it look like Carl is agreeing with Betty, but he isn't. The tense in Betty's utterance of *Jack was smoking* picks out a salient set of past states—those that took place in the break room yesterday. Carl is denying that any of those states were states of an event of Jack smoking being in progress.

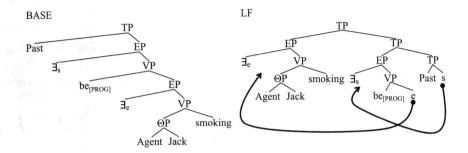

$$\sim\ [\exists e\colon (\text{Agent(Jack)}\sqcap\text{Smoke})(e)]([\exists s\colon \text{InProgress}(e)(s)](\text{Past}(s)))$$

Figure 5.20
Structures and translation for *Jack was smoking.*

Aspectual Classes

• A key component of the investigation into aspect was the evidence for stativity. We relied on narrative progression and other diagnostics from chapter 4.

• Eventualities can be divided into states and events. This division is linguistically significant. Events themselves can be further categorized into linguistically relevant aspectual classes.

Applications

On completing this chapter, you should be able to do the following:

• Assign a <u>base structure</u>, an LF, and a <u>translation</u> to English sentences formed using tense, aspect, transitive and intransitive verbs, adjectives, adverbs, prepositions, conjunction, and one or more DPs formed from a name, a pronoun, or a determiner and a noun phrase. Here are examples of such sentences:

  ◦ *A student from Hampshire College has visited us today.*

  ◦ *Some Canadian farmer will be quietly feeding a donkey tomorrow.*

  ◦ *Gadarine arrived, and Nadir opened a bottle.*

  ◦ *Gadarine arrived ,and Nadir was opening a bottle.*

  ◦ *At least one man had called every woman on Thursday.*

  ◦ *The reporter had investigated a plane crash on Thursday.* (3-way attachment ambiguity)

  ◦ *No lawyer gave Amaya a book about himself.*

• Discern whether a given structure is eventive or stative.

• Describe how discourse conditions influence the interpretation of tense, free pronouns, and the understood ordering of events in a narrative.

Further Reading

Alexiadou, Artemis, Monika Rathert, and Arnim von Stechow. *Perfect Explorations*. Berlin: De Gruyter, 2003.

Altshuler, Daniel. "Discourse Transparency and the Meaning of Temporal Locating Adverbs." *Natural Language Semantics* 22 (2014): 55–88.

Altshuler, Daniel, and Roger Schwarzschild. "Correlating Cessation with Double Access." In *Proceedings of the 19th Amsterdam Colloquium*, edited by M. Aloni, M. Franke and F. Roelofsen, pp. 43–50. Amsterdam: University of Amsterdam, 2013.

Bach, Emmon. "The Algebra of Events." *Linguistics and Philosophy* 9 (1986): 5–16.

Bittner, Maria. "Aspectual Universals of Temporal Anaphora." In *Theoretical and Crosslinguistic Approaches to the Semantics of Aspect*, edited by S. Rothstein, pp. 349–85. Amsterdam: John Benjamins, 2008.

Iatridou, Sabine, Elena Anagnostopoulou, and Roumyana Izvorski. "Observations about the Form and Meaning of the Perfect." In *Ken Hale: A Life in Language*, edited by M. Kenstowicz, pp. 189–238. Cambridge, MA: MIT, 2001.

Kamp, Hans, Uwe Reyle, and Antje Rossdeutscher. *Perfects as Feature Shifting Operators*. Leiden: Crispi, 2016.

Klein, Wolfgang. "The Present Perfect Puzzle." *Language* 68 (1992): 525–51.

Klein, Wolfgang. *Time in Language*. London: Routledge, 1994.

Landman, Fred. "The Progressive." *Natural Language Semantics* 1 (1992): 1–32.

Mittwoch, Anita. "The English Resultative Perfect and Its Relationship to the Experiential Perfect and the Simple Past Tense." *Linguistics and Philosophy* 31 (2008): 323–51.Parsons, Terence. 1 "The Progressive in English: Events, States and Processes." *Linguistics and Philosophy* 12 (1989): 213–41.

Mittwoch, Anita. "On the Distribution of Bare Infinitive Complements in English." *Journal of Linguistics* 26 (1990): 103–31.

Moens, Marc, and Mark Steedman. "Temporal Ontology and Temporal Reference." *Computational Linguistics* 14 (1988): 15–29.

Musan, Renate. "On the Temporal Interpretation of Noun Phrases." Ph.D. Dissertation, MIT, 1995.

Partee, Barbara. "Some Structural Analogies between Tenses and Pronouns in English." *Journal of Philosophy* 18 (1973): 601–9.

Rothstein, Bjorn. "The Perfect Time Span. On the Present Perfect in German, Swedish and English." Ph.D. Dissertation, Stuttgart University, 2006.

Rothstein, Susan. *Structuring Events: A Study in the Semantics of Lexical Aspect*. Malden, MA: Wiley-Blackwell, 2004.Smith, Carlota.*The Parameter of Aspect*. Dordrecht: Kluwer, 1997.

Varasdi, Karoly. "Making Progressives: Necessary Conditions Are Sufficient". *Journal of Semantics* 31 (2014): 179–207.

Zucchi, Sandro. "Incomplete Events, Intensionality and Imperfective Aspect." *Natural Language Semantics* 7 (1999): 179–215.

Notes

Preface

1. Stephen Neale, *Descriptions* (Cambridge, MA: MIT Press, 1990), §2.5. This notation can also be found in: Elena Herburger, *What Counts: Focus and Quantification* (Cambridge, MA: MIT Press, 2000); James Higginbotham, "The Logic of Perceptual Reports: An Extensional Alternative to Situation Semantics," *Journal of Philosophy* 80 (1983): 100–127; James Higginbotham, "Mass and Count Quantifiers," *Linguistics and Philosophy* 17 (1994): 447–480; James Higginbotham and Robert May, "Questions, Quantifiers and Crossing," *Linguistic Review* 1 (1981): 41–79; Barry Schein, *Plurals and Events*, Current Studies in Linguistics, Vol. 23 (Cambridge, MA: MIT Press, 1993); Barry Schein, "Noughty Bits: The Subatomic Scope of Negation," *Linguistics and Philosophy* 39 (2016): 459–440; Barry Schein, *'And': Conjunction Reduction Redux* (Cambridge, MA: MIT Press, 2017).

1 Introduction

1. Keith Laing, "GOP: TSA Scanners 'Thoroughly Useless,'" thehill.com, March 16, 2011.

2. "Q'eqchi' is a Mayan language of the K'ichean branch. It is spoken by approximately one million people in Guatemala, mainly in the departments of Alta Verapaz, Petén, Izabal, Baja Verapaz and El Quiché, as well as in the Toledo District in Belize. This is a huge territory that includes Central and Northern Guatemala, just in between the mountainous highland area in the central part of the country and the low-lying rainforest plains in the extreme north" (Igor Vinogradov, "Irreality in Q'eqchi' (Mayan)," LIAMES: Línguas Indígenas Americanas, 18(1) [2018]: 160–177.). In the writing system used here, "q" stands for a uvular plosive, and "x" stands for a palato-alveolar sound (like the first sound in "shout"). An apostrophe indicates that the sound is ejective; for example, q' is a uvular ejective.

3. World Loanword Database. "Vocabulary Q'eqchi'," http://wold.clld.org/vocabulary/34. Accessed 2/10/19.

2 Symbolic Logic

1. Robert Freidin, "A Brief History of Generative Grammar," in *The Routledge Companion to Philosophy of Language*, ed. G. Russell and D. Graff Fara, 895–916 (New York: Routledge, 2012).

3   Sentences and Determiner Phrases

1. We have endeavored to make our discussion transparent to those with little prior experience with syntactic theory. If more information is felt to be necessary, we recommend the following article, which is is written for a general audience: Howard Lasnik, "The Forms of Sentences," in *An Invitation to Cognitive Science: Language*, 2nd ed., ed. L. Gleitman and M. Liberman (Cambridge, MA: MIT Press, 1995), 1:283–310.

2. For more sophisticated uses and psychological discussion of ambiguity, see Julie Sedivy and Greg Carlson, *Sold on Language: How Advertisers Talk to You and What This Says about You* (Hoboken, NJ: John Wiley & Sons, 2011).

3. Alyssa Sullivan, review of *Allegiant* by Veronica Roth, November 25, 2013, www.uhsecho.com.

4. Gottlob Frege, "Über Sinn und Bedeutung," *Zeitschrift für Philosophie und philosophische Kritik* 100.1 (1892): 25–50.

5. See Lasnik, "The Forms of Sentences," §10.5, for more discussion of ellipsis.

6. Antoine Arnauld and Pierre Nicole, *La logique ou l'Art de penser* (Paris: Jean Guignart, Charles Savreux, & Jean de Lavnay, 1662).

7. Technically, this requires modifying the QR rule so that it begins: "If a node is indexed or has an indexed daughter," instead of "If a node has an indexed daughter."

8. Hans Reichenbach, *Elements of Symbolic Logic* (New York: Macmillan, 1947).

9. This is based on an excerpt from *Vintage Murder* by Ngaio Marsh discussed in Helen Dry, "Sentence Aspect and the Movement of Narrative Time," *Text* 1 (1981): 233–240.

10. These examples are slightly revised versions of those presented in A. Kehler,. *Coherence, Reference and the Theory of Grammar* (Stanford, CA: Center for the Study of Language and Information, 2002), chap. 5.

11. David Hume, *An Inquiry Concerning Human Understanding* (New York: The Liberal Arts Press, 1748).

12. These definitions are simplified for the purposes of this exercises. For a proposal for how coherence relations are defined, see Kehler, *Coherence, Reference and the Theory of Grammar*, as well as D. Altshuler and K. Varasdi, "A Proof of Definitional Adequacy of RESULT and NARRATION," in *Proceedings of Semantics and Linguistics Theory 25*, ed. S. D'Antonio, C.-R. Little, M. R. Moroney, and M. Wiegand (Ithaca, NY: Cornell University, CLC Press, 2015). Una Stojnić, "Context-Sensitivity in a Coherent Discourse," Ph.D. Dissertation, Rutgers University, 2016.

13. While this may be counterintuitive, Hume's idea is that there is one psychological process by which we identify things as either resembling or not resembling.

14. This generalization goes back to work by Jerry Hobbs, "Coherence and Coreference," *Cognitive Science* 3, no. 1 (1979): 67–90.

4   Events and States

1. G. O. Curme, *English Grammar* (Harper & Row, 1947).

2. To appreciate this use of the technical term patient it might help to think of the noun *patient* as it occurs in *The doctors examined the patients*. The doctors are doing something: they are the agents. Those who are being examined are having something done to them: they are the patients.

3. David Dowty, "On the Semantic Content of the Notion of 'Thematic Role,'" in *Properties, Types and Meaning. Volume II: Semantic Issues*, ed. G. Chierchia, B. H. Partee, and R. Turner (Dordrecht: Kluwer Academic, 1989), 110.

4. For examples of these phenomena and discussion see Alexander Williams, *Arguments in Syntax and Semantics* (Cambridge, UK: Cambridge University Press, 2015), §11.2.5.

5. Christopher LaTerza, "Distributivity and Plural Anaphora," Ph.D. Dissertation, University of Maryland, 2014, §2.1.3.3.

6. Lisa deMena Travis, *Inner Aspect. The Articulation of VP*, Studies in Natural Language and Linguistic Theory, Vol 80 (Dordrecht: Springer, 2010), 75–87.

7. Richard Larson, "On the Double Object Construction," *Linguistic Inquiry* 19 (1988): 335–91. See also Howard Lasnik's discussion of *have* and *be* in "The Forms of Sentences," in *An Invitation to Cognitive Science: Language,* 2nd ed., ed. L. Gleitman and M. Liberman (Cambridge, MA: MIT Press, 1995).

8. Richard Larson, *On Shell Structure*, Routledge Leading Linguists (New York: Routledge, 2014).

9. Stephen Neale, *Descriptions* (Cambridge, MA: MIT Press, 1990).

10. Such as Elena Herburger, 2000. *What Counts: Focus and Quantification* (Cambridge, MA: MIT Press, 2000); James Higginbotham and Robert May, "Questions, Quantifiers and Crossing," *Linguistic Review* 1 (1981):41–79; Barry Schein, "Noughty Bits: The Subatomic Scope of Negation," *Linguistics and Philosophy* 39 (2016): 459–540.

11. The SL statements above use the variable '*s*' for states. Oftentimes, states and events are collected together under the heading *eventuality*. In that case, despite the confusion, authors will use '*e*' for eventuality and you can find: [∃e: State(e)] ((Hold(Gadarine) ⊓ Own ⊓ Theme(Fido))(e)).

12. Graham Katz, "Manner Modification of State Verbs," in *Adjectives and Adverbs*, ed. L. McNally and C. Kennedy, 220–248 (Oxford: Oxford University Press, 2008).

13. These examples are from Susan Rothstein, "States and Modification: A Reply to Maienborn," *Theoretical Linguistics* 31 (2005): 375–381.

14. These examples are from Katz, "Manner Modification of State Verbs."

15. Not included here are the rules of translation and SL interpretation introduced in the discussion of relative clauses in section 3.5.

5   Tense and Aspect

1. Barbara Hall Partee, "Some Structural Analogies between Tenses and Pronouns in English," *Journal of Philosophy* 70 (1973): 601–609.

2. Lauri Carlson, "Focus and Dialogue Games: A Game Theoretical Approach to the Interpretation of Intonational Focusing," in *Cognitive Constraints on Communication*, ed. L. Vaina and J. Hintikka (Dordrecht: Reidel, 1984), 295–333.

3. See, for example, Hedde Zeijlstra, "Negation in Natural Language: On the Form and Meaning of Negative Elements." *Language and Linguistics Compass* 1 (2007): 498–518.

4. Hans Kamp and Uwe Reyle, *From Discourse to Logic: Introduction to Model-Theoretic Semantics of Natural Language, Formal Logic and Discourse Representation Theory* (Verlag: Springer, 1993), 547.

5. There is a discussion of this syntax on page 299 of Howard Lasnik, "The Forms of Sentences," in *An Invitation to Cognitive Science: Language*, Vol. 1, 2nd ed., ed. L. Gleitman and M. Liberman (Cambridge, MA: MIT Press, 1995). Exercise (4.7) on ditranstives illustrates another case where a verb takes a VP complement.

6. The name *Vendler classes* is based on work by Zeno Vendler, *Linguistics in Philosophy* (Ithaca, NY: Cornell University Press, 1967).

7. The perfect is formed with the verb *have* followed by the past participle. *Spoken* is the past participle of *speak*. Similarly, *fallen* is the past participle of *fall*, as in *The sky has fallen*, and *sung* is the past participle of *sing* as in *Rihanna has sung a song*. For *visit* and many other verbs, the past participle is identical to the simple past. Compare *Rihanna has visited us* and *Rihanna visited us*. There may be dialects in which the simple past and the past participle forms are always the same; in dialects where they are different, for some verbs, speakers are unsure what the past participle form is.

8. See Lasnik, "The Forms of Sentences," 299.

9. The word *perfect* usually means "ideal," but it can also mean "complete," as in *that makes perfect sense* or in the phrase *perfectly reasonable* meaning completely reasonable. . The completeness meaning is the source of the grammatical term *perfect*.

10. This example comes from James Higginbotham, "The English Perfect and the Metaphysics of Events," in *Time and Modality*, ed. J. Guéron and J. Lecarme, Studies in Natural Language and Linguistic Theory, Vol. 75 (Verlag: Springer, 2008), 173–193.

11. This example is based on Renate Musan, "Tense, Predicates, and Lifetime Effects." *Natural Language Semantics* 5 (1997): 271–301.

12. Seth Cable, "The Implicatures of Optional Past Tense in Tlingit and the Implications for 'Discontinuous Past.'" *Natural Language and Linguistic Theory* 35 (2017): 635–81.

13. For more on the syntactic similarities between perception verbs, causative verbs, and aspectual heads, see Susi Wurmbrand, *Infinitives: Restructuring and Clause Structure*, Studies in Generative Grammar 55 (Berlin/New York: Mouton de Gruyter, 2001).

Index